PRAISE FOR KERRY'S ADVOCACY & MENTORSHIP

"Coming from unimaginable depths of OCD, Kerry's entire life was completely entangled in her intrusive thoughts, and almost every hour of every day was committed to neutralizing her fears and anxiety through hundreds of compulsions. After committing herself to intensive OCD treatment, Kerry has risen to improbable heights. Not only has she learned to live free of OCD, she has written a beautiful memoir about her personal journey, and is leading a website that has reached thousands of people that are continuously learning and benefiting from her experience. Kerry is a testament that if one dedicates themselves to treatment; one can overcome this dreadful disease in an overwhelming fashion. I am immensely proud of her progress along with her commitment to disseminate her knowledge for the benefit of others suffering from OCD."

-Jim Sterner, LMFT
Founder, *The Gateway Institute*

"Kerry so vulnerably came onto my podcast and laid it all out on the table, holding nothing back. The honesty in sharing her story was refreshing and relatable for my listeners and myself. Being a guest on my show, she created ripples in my community empowering other women to also own their brokenness and become an example of what it looks like to overcome extreme obstacles. I am beyond proud to watch Kerry trailblaze a new way for mental health while also creating a path for others. You won't regret hearing her story."

-Sarena Hess, Founder, *Women For Greatness* Podcast

"With *The Obsessive Outsider*, Kerry Osborn has the potential to reach millions of other 'outsiders' who feel alone in their experience. I believe this book will change the way people view OCD for the better."

-Rudy Caseres, Host on *The Mighty* Live Streams and Mental Health Public Speaker

"Having lived with Obsessive-Compulsive Disorder most of my life, I hit a point where I knew I couldn't live with the OCD demons any longer; that's when I found Kerry and her website, *The Obsessive Outsiders*. With her help and knowledge about the disorder I was able to get a handle on the disease that had stopped me from accomplishing so much in my life. Thanks to Kerry, I could finally talk to someone who knew what it felt like to live with OCD and knew how to conquer it, I no longer felt like that once hopeless outsider!"

-Danielle Saluan, Fashion Blogger and OCD sufferer

"As a mother with two children that suffer from severe cases of OCD, I have met my fair share of individuals involved in the mental health industry. But Kerry stood out more than the rest. After watching her speak and getting to truly know her, I think she is a major voice for OCD awareness. She helps the community everyday and is such an amazing young woman. I look forward to seeing the bright future that lies ahead for her and cannot wait for everyone to read her book."

-Dana Yuran, a mother of two adult kids with OCD

"The best way to educate the world about OCD is by sharing our stories. Kerry does that beautifully, and I'm so glad she decided to write this book."

-Stephen Smith, Founder and CEO, *nOCD app*

THE OBSESSIVE OUTSIDER

ONE WOMAN'S JOURNEY FROM SEVERE
OBSESSIVE-COMPULSIVE DISORDER TO A LIFE
LIVED ABUNDANTLY

KERRY ALAYNE OSBORN

DEDICATION

This book is dedicated to every single individual who suffers from the
ruthlessness of Obsessive-Compulsive Disorder,
whether diagnosed or undiagnosed.
I see you. I hear you. And I wrote this for you.

"For my thoughts are not your thoughts, and your ways are not my ways. For as Heaven is higher than the earth, so my ways are higher than your ways and my thoughts than your thoughts." Isaiah 55: 8-9

This Bible verse belongs right here, before the book begins. For me, this verse is a vivid reminder of how small my thoughts are, and how much greater God's are. We often get so caught up in our OCD-cycled brains, we forget to take a moment, breathe, and reflect how much bigger and higher God's reasons and plans are. It helps me remember to put my thoughts and my ways into perspective and give it all to God - where I belong.

A NOTE TO YOU, THE READER

This book was intended to be strikingly different from any other book you would pick up on Obsessive-Compulsive Disorder in years past. When I first began writing this book, there were not many books on OCD that were written from a patient's perspective in recovery. Therapists, researchers, and psychologists wrote most books on the market when I had the idea to write about the nitty-gritty, not-so-pretty details of the onset of OCD at the age of seventeen, years of adolescent frustration and intensive therapy programs, and ultimately trying to put on paper what led to my state of ongoing recovery today. The stigma of living with Obsessive-Compulsive Disorder and the taboo of outright discussions on mental illness have come leaps and bounds from where they were when I embarked on this written journey, and it brings me such joy to think I could have played even the smallest role in that progress with my mental health platform and various stigma-shattering projects over the years. It really started to snowball once I mindfully set the intention of stepping out of my self-protected stigma zone and decided it was okay to be a face of the disorder, a trendsetter, and an unfiltered, living example of what non-traditional OCD can look like and how the worst of it can undoubtedly be worked through to live a life of self-proven quality many sufferers didn't know was possible.

So here goes...everything. The perspective of this book is from a real patient, a true sufferer, and an overcomer — not a therapist or doctor with a high level of education relaying information to you. I believe it's key to hear both perspectives. My dream for my readers and my peers is to take everything from this book — my story of imperfections, my unwelcomed imagination, my perseverance, my triumphs, and my firsthand experience — and use me as inspiration to consciously improve yourselves. I have no problem exposing the depths of my unhealthy mind in order to help you see how bad OCD can get if you continue to allow it to burrow and fester in your mind. Let me tell you, I have been at my lowest low with severe OCD and right now, my highest high. My goal is to tell you about the path I chose or that chose me. I still can't figure out who picked their poison. I will spell out the lessons of dignity that it took to stand at the base of a mountain with no courage, powder my climbing hands, and get ready for a climb many do not surmount. With the tools that are proposed here in my book, I guarantee you, you too will be a lot closer to climbing without a lead.

Once I learned how to manipulate my OCD right back on itself, it became very important to me to write a patient-to-patient book to my fellow obsessive outsiders. That's what we all are, right? We are outsiders because we are constantly separating ourselves from the rest of the world to be in our own obsessing world. You didn't seek to create this world, yet you are contributing to the growth of this world with each and every compulsion you perform. Chances are, if you have purchased my book, you have purchased countless other self-help books on OCD. That is exactly what I intended this to be – a self-help book — because it's time you learned to actually help yourself rather than everyone trying to help you. It's time you received the tools, undeniable inspiration, and most of all, courage and perseverance to truly and unequivocally help yourself.

I set out to write this book to give you an easy read for once. I am not going to break down the analytics of OCD and how it all works with a bunch of medical jargon. That's not what you need. What you need is a simple, inspiring piece of work from someone who has lived through all of the emotions that come along with OCD and has found a way to make sense of it all. Although researching the scientific analytics of what is actually malfunctioning in the mind of someone with OCD is extremely helpful and relieving, at the end of the day we are looking for solutions, not just a continuous breakdown of what we already know. You need to be able to get to a point of action. But before you can get there, you need to be inspired enough through simple terms that worked in success stories, which, in turn, will work for you. So here I am.

On the other hand, I am happy to give a simple education on the basis of OCD for anyone reading this without a proper understanding of the disorder. OCD is a disorder rooted in one receiving consistent, unwelcome, disturbing, and intrusive thoughts. In order to get rid of or prevent these thoughts from coming to fruition, one in turn performs compulsions. These can be mental or physical routine acts that vary from person to person. The more enabling compulsions performed, the stronger the obsessions become, and the tighter the grip the disorder will have on you. OCD is a constantly revolving circle that can be very hard to commit to break free of, but it most certainly *can* be done. Breaking free from this ongoing circle of constant torture will create a life of free will you didn't know was even possible for you.

When I was battling OCD at my worst, I wish I had been able to open up a book written from the perspective of someone who had severe OCD. If only I had been able to get my hands on a rulebook, lessons, or comforting guidelines from someone who related throughout my intense battle, to feel some sort of comfort. It just didn't exist at the time, at least to my knowledge. So, I created one. I wrote this book mainly for people who may not have the exact same battle as me (since OCD has many different subtypes and themes), but who have had the same struggle, which is the core of what we can all relate to. I have achieved a measure of success at a young age, but I am not merely speaking financially. I believe that there are many versions of success in life, and to each of them we owe the same recognition — putting up a fight. The catch is that I had very severe Obsessive-Compulsive Disorder during all of my small successes. My biggest success, by far, has been overcoming the depths of this disorder to lead a fully functioning life, an often rare feat for people who live in constant torture of severe OCD. My goal for each and every one of you is to tell you my story as pure insight for you, whether you have OCD or not. For those of you reading this without OCD, use me as inspiration to the fullest extent for you. If I can be a success in this world *with* severe OCD, imagine what you can be without it. If you are reading this and you do have OCD, then this is your opportunity to hear trials, tribulations, and triumphs from a fellow suffering patient, so that you, too, can feel like you have a guide that you can actually relate to. When I was at my sickest point, not a single soul could relate to me. No one. Nothing. I have never been so alone in my entire life as I have been at the lowest points with my OCD. Yet, I never recognized how alone I really was because I was so isolated in my never-ending thoughts. I would love for this book to be the lifeline that you feel like you don't have right now. I want you to highlight parts that stick out to you, tear out sections that you want to live by, and most of all, treat this book as the friend and fellow sufferer that I never had.

Part One of this book is my entire story: everything I went through from the onset and acknowledgment of my OCD, how I initially dealt with it, and finally, how I am successfully living with OCD today. The reason I am about to take so much time to share my story with you is to gain your trust. If you have OCD, the only way you will actually take my advice is if you trust me. We are woven from the same cloth. Once I have gained your trust, and you understand we are not all that different, I take Part Two of the book and break down my detailed approach to leading a fully functioning life amidst OCD.

At the end of every chapter, I provide a personal note of realness, as if I am talking directly to you. Each note wraps up the chapter, just as I would if we were in person.

Although I believe if you have OCD you will identify and enjoy reading my story, if you should decide to at any time, feel free to skip my memoir to Part Two. This is where my story ends and yours begins. Part Two is when I begin getting into the details of how to actually take measures and do something about your OCD. If you find yourself not relating to or interested in my personal story, I challenge you to skip to Part Two and give it a chance before you close this book. I truly believe this section will resonate with each and every obsessive outsider.

As I wrote this book, I envisioned the guy from my support group who washed compulsively to the point where he could rarely leave his house. I envisioned the sweet woman who lost out on some of the most important years of her children's lives because she couldn't take them to school for fear she would hit pedestrians. I pictured the man whose deepest fear is that he will use any sharp object near him violently on a loved one for fear he has the potential to be a murderer. I saw an old peer who lies awake every night, wondering over and over again if the stove is turned off and if her family will be dead in the morning because of a gas leak or the house catching on fire. I felt for a young girl who believes every time she signs her name on any document, she is signing her soul away to the Devil. I mourned deeply for the loving teacher who received intrusive sexual thoughts about her students which had no correlation to her or her desires. I cringed for the new mother who suddenly receives violent images of hurting her beloved baby or husband and has no one to talk to in order to find out what is suddenly happening in her mind. I replayed the thoughts someone once shared with me about the role OCD played in their intimate relationships — thoughts I uneasily dealt with myself. I thought about the girl who I once was, who couldn't even take a single, solitary step without receiving intrusive, painful thoughts. These are the people — people I imagine are just like you — who I envisioned as I wrote chapter after chapter. These are the people I want to touch. I allowed myself to feel the life-sucking, debilitating pain inside each of you, which I know all too well, as I wrote every word, in hopes to get through to you.

Take a walk with me through the content in my book. Trust that I know what it's like to see the light but never truly believe that I could get there. Until I was there — in the light — living a normal life with OCD. Trust me that "OCD Recovery" *is real*. It doesn't mean cured. It means that I am in active recovery, living a life so normal there are days I forget I even have the disorder. Many OCD sufferers are skeptic of the term, "OCD Recovery," and rightly so. If I had never experienced it like I do every single day and have for years, I would be a total skeptic. But instead, I am a walking, breathing example of the truth behind OCD Recovery.

However, I didn't just keep walking through the tunnel until the light got brighter and bigger. I started running once I saw how my tools in therapy were working. And for those that I didn't yet see, I took the chance. I put up with the many uncertainties. I turned around and looked OCD square in the face — and then, I turned back around and kept living my life. I am so proud to honestly say that OCD doesn't control me anymore. Do I still have OCD? Absolutely. But it doesn't consume me because I don't allow it to. I have to continually make a conscious decision for this to happen, but boy, is it worth it if you stick with it.

I put up a serious fight and never went down easy. Since I went through everything I have and still go through daily, I may as well document it and entertain someone along the way. And if I happen to help <u>one</u> person become inspired enough to run instead of walk through the tunnel to see life on the other side, having OCD will officially be the best thing that has ever happened to me. And no, OCD — that is not a compliment.

PART I

1

"MY END ALL, BE ALL"

I couldn't breathe. No matter how much I gasped, I couldn't get a single breath. I opened my eyes, slapped down my air bag, and looked at the black smoke and fire only two feet from my face. The engine was on fire. Every second that passed was another second closer to the car being left to nothing but ashes. I faintly heard my friend, next to me in the driver's seat, crying out. Was she hurt? I knew if I looked over at her, I would faint. I often faint in times of trauma or at the sight, sometimes even the thought, of blood. I instinctively knew the second I looked over to her to assess her situation, I would be out cold, and we would both be stuck inside the enveloping car. I forced myself to keep looking straight ahead, undid my seat belt, and with all of my might, tried to open my passenger side door. It was as though the silver handle led to nowhere. It didn't budge. It was jammed shut from where the other car had struck my side. My head was so fuzzy — yet so clear. We have been in a car accident. The first accident I'd been in, and my head kept obsessively repeating one thought. "I need out of this car...*now*." Within one second, I had climbed over the console towards the back and tried the next door. It opened. I fell out of the car into the outside world and began to run across the highway through oncoming traffic to the grassy knoll of a park on the other side. As soon as I touched the grass, I collapsed. I still hadn't been able to take a breath. It was as though I had the airway of a straw but couldn't suck in as much as nearly half of a straw. As I collapsed on the grass, my blurry eyes saw the outline of a familiar frame and face running towards me. "Who was he? I know him... How do I know him?" The thought trailed off...

Before I knew it, he was hovering over me, and he began to pray over me. It couldn't be...This familiar man was the pastor of my church.

Allow me to set the scene and narrow down the irony of this one hundred percent true miracle for you. We had crashed near the outskirts of the most deserted part of the park where people rarely are. It was a tiny, grassy knoll in between office buildings and parking lots. My pastor had been walking on the bike trail and happened to be passing the exact nook of our crash at the very moment I was running from the car. He was sent by God Himself to save my life. The best part? He knew exactly who I was, knew my mother, and immediately called her. Mom...I just wanted my mom. I needed that familiar face to remain conscious and fight until I could get my breath back. Fleeting thoughts continued, "Why can't I breathe? It's like my lungs have been crushed... Is it from internal injuries or could whiplash really be this bad?" Within seconds, my mother's face was hovering above me. "Mommy!" A small breath started to come back to me at the sight of her. I looked back at the street to the crash site. The car was no longer a car; it was pure fire, ashes, and black smoke that brought our whole town to a halt. "...where was my friend?" And there she was, standing over me, holding her arm dripping with blood. "KERRY! KERRY! ARE YOU OK??!?!!" I shielded my eyes from looking at her. I couldn't let myself faint; I needed to stay awake. She was ushered away, and I didn't see her again until the hospital. It was all so fast, so confusing. Had we both made it out of the smoldering metal of what used to be a car...alive?

Perfect weather had paved the way for our drive home from school that day. We jetted off campus and headed down the familiar highway we used daily. As we cruised down the highway, she had been updating me on the latest with her boy, and I was eagerly listening. While she was talking, I vaguely remember a car full of boys driving parallel to us. My friend, all of a sudden, overcorrected to avoid a collision with them during a mutual lane change, and with the distraction, lost complete control of the steering wheel. The front left tire bounced and skidded into the median, becoming stuck in the gutter, causing the steering wheel to lock. All at once, we were airborne over the cement and tree-filled median, landing on the opposite side of the highway. The car landed so that the passenger side where I was sitting was facing on-coming traffic, which was coming full speed ahead with no time for anyone to hit their brakes. The last thing I saw before I felt the impact was a white Dodge SUV coming for my face. And there it was — the climax of my life before my very eyes.

I was ending my junior year in high school. I was *that* girl. The girl that had everything every girl in high school wanted. I had the entire package: Daddy's little girl, a neck-breaker, actual blonde brainpower, no concerns of money, and a future about as bright as a valedictorian. I was wise beyond my years, providing those around me with the notion that this young lady was going places. BIG places. I was preparing to submit my college applications for early admission. I had a few schools in mind and couldn't wait to finish high school and show the world was I was made of. Little did I know that my self-fulfilling plans were not registered in God's plan for me.

I was the only one to walk away from our multi-car crash with no major injuries. At the time, everybody was relieved; yet, no one had any idea what was really going on inside me. What nobody knew at that moment was that my injuries were far beyond that of a physical nature. Mine were psychological. *Seriously* psychological. People tend to always recognize and register physical injuries; oftentimes not realizing people can be just as injured internally (psychologically) as externally during catastrophic events. I, you will soon find, am Exhibit A.

Author's Note: "If you find a path with no obstacles, it probably doesn't lead anywhere." –Frank A. Clark.

This was the quote that began my college entrance essay, fresh off of being diagnosed with OCD, although I hadn't yet registered what OCD even was. To this day, my greatest obstacle has been living with my OCD as an adolescent, by a long shot. Has OCD been your greatest obstacle? Today, I thoroughly believe every obstacle can be overcome, which is why they are placed in our paths. Instead of looking at this disorder with a pitying outlook (which is very normal and common), take a moment to intentionally try to mentally separate yourself from the disorder. There's YOU (insert name here), and then there's your disorder (insert disorder here). The goal of this book — every chapter, every story, every word — is to help you see you can overcome this chronic disorder to live a much more manageable life. *I am living proof.* It may be a slippery obstacle to navigate, but you owe it to yourself to allow you the time to step back and assess the tools that are available that you can use to move past this obstacle. The biggest and most powerful tool you will find you have is <u>yourself</u>. It doesn't feel like that right now — trust me I know — but no tool, no therapist, no medication, no leaning on ANYONE for support will ever come remotely close to what you can do for yourself. In order to overcome the worst of OCD, you have to change your mindset. You are much more powerful than you give yourself credit for when it comes to OCD. You can absolutely overpower parts of your mind, *but you must first find the courage and targeted mentality to make a change.*

Let's do just that. Take a second right now and silently say to yourself — whether you believe it or not — "I, myself, just as I am, am solely the most powerful tool in the world for mindfully and intentionally overcoming my disorder."

2

"THE ONSET"

When I say "psychological," I'm talking the same page as Schizophrenia, Body Dimorphic disorder, and Obsessive-Compulsive Disorder to name a few. I'm talking about the kinds of disorders where people seemingly cannot relate to you in any way, shape, or form unless they have the same disorder. I used to be one of those people...until all of a sudden...I wasn't. Soon after the accident, I developed Obsessive-Compulsive Disorder faster and harder than I ever could have imagined.

How and when my OCD truly started to surface is still somewhat a mystery, as it is for many people. OCD can arise through many different situations. Some are genetically predisposed to the disorder, as it can run through a family's history. For others, OCD can be onset by traumatic and environmental events. These events can be emotional, such as seeing your beloved pet get run over, or physical, such as hitting your head. Although there are no known cases of OCD in my nuclear or extended family, looking back, I believe I was pre-disposed to elements of OCD tendencies all my life. I have always been very rigid, inadaptable, and very literal. There are sporadic instances I can remember, small flashbacks, where it makes sense only now that I had OCD engrained in me all along.

I think back to a time in the second grade, at the end of the school day, when my teacher went around the class and asked what we had all individually learned that day. The circle came to me, and I realized I technically hadn't learned anything brand new that day, just expanded on subjects I already knew. I took the question so literally. When it came around to me, I remember just using a reason the other kids used ("I learned more times tables," or something of the sort), and immediately felt a pang in my stomach. I thought I had lied because I hadn't felt like I technically learned anything I hadn't already known. I remember after school was dismissed, I couldn't allow myself to go home, knowing I had lied to my teacher. Twenty years of my life have gone by, and I can still feel that sickly feeling of deep ridden guilt running through my gut. I followed my teacher around on the playground as all the kids were leaving school and tried to explain myself in my round-about second-grade language, so she would know I deeply regretted my "lie." I couldn't allow myself to not tell the *entire* truth. I was afraid if I didn't tell the whole truth, and left any part unsaid, I was not doing my teacher justice.

That story explains my OCD and me perfectly. I was obsessing so badly my stomach hurt. I, still to this day, am exactly the same. I can't live with myself if I lie. I need to describe and perfect things to a "T," and I must say everything I am thinking. I can't let go of anything. I dwell on every detail and must do everything possible to explain myself and do my very best. My poor little heart couldn't bear the burden of not thoroughly explaining myself to my teacher that day. This is just one of so many examples of looking back at elements of OCD in my early life.

In middle school, I remember I went through a phase where I had to say, "I think," at the end of every sentence I said. If I didn't end my sentence with the phrase, I was afraid I would be held responsible for any part of my statement that could be refuted. Just in case any part of my sentence could be argued or inaccurate, I had to have the leeway of saying it. I thought if I ended every sentence with this phrase, for any part of my statement that was not absolutely perfect, I would be excused. I wanted to lay everything out onto the table, for fear of something happening later. To this day I have the exact same mentality, sans the compulsion! I want every detail discussed, so nothing can happen later to cause an argument or surprise. I go to unthinkable lengths to try and prevent something bad from happening or letting something I previously said haunt me later.

In Junior High school, I was honest to an actual fault. Truly. I was still terrified of not telling the entire truth, even though I spoke nothing but the truth. It became a problem when our school entered into a national writing contest, and I worked for weeks on my essay. I researched, dug creatively, and wrote the best essay I had ever written. A few weeks later, my teacher announced to the class that the essays had been submitted to the city. Out of everyone who entered, my essay won to go on to state finals. I was shocked and filled with excitement, but the excitement soon turned into fear. My happiness was quickly veered. I feared that I had plagiarized, even though I had done no such thing. I took plagiarism so seriously; I thought there was a chance I had taken even a few words from someone else during my research. I couldn't think of a certain phrase or sentence I had taken, but I couldn't let it go. As if using the word "the" was plagiarism! I couldn't allow myself to just be ecstatic in the moment and realize I had truly, honestly won. A month or two passed, and one day during a school wide auditorium, the principal said he had an announcement. He went on to say that one of the students in the school had just gone on to win the state of California finals for their essay. It was *me*. I walked up in front of my entire school and accepted my award of twenty dollars. As I walked off the stage, I saw my mother had been called to come and watch. Fear began to set in. What if I didn't deserve the twenty dollars? What if everyone thought I was capable of such an accomplishment, but I wasn't? I then made a huge mistake. I couldn't sit with the thought that I might not deserve this award. I went to my teacher who had assigned the essay and entered us into the contest. I explained my fear to her — that I thought there was a tiny chance I had plagiarized. I think back today what she must have thought when one of her students who had just won the state championships told her they thought they had plagiarized. She questioned me a few times, but of course let it go. She knew I hadn't plagiarized. Everyone knew me better than I knew myself.

Before the car accident in high school, I never had any specific linked obsessions or performed any notable compulsions. I had the urges to do the things I mentioned above, but they were not dead set intrusive thoughts and vivid compulsions. They were just faint, deep feelings that were simply who I was. It seems somewhere between the emotional and physical trauma of the accident, the true obsessiveness began to set in. I don't recall hitting my head in the accident, but something triggered me that day. I developed a somewhat acute case of post-traumatic stress disorder. Post-traumatic stress disorder can then stem into many other disorders as the ones previously mentioned, and in my case, it was Obsessive-Compulsive Disorder. The *real* kind. Not the kind everybody thinks they have when they want their pencils lined up correctly or have little rituals or preferential tendencies, which make them think they are all of a sudden "ridden with OCD." Some say everybody has elements of OCD tendencies in them, but the difference lies in that most people do not feed into and believe their unwelcome thoughts with every fiber in their being. Whereas a person with OCD can take one triggering experience, one thought, and give what we call "credit" to it, and then believe it wholeheartedly. That person will begin to obsess about it, perhaps trying to un-do the thought, make it go away, or prevent something from happening by performing compulsions. The compulsions give a sense of control to the person with OCD to momentarily relieve the associated anxiety.

By the end of the short summer after the accident, as I was heading into my senior year, my mother says she had "a different daughter." The frame of time where the OCD developed full swing was around a couple of months after the accident. For some people, whether a physical or psychological trauma, OCD can develop overnight. For others, it can take years. I will never know what truly brought on the onset of my OCD, and I don't try to figure it out anymore. Something among the trauma of my car accident, my teenage hormones, and perhaps pre-disposed OCD traits set in, and I was going full speed ahead on a road with no sense of direction to where I was headed.

Author's Note: The onset of OCD at any age is incredibly difficult to face. Developing OCD as a child starts life off in a very complex and complicated bubble. The onset of OCD as a young adult can take an already confusing and constantly changing time in life and complicate it even more. Learning to navigate newfound OCD as a mature adult can take a life you may have felt sure of and cause you to begin to question who you are and everything you know. OCD doesn't care how old you are, how inconvenient your life is at the time, or how drastically your life is going to change. No matter what stage of life you are in, OCD will try and take every joy, passion, and love in your life and compromise it to a point of destruction. You won't feel prepared. You won't feel sure of anything, and you certainly won't feel control. It's a slow, grueling process of feeling like you're watching your life turn upside down as fast as an upturned snow globe. No one is ever prepared for this radical change, and it often brings with it angry tears, crippling breakdowns, and thoughts of giving up. Since we have not chosen to be victims of OCD, we must learn to take this confusion and anger and channel it to *accept, face, understand,* and *fight* the OCD. Do not doubt for a second that this hopeless, bottomless pit you feel deep inside cannot arise to the surface again. With the proper tools to fight your OCD, you not only can build a ladder to climb out of the bottomless pit, but you can then fill the pit in with dirt and stomp on it. Exposure in light of your fear is the best place to start on your path to overcoming the dominance of OCD. We will get deep into what that means a bit later. I have to finish spilling my ridiculously embarrassing story first. Thanks for listening, by the way!

3

"BEAUTY BECOMES A BEAST"

I still remember the day when I first realized something was wrong. *I was losing too much hair.* It was towards the beginning of my senior year in high school, and I knew something wasn't right. I regularly dyed my hair bright blonde and straightened it every day. I like to think that something in the midst of that routine, weather changes, and perhaps nesting hormones made my hair fall out at a much faster rate than I had ever noticed before. I would brush my hair, unknowingly look at the brush, and be hit with the realization there was simply too much hair in the brush.

I began to go to every length I could to save my hair. I was going to health food stores and buying every natural hair growth product on the market, switched over to silk pillowcases to lessen nightly hair tugging while I slept, even to blatantly refrain from hugging people because the chances of my hair getting pulled on was always high. I began to notice when I brushed and washed my hair, I would lose a tremendous amount, so I slowly backed off on both. I wore hair wraps to bed because I didn't want to see hair on the pillow in the morning. I treated my hair like it was a foreign silk, where every move and decision I made, I considered whether it would affect my hair or not. I didn't allow myself to do anything where I could sweat, for fear of losing more hair in the process. I went as far as getting my blood drawn to see if there was anything internally abnormal. Anyone who knew me well fully understood that no amount of money on planet Earth could get me to get my blood drawn. Yet that's how serious I was about figuring out the source of my hair loss. In fact, I honestly don't know if I had had my blood drawn since I was a small child! After all of that, the doctor found nothing distinctly connected to why I might be shedding more hair than normal.

I was at a loss. I wanted a tangible reason to link my hair loss to, so I could fix whatever it was. But I had nothing. I had done everything I could think of.

I must have been subconsciously looking for an out, a way I could stop this process from the inside since I was already doing everything I could on the outside. This is where I believe my first ever distinct OCD came in. It started more as an overall obsession, not as discrete thoughts and repetitive compulsions. It wasn't like loads of wild thoughts were entering my mind in the beginning; it was just the intense obsession I had with my hair. I didn't feel like my mind was telling me to do anything beyond what any person would do who was losing more hair than usual. The intrusive thoughts began slowly for me, so I had no idea what or where my thoughts were coming from. They seemed so natural and definitely not intrusive, just an overall icky feeling when my head went to these bad places. This usually happened as I looked down at the hair that had fallen out. I would spend most of my waking moments just staring in the mirror, looking at the texture of my hair, treating it like a specimen to see if it looked thinner. I began counting the number of hairs on my brush. "Is there too much hair on my brush? How much hair used to come out on my brush? How much has this number increased? WHY didn't I used to pay more attention to the hair in my hairbrush in the past so I could decipher?!"

As I would go about my days, I started getting brief thoughts that shot through my head. They would be horrible thoughts about my hair thinning, or I would see images of me losing my hair. I would briefly picture myself with thinning hair and the possibility of being almost bald. I *had* to find a way to quickly erase these images from my head because my heart would literally sink to my stomach at the mere instant they entered my mind. My hair was my best asset. My looks meant everything to me. Learn this now — *OCD will always target what means the most to you.* Losing my hair was like losing my eyes. In fact, I would have rather lost those. You see, I figured that if you're going to be the best at anything, especially the best looking, you must have the entire package. Hair was obviously the key factor in my package. Other than my hair, I didn't feel there was anything about me that was special or set me apart from anyone else. Without my full head of thick, blonde hair, I saw my life crash before my very eyes as a seventeen-year-old girl. I couldn't get it out of my head that I wouldn't be pretty or worth looking at any longer unless my hair remained how it always had been. Rather than allowing myself to think about the bigger picture, how there were solutions if my hair had really been falling out to a point of baldness, I just focused on the intention that I had to stop this process altogether. *NOW.*

As soon as I would get a negative thought related to my hair or see a vision that I was ugly with thinning hair, I would get this innate trigger that I had to do something about it. I couldn't let the thought just be a thought and move on. A thought in passing was as good as it being actual reality to me. *Sound familiar?* It was as though I could cancel the thought if I did whatever my brain told me to do next. The obsessions seemed to be based upon my anxiety level at that time. Heightened anxiety probes for more intense obsessions, which led to my next action: find a way to cancel the thoughts so they cannot come true. These compulsions would vary every single time. They were so random, so miscellaneous. Sometimes I needed to touch something multiple times or go back and do something once more, like walk back and re-shut a door again. Other times I had to walk in a certain path or feel the urge to need to touch something in particular. The compulsions changed based upon my surroundings. The obsessive thoughts followed me everywhere I went and adapted to wherever I was. I started to believe that as I would perform the compulsion, I wasn't losing as much hair — or so I thought. Looking back, I realize what actually happened. In my head, I had cancelled the thought via the compulsion, so I didn't believe it could come true. Since I so intently believed that I had cancelled the thought, I would literally think that I was losing less hair because I performed the compulsion. Even if I didn't fully believe it, I still felt like I was at least *doing something about it*, rather than feeling that constant loss of control.

I didn't ever think my behavior was even abnormal. I was just doing what everyone would do who cared as much as I did, right? I didn't see at the time how bad this thought process could hurt me. I had no idea I was constantly and repetitively feeding the source that caused my pain. My brain triggered my eyes to see what I believed. On a repetition and repeat basis, I continued to perform these compulsions for every obsessive thought I had. Perhaps it started at 20 bad thoughts a day and soon moved to 50. A few weeks later, I was at 100. Pretty soon, I was performing hundreds of compulsions a day. With time, it came to a point where I couldn't make a single decision in my life without "consulting" my OCD at every given second. Except, I didn't know it was OCD. It never even crossed my mind. Since my compulsions were completely miscellaneous and random, when I received an intrusive thought, I immediately did whatever I felt compelled to do in that instant. I eventually let my OCD guide me in what I would wear everyday (I would get bad thoughts about wearing certain colors or types of fabrics/clothing that I desired), and what I would eat at every meal (every time I looked at a menu I would be forced to choose the one thing that I didn't get a bad thought about when I saw the words, regardless of whether I wanted that or not). I let my OCD tell me which lane to drive in, when to wear or not wear my seatbelt, which exits to take (whether they were right or wrong), who to talk with, and who to blatantly ignore — even if they were speaking directly to me. I would get thoughts that I had to physically touch random people with good hair to help stop the hair loss, so I would pretend to bump into them, doing all sorts of weird behaviors that would make me feel better inside. I let my OCD tell me which letters to select on multiple-choice tests, even if I knew they were wrong. For example, if I knew the answer was "B," I pictured thinning hair, so I chose "C," which meant less hair loss. Inside my tortured head, I thought that I couldn't get through the rest of the day or the rest of the test knowing that I would lose too much hair later if I selected a certain letter. It wasn't worth it. I needed to feel that instant calming sensation I knew I would feel if I gave in to the OCD. I began to spell words improperly because as soon as I would get to certain letters, I would get a bad thought and stop mid-word/sentence. My grammar began to suffer immensely because I would have to reverse or skip words and purposely mess up sentences to a point where they made no sense. Every letter, every number meant something that I could use to my benefit or suffering. I didn't allow myself to say many of the brilliant ideas I had in my head on essays, in class, or in everyday life. I would get intrusive thoughts that if I verbalized them, I would lose more hair. The things I could have done in this world if I had allowed myself to just speak my mind without letting the obsessions stop me!

I began to do whatever "it" told me to do regarding every move I made. I referred to my OCD as "it." I will later explain the danger of me isolating and calling my OCD, "it." I let my OCD control everything about me — manipulating everything. There were so many activities and opportunities that I wanted to participate in that I would have bad thoughts about, such as if I went or participated, more hair would fall out. I look back as I write this and realize how much time I really lost during my adolescent years. The opportunities I missed out on and the chances I lost. The friendships and relationships that never lasted because of the OCD. The life I lost.

My hair was, of course, still shedding, but I thought that I was probably helping the process of keeping my hair in longer by obeying these thoughts. *I believed there was a direct connection between the thoughts inside my head and my universal reality.* The logical side of me knew that maybe the compulsions weren't completely stopping my hair loss but that performing them couldn't hurt. I wanted to know I was doing everything humanly possible to stop hair loss, which included externally (physically doing anything I could to stop it such as targeted hair products and vitamins) and internally (obeying and performing my compulsions at every given chance). I ultimately just wanted that part of my stomach that seemed to be directly linked with my OCD brain to "feel" better. Performing the compulsions just made me feel more comfort and relief in the moment. At times I wouldn't even have a specific thought, but I would pass by something and need to touch it or walk in certain familiar pathways, just because it felt right. I couldn't always pinpoint why I felt the need to walk in certain patterns or brush by certain things, but I did it anyways. My safety blanket of OCD was stronger than ever, strengthening with each and every compulsion I performed.

Everyone around me thought that I was absolutely insane. Most people had no idea I had OCD and just saw me do these random and peculiar things. People just thought I was a lunatic. My family also thought I was crazy. They still saw a full head of hair on me. The truth was you couldn't see a huge difference in my hair even though I was shedding as much as I was. I saw exactly what they saw, but I lived in fear that any day now the hair loss would be obvious. It was that very day I was working so hard to prevent by performing my compulsions. I was constantly complaining and crying violently about losing my hair. I thought the only reason that I still had that much hair was because of the compulsions that I was visibly performing. I thought about how I couldn't bear to stick around to see what would happen if I stopped performing the compulsions. I simply thought that I was doing myself a favor. I didn't necessarily think I was going bald, but I knew I was losing more hair than I was comfortable with. That was enough to send me to great lengths. I would complain to my parents every single day about hair loss, and they didn't believe me. They thought I was obsessing about something that wasn't real, but I knew it was. I truly was shedding more hair than I ever had before, and because of that, I was losing my mind. My OCD had latched onto my hair with a grip unlike anything I had ever known.

One day, I took my mom by the hand and dragged her to my room. I made her sit and watch me as I brushed out my hair and began making a huge pile of hair. I hoped by showing her how much hair was coming out, she would finally believe me. She didn't. If she did, she didn't admit it because she didn't want to feed my "obsession with my hair." She sat there and watched me, and even though she saw the huge pile of hair, she still told me it was all in my head. That was what hurt the most — not being believed, not being understood or identified with by those I loved and trusted the most. I knew I was taking this hair loss obsession to the next level and cared more than most people ever would by this point, but the reality that I was losing more hair than normal was very real. So I continued brushing my hair less and less. I continued washing it less and less. Dreadlocks? I dare to say, yes.

Take a moment to envision this very sad reality. I had very long blonde hair. For a girl with my kind of hair to stop brushing and washing it — it was just not socially acceptable. But at that point, I had stopped caring what was socially acceptable or not. I was so focused on saving my hair. Yet I couldn't take the pang in my stomach when I would walk past someone, and they would look at my hair like I was homeless when they were more than aware of who I was and that I was definitely not. I began to train myself to block all my emotions so I couldn't feel how people perceived me. I knew how socially unacceptable I looked and acted when I visibly performed odd compulsions. As I closed off my emotions, I no longer felt excitement or happiness. I numbed myself to focus on nothing but preventing hair loss through my compulsions all day, every day. All I wanted was to be pretty, and as far as I was concerned, being pretty involved hair — and not thin hair. It was more important for me to keep that hair in my head and have a complete rat's nest than to fear the idea that I may keep losing it; and furthermore, that I was doing nothing about it. So the compulsions continued.

It only became worse. I became indifferent to what I looked like, and my emotions continued to deflate. I craved the feeling of relaxation when I performed the compulsions regarding my hair. My stomach was always getting in knots when I got a bad thought. The knots never went away until I somehow got rid of that thought — no matter what it took. Performing whatever compulsion in that moment that shot through my head would calm my stomach. I *needed* to feel the relief. I would look to whatever was around me to help calm my obsessions. I could feel my obsessive thoughts throughout my entire body. My nervous system seemed to be directly linked to my intrusive thoughts. At times, I would momentarily lose my breath when I was hit with a brick wall of obsessions. As soon as I would perform the compulsion, my stomach would calm, and breath would actually start to come back into me.

OCD is fundamentally black and white. Numbers. Colors. Distinctiveness. Literalness. Intenseness. Dedication. Obsession. Most of the time, my OCD "number" was eight. It seemed like the most rounded number in its shape. As soon as I looked at an object, any object I felt had energy, I would stare at it intensely until I saw an image of a full head of hair. I would then touch that object eight times, swallowing on the eighth touch. If I didn't swallow, it didn't count. Oftentimes this varied to stepping on something eight times, staring at something and counting to eight seconds without blinking or swallowing. As soon as I would do these things, my stomach would go back to normal until the next few seconds when I got another bad thought. Throughout my battle with OCD, I can't tell you how many "numbers" and "colors" I have had. Most of the time, they were even numbers because that meant thicker hair. Other times, I needed to use odd numbers because that meant that I was losing less hair. I knew I was doing everything to keep as much hair in my head as possible. I *needed* to know that. I became so depressed; I lost myself as a person. And man, has it been hard to find myself ever since. My OCD led my entire life. Everything I said and did was based on my disorder. Sound familiar?

And so I went. A top-notch girl in her prime, soon to fall off every-one's radar.

Author's Note: If you ever feel like you're losing the **core** of who you really are because of your OCD — stop. Stop right there, right now. Once you lose yourself, it can feel impossible to find yourself again. But I've done it. I have found myself again. So can you. It's a good idea to mindfully take a step back out of the chaos and regroup. Rather than shoving all that OCD dust under the rug, shake that shit and look into it. Rip that mushy rug apart and figure out the essence of your anxieties so that you can be in touch with them instead of shunning them. This is called exposure, and it is key to recovery. Force yourself to do activities and joys that remind you of what you love. Give yourself a moment to smile, a reason to laugh. Always strive to regain self-awareness of who you really are — separate from your OCD. I watched myself losing the core of who I was with every intrusive thought and with every compulsion but never stopped and looked down from 30,000 feet at myself to notice my downward spiral. I didn't analyze how quickly OCD was ruining my life because I was too busy enabling it. I had no self-awareness that my health and my very being were declining. I didn't stop to think my thoughts might not be real. I just kept scratching, searching for anything and everything that would give me reassurance, a moment of peace. I didn't know to look at the forest; I just wanted to focus on getting reassurance from the tree in front of me. If I had known to recognize my abnormal behavior early on, reflected on the changes I was going through, and spoke to someone about them, I would have possibly prevented everything you are about to read.

4
_____

"OBLIVIOUS BLISS"

My parents knew something was very wrong. They noticed all kinds of different behaviors from me, and they eventually caught on to most of my compulsions, although they didn't understand what they were. They started to have a really hard time with the interferences of my compulsions in their house and in their lives. I began to verbally say "No!" out loud after obsessive thoughts shot through my head. Oftentimes this would "replace" my physical compulsions, as I would say "No!" and the obsessive thought would disappear. But I was still performing a mental compulsion. Obviously, my parents would always ask me why I was randomly saying "No!" out of the blue all the time. My poor mother clearly thought I was hearing voices in my head and started to get a bit skeptical, asking me why I was doing that. I would do all kinds of random things around the house — from going out of my way to physically touch or tap random items throughout the rooms as I walked to leaving random pieces of food everywhere. I would leave everything, from crackers to parts of my dinner, all over the house. I would even take food and put it under my pillow. I hardly remember many of these compulsions, but my family oh so kindly reminds me. These compulsions were affecting them and their lives. I did every kind of random act you could imagine, mainly because I just had an inclination to do them, and it made me feel better and calmer in the moment. I would look at just about anything and need to change something about it or at least touch it to make myself feel better. All of these compulsions were typically in response to intrusive thoughts of my hair falling out. I was constantly and consistently looking for a sense of control, and my compulsions were as close as I could get.

My parents began demanding that I stop leaving things all around, messes that I couldn't bring myself to clean up, such obvious randomness. You should know there is nothing random about my family. They are levelheaded, mainstream, very stable people who didn't understand the first thing about mental disorders. They were the epitome of me before I had one. I'm sure they saw some sort of correlation between my obsession with my hair and my weird behaviors. We would have wild arguments, and I would face consequences because I wouldn't stop my interrupting behaviors. Worst of all, my parents would fight over how to handle me. How were they expected to know and agree on how to handle their child who had developed such crazy behavior out of thin air after seventeen years? It began to tear my family apart. I was the center of all conflict in the family, and we had plenty of it. What hurt the most — my family didn't understand me. They couldn't relate and had no idea what was happening to me, what I was going through, or how to properly deal with the situation. And neither did I.

What all of this really came down to was my OCD being firmly based in "magical thinking" paired with miscellaneous compulsions. I truly believed that my compulsions had an effect on my reality and the world around me, as if I could magically alter things from happening. I would get an intrusive thought and have to prevent or make it happen in reality, so I performed my compulsions as a response to these thoughts. Mind you, at this point in time, I still didn't know any of this was OCD. None of us correlated the behaviors to anything in particular. These are all of the realizations that were pieced together years later.

My parents knew they had to do something. They had no idea

what had so significantly changed in my life, or why I was suddenly acting so insane, so unlike myself. Most of all, they knew they were not willing to live with whatever was going on with me. My mother and I were fighting non-stop. It was terrible. My mom found a local marriage and family therapist, hoping it would shed some light on her "troubled daughter." I spent weeks attending regular therapy, and I could not tell you what it was or what she saw in me, but that therapist was the first person who surfaced that I may have OCD. I still have an image engrained in my mind of when she first said it, "I think you may have something called OCD." I didn't know what it was — a disorder?

I was then connected with a testing center to get to the bottom of what was wrong. I took a series of tests one afternoon to test me for OCD and many like disorders. After the data had been analyzed, I was connected with a local psychiatrist who would be able to prescribe me medication. All I remember about going to see the psychiatrist was how awful my experience was. We did not click on any level, but I was put on different anti-depressants over a period of time. I couldn't honestly tell you if any of them worked because I couldn't take them properly. The first reason was because I didn't want to consume anything that could potentially make my hair fall out. I had heard that certain medications could cause some hair loss, and I was not willing to stick around to find out. The second reason was that I would get obsessions right as I would put the pill in my mouth. I often immediately hid the pills or collected them, whatever my mind told me to do to get the bad thought away in the moment. Some days I would be able to take the medication without getting an intrusive thought and some days I just couldn't. Clearly, the path I was on was ineffective and something needed to change. I continued seeing the same marriage and family therapist for a few weeks until my parents realized that although she may have hit the nail on the head with my diagnosis, she was not able to help me fully attack my OCD or even deal with it for that matter.

All the while, I couldn't have cared less about my diagnosis. I felt nothing, absolutely no emotion about it. The truth was my parents cared more about it than I ever did at the time. I went to therapy and through the ropes of testing and medication like a cow in a cattle herd. Just take me where I need to go, and I'll follow. I didn't care that I had a disorder. I didn't care about the results of the testing, and I certainly didn't care about figuring out what I needed to do to get healthy. All I cared about was stopping my hair from falling out. I didn't understand what OCD really even was or how it had anything to do with me. I wasn't connecting the dots that my hair shedding was completely separate from my OCD. My mental disorder just grabbed on to the one thing that mattered most to me and then got as inter-twined and twisted in it as possible, sucking me out of touch and out of my mind. It was only because of my parents that I got up in the morning. They certainly weren't going to let me live the way I was any longer, which meant *I* wasn't going to live that way any longer. So, I went where they told me to go like the emotionless being that I was.

When I reflect back on those days, I wonder why I didn't care enough to even Google the disorder. Nowadays, I would have gone right home and researched it, figured out any correlations, welcomed testing and treatment, and would try to find support groups and a therapist specializing in OCD. It just never occurred to me. In 2009, OCD just didn't seem like a topic that was ever discussed. Mental illness and mental health talk were practically non-existent, and that may have been part the reason I just brushed everything off, delaying my progress. I honestly don't think I ever really associated the two together: I, Kerry Osborn, have a chronic mental disorder called Obsessive-Compulsive Disorder. All I associated was: I, Kerry Osborn am losing too much hair, and I have to stop this process before my hair becomes so thin that I might as well just be invisible. I was just a senior in high school, about to embark into a college experience where I wanted to be noticed. I wanted to be pretty. I wanted guys and girls to do a double take. I put my identity in my appearance. I've never been thought of as a vain person, but somehow at that age, having the satisfaction of being beautiful (which I didn't believe was possible without thick blonde hair) meant almost everything to me.

Through a lot of research — on my parents' end and whoever else

— I was connected with a local psychiatrist who handled both therapy and medication. I continued seeing this doctor very regularly, throughout my senior year of high school. He was a strange, distant, older man, but we got along very well. I would come into his office week after week, telling him my latest problem, my latest fears. He helped me walk through and face them very well, but we never truly attacked my disorder. He was mostly an ear that I needed with sound advice. He didn't provide any reassurance, but he did probe as we both tried to figure me out. My parents would occasionally sit in on therapy with me, and he would find ways to help my parents and myself find insight into my world. One instance that stands out and continues to be a huge motivator in my life was the day he looked right at my mother and said, "There is no telling what this girl could do in this world if she didn't have OCD." To this day, my mother still brings this up. It was one of the most profound statements either of us had ever heard, and I believe that is partly due to the fact that we both know it's true.

Although my parents have been with me throughout everything over the years, my relationship with my brother was severely affected. I looked up to my brother as an idol my entire life. All I ever wanted was to be accepted by him. Unfortunately, my brother went off to college during the thick of me at my worst with OCD, before we had a grip of what was going on with me or how to deal with it. He left during an all-time high of conflict in my family, and I was the root of it. He left seeing his little sister a distraught and confused physical and mental mess. He left with the memory of his little sister tearing his family apart every single day. To this day, I remember finding one of my brother's journals in his room from during that time, and he privately wrote about how he swore my OCD "was the devil's way into our family." Those words have stuck with me for a long time because it brought to light all of the resentment and blame he has had toward me over time. Our relationship struggled for years, as we only saw each other a couple times a year, if that, on holidays after we both went away to college. He never got to see the person I was underneath my OCD. He just continued to see his sick little sister on the few occasions we were together. It has only been recently that our relationship has been able to build again, once I began to lead a normal life amidst my OCD.

My parents began to look into OCD institutions behind my back. My mom researched for weeks and weeks, looking up the finest places around the United States for me to get the help they thought I needed. I later found out my mom was in close communication with one of the highest held standard institutions in OCD treatment — and there was a six-month waiting list. In order to get on the waiting list, it was crucial the patient could fill out a very large document of preliminary paperwork. My mother knew there was no way I would be able to properly fill out the paperwork with my compulsions. The staff let her know that if I was not able to fully fill out the paperwork by myself, I was not ready to be a part of their program. At the time, my mother, of course, was in shock. How could such a prestigious institution not understand filling out the very paperwork was part of my exact problem, the reason I was seeking help? I look back now and realize the exact reasoning for accredited institution's rule. The patient has to be fully ready to attack the OCD and truly *want* to get better before they enter the institution. If they are not willing to take the steps to fill out the very paperwork, they are not ready for true combat against the OCD at the institution provided.

So I continued to live my life throughout my senior year, obsessions and compulsions in tow. The worst days were days when I washed my hair. My entire school day would usually be ruined because every single time I looked down at my clothes, they were covered in hair. Those were the days I wasn't my typical hilarious, fun self. I began to wear my hair up so I couldn't see how much hair I was losing throughout the day. I started to lose my spark in everyone's eyes. My bubbly self would go from being so happy one minute to looking down at my hair loss, and I would immediately deteriorate before their eyes. It was my every conversation, and anyone who hung around me knew my obsession with my hair. One of my friends in my high school pre-calculus class would tell me almost every day my hair was not falling out. He had heard me complain one too many times. One specific morning when I had washed my hair, I lifted it up above my sweatshirt and showed him all of the blonde hairs stuck to my back and my chair. He looked right at it and said, "Maybe your hair really is falling out."

I couldn't pull myself together. I lived each and every day with a sunken heart, searching for anything and everything that could help relieve my pain. My OCD seemed to be the only reassurance I had in my life, the only thing I could grasp onto with any connection in the world. The truth was, I didn't want to live if my life was going to be like it was during that time. I wanted an out from the suffering. Amidst everything going on in my head and soul, I didn't see how I could keep facing life at the rate I was going. It was more than just my hair at that point. I had lost who I was. The bottom line was that I felt trapped. I felt trapped in my body, and I was suffocating under the control. I remember a night I was sitting on my bed, crying, listening to the song, "Come On Get Higher" by Matt Nathanson. The lyrics that resonated with me were: "I miss the sound of your voice," because I missed the sound of my old voice. "If I could tell you what's next," because I desperately wanted to know what would be next, if times would get better. "Make you believe, make you forget," because I so deeply wanted to believe these times were over, and I would make it out of this phase. And, "I see angels and devils and God when he calls," because maybe, just maybe God was calling me...home. That night, right then and there, I Googled different ways to commit suicide. I knew I wouldn't be able to inflict any pain on myself, so I wasn't able to take it seriously. It was a matter of thought that I would be away from this pain. I have often thought that same thing. What I would give to be out of this body and out of the momentary pain of OCD. It was only a year or two ago when I was going through a very, very hard time which will be discussed in the second half of the book, that my mom spoke words I never knew of at this time in my life. She was worried about me being emotionally unstable and accidentally shouted how she used to sit (and sometimes sleep) outside my bedroom door at nights my senior year because she was so worried. She knew a part of me didn't want to live anymore, and she didn't trust me. I had absolutely *no* idea she ever did that. As I've said, much of this time period I have blacked out. My parents struggled so much with how to handle me and how to help me. My dad started asking me if I wanted to drive to LA on Saturdays and have lunch and walk around. LA is a two-hour drive one way from my hometown, and my dad and I made this a bit of a tradition during some of my darkest times. He knew how much I loved to be in the ambiance of celebrities and the lifestyles they lived. So he would take me to all the hottest LA brunch places, and I would just be in awe of everything around me. This is when my love for fashion started budding. My dad helped me find designer thrift shops and really cool places to shop in LA and would get me a few new goodies every time. I started to put a lot of effort into the way I dressed and incorporated fashion risks into my life as a subconscious distraction from my hair. I think a part of me thought if people were staring at killer outfits, they wouldn't notice my hair. Wrong. Looking back, it was times like this with my dad that kept me going. Little things to look forward to on the weekends, to be different and experience a new world helped me come out of my own, even if it was only for a few hours. To be honest with you, if it wasn't for my parents and the thought of what it would do to them, I don't know if I would be here to write this book that I pray resonates with you.

The year went on, and it became time for me to get serious about college. There wasn't a doubt in my mind that I was still going to college, right on track with the rest of my class. If I was going to stick around, I needed to keep up with everyone else my age. I didn't care if I was on my deathbed; no one was going to stop me from staying on my academic track. Although I could tell everyone around me was silently questioning if I should take such a leap at such an unhealthy time, I paid no mind. *As if I was able to go to college with my hair looking like Chewbacca straight out of Ace Ventura's jungle.* None of us had any idea that the severity of OCD I had at the time was nothing compared to the severity it would become in the following year. Regardless, I was on track, applying and anxiously awaiting my acceptances. I ended up deciding to attend Concordia University of Irvine, California, about three hours from my hometown. My doctor knew if I was going to go full force with going away to school, dramatic measures needed to be taken. He helped my parents and I set up everything we needed with the schools' Disability & Services Center and went as far as to help me get my own dorm room. I remember sitting across from him one day when he made the first call to the University, telling them my situation, and why I simply could not live in the same room as another person. I took all of the tests and precautions I needed to in order to get the help I would need in school. I was able to get my own dorm room, a student note taker, and was authorized to take all of my exams in a private room, free of further distractions. He also helped me find a local therapist near my school. Since the mediation route hadn't really worked for me (also due to my inability to take it), I no longer was on medication, and I was happy to continue my therapy without it. My plan was to go off to school like I was no different from anyone else. I think that may have been due to the fact that I didn't really believe I was all that different.

But I *was* different. I was nowhere near healthy enough to be on my own, especially at a time when grades, education, adolescence, and peers were so important. I was at a crucial growing and developing age, and I should have stopped my world to get the help I needed to attack my OCD. But to be honest, I didn't know attacking OCD was truly an option at the time. I had never been introduced to or taught a proper approach to attack my OCD. I didn't know there were ways to live a better quality of life through the right kinds of therapy. I had only ever had therapists probe and ask me questions, never truly getting to the bottom of how they can help me manage the OCD. I didn't see a real reason to not keep on track with my life and education. I thought as long as I was scheduled to attend weekly therapy, I was doing my best. Wrong.

Author's Note: Muddling through the initial onset of OCD and how to navigate through it alone is incredibly difficult. You can't actually address your OCD head on if you haven't even wrapped your head around it. Don't be afraid to go through the process of finding the right therapy for you. You can't keep living this way. It only gets worse, my friend. Finding the right therapist, psychiatrist, and supportive team around you can be discouraging at times, but it can most certainly be done. I would say if it feels right, then you're in the right place. But since you most likely have OCD, I can't say that because everything that "feels" right is typically wrong. The point is, getting clinically diagnosed with OCD and finding the team you will move on to fight with is very important. Thankfully, there are resources now such as the International OCD Foundation website which can provide therapists that specialize in OCD in your area immediately. You can always take an assessment and have a consultation with as many therapists as you need until you feel comfortable moving forward with the uncomfortable. The earlier you get the help you need, and furthermore for that matter, *trust* the help you have, the sooner you will get to wrapping your head around the world you and I unfortunately are living in — and what we can do about it.

5

"HER"

After a long summer of allowing my hair to become dreadlocks, I was only a few weeks away from stepping foot onto my new college campus. The knots in my hair were the worst underneath, in the back of my head. I had somehow concocted a way of making the first few layers of my hair cover the knots, while underneath was an Amy Winehouse beehive. Seriously, a beehive is a perfect description of what it looked like. The knots had tangled into one massive knot at the lower half of the back of my head, and I just let it get bigger over time. Everyday it got worse, and it was to a point where there was no untangling it. It was out of control. I was still losing hair, but it was getting caught in the knot. So I deceived myself into thinking it wasn't falling out as much. I never let myself see the back of my head. I tried to stay focused on the front (as if it was any better). As long as the front looked how I liked it, I thought I was good to go. Judge me — I'm used to it.

Although my hair was clearly not brushed and had an obviously different texture when I entered college, I will still in a stage where I was considered pretty. Yes, something was different about my hair, but overall, I still looked like a normal girl as long as I wasn't performing visible compulsions. My makeup was always done, and I dressed up every day. I was convinced that even though my hair was in the state it was, it was still more appealing than if I had thin hair from having to cut my knots out and brush it out. I didn't think I was pretty or anything worth looking at without all that hair. I was a walking illusion. I went about my new college campus and made a few initial friends and somehow got the attention of a couple boys — one of which I started "dating." Except it wasn't an actual relationship. We didn't communicate well, and that was due to the one thing I never told him about — my OCD. It was a compulsion to NOT tell him I had OCD. I was very good at covering up any compulsions around him, but there were certain aspects he and his friends questioned about me that I couldn't explain. There was no doubt about it. Something was very off about me, and they knew it. I was unable to hold a normal relationship. I wasn't even in touch enough to have a relationship with myself. I just moved through life and didn't reflect or question anything other than the obsession and compulsion to perform right in front of me. A couple of weeks later he called me and let me know it was no longer working for him. Shocker.

I continued on a downhill spiral for the rest of the year. My hair was just impossible to deal with. I couldn't hide the knots underneath anymore. My hair became so off-putting. People looked at me funny at first, but after a while, they looked at me like I was a downright homeless looking freak. I eventually lost the few friends I had made because they believed I was actually a freak of nature and something was clearly wrong with me. Looks and reputation in college were seemingly everything. For a girl like me, who based the majority of my happiness on my physical appearance, there was almost no way out. With OCD, right as you think there is no way out, your OCD creeps back in to try and save the day. Right when you feel complete loss of control in your obsessions, your compulsions give you that control. Turns out the compulsions may have quite often "saved the day" of momentary pain, but they ended up ruining my life.

I started performing compulsions that I thought could change my appearance. I would get an obsession as I walked by someone, and if I performed the right momentary compulsion, I thought to a certain extent they would see me with normal hair. I actually started getting some thoughts that people could see me differently than how I really looked if I performed my compulsions correctly. I thought that if I would step in certain places and swallow at the same time that people would see me as a normal, pretty girl. As if I could change their vision! Magical OCD thinking at its finest. Sometimes I would even look in the mirror and see less tangled hair, and I thought it was because I combined "energy" with my steps and was able to change my reality. After a while, I would start to see certain places to step, and I would get a thought that if I stepped there, I would somehow, miraculously and magically, gain the appearance of more hair. So I tried it — stepping in certain places that would "help me gain more hair." I actually would pull on my hair and none would come out after my steps. I would look in the mirror, and my eyes actually saw more hair. I was sold. I was so convinced that the way that I walked would change my hair loss, and in turn, give me the "dream hair" that I always wanted. In my eyes, it was worth a try. Eventually, I thought I didn't need any hair care regimen at all and just relied on my compulsions to take care of it.

Energy. This was when I started to confuse the power of the universe with my OCD. This is where my magical thinking OCD really found its home base. I really believed that if I stepped in certain places that felt energy-filled, I was able to actually take it from the ground into my body. I would get thoughts that this universal force was going to make me prettier, make my hair stop falling out, live a better life, become more successful, etc. By performing the compulsion of stepping in a certain place, at a certain time, then swallowing, I was accepting the energy the universe was giving me in that moment. I thought I could control my positive energy and surroundings by using my OCD in conjunction with this power.

My OCD got wrapped up in similar ideals as the book, "The Secret," and I thought my compulsions were granting me things I couldn't grant myself. This was scary first and foremost because I am a Christian, but also scary because my OCD had intertwined into an area I was truly afraid was real. I feared if I didn't give into these obsessions by performing my compulsions, I was missing out on incredible opportunity from the universe. The kind of energies celebrities, very successful people, and believers of "The Secret," were subjected to. Because I have OCD, I take things I hear or read that have a very fine line and obsessively misconstrue them. Things like this area are very fuzzy to me because of the infamous OCD thought, "What if?" I questioned if I could use the energy of the universe without my OCD, *or if I needed* my OCD to be able to receive certain blessings or opportunities in life. I didn't realize you could have positive energy and good thoughts without controlling everything with OCD. There was a very fine line between OCD, energies, and magical thinking to me. And quite frankly, it's a very tricky and scary territory if your OCD infuses into your thinking pattern. It's a fine line that I honestly still struggle with and discuss with my therapist at times. During these times, I have to bring myself back to the separation of OCD from everything else. I don't mean magical in a weird and creepy way. I'm a very smart girl with good common sense, and I don't believe in things that aren't tangible. But OCD has a way of finding thin cracks of potential questions throughout areas I believed I was uncertain in. There is a constant battle of my own logic versus my illogic. I have to continuously remember my OCD will do everything in its power to creep in on anything I am fearful of or skeptical about. Damn you, OCD. Damn YOU.

I knew that at this point my hair would never come out of the knots I had allowed to form. I had been desperate to not touch my hair, and it showed. It either would keep getting worse, or I would have to get it all shaved off, neither of which were an option in my book. But the thought of having somebody touch, let alone brush through my hair, was outlandish to me. I would have rather died, literally. That's how utterly important this obsession was in my catastrophized mind. I honestly figured since that hair was on a beautiful girl with a killer body, people might overlook the hair issue. WRONG. People began avoiding me like I was a homeless man about to interrogate them for their bank account number. For somebody that was used to positive attention for years, I just couldn't take this. I couldn't look at myself in the mirror. My gut-wrenching compulsions seemed to become worse by the hour. OCD was affecting how I talked, the way that I was walking, and the number of times that I blinked. My OCD was still deeply affecting the foods I ate and didn't eat, or how much I could eat of the things I wanted to. Regardless, I typically wasn't eating enough. I was already a rail, so this was obviously an issue. I also had no friends to go eat with in the school cafeteria, and at the end of the day, I still had too much pride to go alone. I would try to meet new people just so I had someone to go and eat with, so I wouldn't have to sit alone. These were all short lived.

My walking rituals proved the biggest and most obvious problem, other than the appearance of my hair. People didn't know about the "little things" such as how my OCD controlled my deciding what to wear or how I ordered my food, but boy, could they see me walk. I would stare right at the ground everywhere that I walked, looking to step in all the "right" places that would prevent my obsession from coming true. I hopped around like the damn Easter bunny avoiding certain cracks and ridges and pieces of gum stuck on the ground. As much as I knew I was walking ridiculously, it still killed me when people would constantly stare at me, whisper, and laugh. Two years before that, I would have seriously done the exact same thing they had. They had no idea what I was going through or what was wrong with me. <u>But it meant more to me to perform the compulsions and feel the release of the mental pressure and stomach knots for that instant than to care what other people thought about me.</u> Somehow, I would feel much better after not stepping on certain cracks or special places. I would get this sense of momentary peace that would last up until...the very next step.

My emotional numbness became even greater. I couldn't face what I knew they were saying about me. Adolescent college kids can be so cruel, such bullies. They have no idea what you're battling, and what's worse, they just don't care. I would just mentally numb any sadness I felt, especially when I knew people were talking about me as I walked by or saw my hair. I began to function at the most minimalistic emotional state as humanly possible. I was so un-emotional I became downright rude. I was rude to practically everyone and anyone on my campus because I never knew who made fun of me and who didn't. It seemed like everyone was against me in that small, private university. I stayed clear of as many people as I could. I walked to class and back to my dorm room. I had no business with anyone, and no one had any business with me. I would self-deteriorate like a stick of melting butter as soon as I walked out of my dorm into public. When someone would say a simple "Hi" to me, I would just dismiss them and walk away, knowing they were being facetious. I thought if I was a bitch, it would prove that I still was with it and that people wouldn't mess with me. In reality, all it did was make people talk even more, so I was now the homeless *bitch*, instead of the homeless *freak*. Being rude was my defense mechanism, and it has taken me years to realize my effect on people. I spent my days practically glaring at anybody that had legs. I was so hurt by their words and their darting glances. My defense was 24/7 bitch mode, if it hadn't been before. I gave practically everyone who didn't already hate me, well, reason to hate me.

There were times where I would get flashbacks to what I used to look like before I was so sick and how I desperately longed to look and feel that normal again. That period of time felt like another lifetime — yet it was only two years prior. I was still somewhat logical. I knew that I had all the goods underneath. I thought if my hair would stop falling out and the knots were untangled and were taken care of, I would be back to my old self. I believed fixing my hair would be the answer to all of my problems. I kept a senior picture of myself from high school before the disorder really set in beside my bed. I remember crying, looking at that picture on countless nights. I wondered if I would ever get back to "her" in this lifetime. She seemed so beautiful — so peaceful. I didn't identify with her any longer. It was like I was looking at a random girl I so desperately wanted to look like. When people would walk into my room, almost everyone squeezed in a comment with a smirk that I slept next to a picture of myself. Little did they know that this picture was what kept me going. Knowing who I once was and how I just wanted to be "her" again. I always referred to the girl in the picture as "her." To everyone, including myself. I couldn't fathom that I was even still the same girl. I looked in the mirror at a completely different person. I was ashamed and shocked that I could still be the girl in the photograph. She had everything going for her, and I was so far gone. My goal became to just become "her" again. Fast-forward eight years — that very same photograph still sits by me today. "Her" is now "Me."

Author's Note: Most people aspire to be like a famous icon, a trailblazer, or celebrity who has inspired them in some way. I sat on my bed every night just aspiring to be myself again. My old self was enough for me. I became my own inspiration. The truth is, although I feel more like "her" today than I ever did during these rough times, I am so much better off now than she ever was. Today, I have surpassed every expectation, mentally and physically, that I had of that sweet 18–year-old girl and beyond. That girl has been challenged in ways many cannot understand, and she had to fight to live, fight to breathe, and fight to feel peace again. Bottom line? You need to set yourself as your own inspiration — today. You should aspire to be yourself in every way, just without the constant demand of OCD. You can't be your best self while allowing the OCD to control you when you know there are ways to get help and manage it. I still feel the demand of OCD every day, but I also feel a sense of control I never felt when I was so sick. A sense of control over my mind, an area I used to cower away from. All of this is because I put up the fight I will shortly share with you. Try to remember a time in your life when you were happiest, when your OCD didn't feel like it owned every cell in your body. I hope you can remember back to a time like this. Use a healthy YOU as your icon because this disorder has certainly made you a trailblazer if I ever saw one. *I owed it to HER to see life on the other side of this disorder — and you owe it to YOU.*

6

"ALIVE"

The one thing I did know for sure, if I just got my hair back to normal, I would be able to start feeling somewhat attractive again. It was no longer just about my hair falling out; it was more so about wanting my hair to be thicker. The less I touched my hair, the better I felt, and the more I thought my hair had a chance at being thick. I didn't even own a hairbrush at this point. I only liked the consistency of my hair about four days after I washed it, because only then did it feel thicker. It was unsanitary and something needed to be done. Given the state of it, there was no way I could untangle it myself. I vividly remember any moments I wasn't getting pounded with obsessive thoughts, I would be staring at pretty girls and gawking at their hair. I would stare at their hair, analyzing it, depicting it, and trying to figure out how I could get mine to look like theirs. I constantly wondered why their hair in general looked so effortless on them and took note how they didn't even seem to care how lucky they were. Oftentimes, given that I was staring at these girls like I was their jungle-haired stalker, they would notice. I would either look away quickly or quickly ask them a question or compliment their hair. I remember a time when I complimented a girl's hair in my class and asked her how she styled it to look so thick. After she answered me, I'll never forget standing in the hallway outside our classroom auditorium and her saying, "What about you? Your hair has an...um...interesting texture to it? How do you style it?" I came up with some ridiculous comb teasing story when in reality I should I have just said, "Oh you know, the good ole' no wash, no brush, step in front of an industrial powered fan and let it get alllllllll nice and tangled, and then take a weed whacker to it and just stop halfway through." If only I had the confidence to use my comedic relief out loud at the time.

I had extended family less than an hour away from my campus, and I would go over to their home on weekends because I was desperately lonely at school. I would sit on the floor of my cousin's room on Saturday nights and beg her to try and untangle my hair. I trusted her to touch it because she was so gentle, and I was able to watch what she was doing the whole time in the mirror. Bless her heart, she would sit there and pick and prod at it but never got anywhere. I was so desperate. Desperate to be and look like myself again. I knew I needed a professional but finding a hairstylist who was willing to sit for hours and untangle my practical dreadlocks was nearly impossible. I knew deep down they would take one look at me and tell me we needed to cut almost up to my scalp. I remember thinking to myself every single day that I would pay every single penny in my bank account, regardless of the cost, if someone could untangle my hair without cutting it off.

My extended family used a hairstylist in the area that they had been working with for years. I had always heard about what a wonderful woman and hairstylist she was. I knew if I was going to even attempt going to a hairdresser, she would be the one. It was just about getting the nerve to call her, to even address the embarrassing situation out loud. After a few more weeks of living in pure insanity — I did it. I made the phone call, briefly and lightly explaining my situation. The appointment was set.

For the next two weeks before the appointment, I lived in complete hell. Every single obsession went into double-time and revolved around the upcoming hair appointment. Intrusive thoughts would shoot through my brain like shooting stars, coming and going so quickly, and I had to keep up. "If I step here or there, I will have to shave off tons of hair. If I touch this or that and swallow at the same time, she will have magic in her fingers, and my hair will become untangled without cutting anything out." I obeyed every single obsession during the waiting period and was incessantly devoted to each compulsion. This appointment meant the entire world to me, and if I came out on the other side of it with short hair or hardly any hair left, my perspective and vision of life would be over as I knew it. I couldn't fathom cutting off my hair because I would lose anything and everything left about me that was somewhat pretty. A wig and extensions were not an option. I needed to keep my own hair. I was obsessed to a point where my life literally depended on it.

Finally, the day came. I had called my mother and begged her to drive down for moral support. No one actually had any idea how incredibly crucial this appointment was for me. I had my mom sit in the sitting room of the salon for the entire appointment. I hadn't been inside a salon for what seemed like years. Ahhh, the smell of beauty that had become a faint memory. I remember taking in the smells of the salon, the faintly familiar smells I used to love. I sat down and begged and pleaded with my hairdresser. I explained my desperation to her, how important it was to me to get my hair completely untangled. I went as far as telling her these exact words, "You have the ability to save a life today." I'm sure she thought I was joking — but I wasn't.

Three straight, solid hours. She worked. She pulled. She prodded. She cut little, impossible pieces. I cringed for three hours, to the point where my neck muscles were completely in spasm. No hairdresser in the world would sit down and untangle dreadlocks. But she did. I remember seeing her through the mirror make a face at another stylist halfway through. A face that screamed, "NO AMOUNT OF MONEY IN THE WORLD IS WORTH THIS." I died inside. I kept sitting there, with nothing to say. I was mortified. I felt so bad for her, but I was so angry at the same time that she was making faces at other people that screamed, "Help me! Why did I agree to this? This girl is nuts."

Hours later, after I had secretly obeyed every single obsession and performed every single compulsion, she was able to fully and completely brush my hair, just enough for me to make it out of there alive. ALIVE.

On the outside, I was a new woman, or so I thought. I hadn't felt that light in as long as I could remember. I felt like I weighed two pounds in that final moment. I ran over to my mom and said verbatim, "I'M BAAAACK!" My mom's jaw dropped. She couldn't believe it was possible to get the knots out. I didn't get any more obsessions in the salon that day. I was floating. Man, that feeling felt like years, even though it had only been a few minutes. I mean, *hello*, she had just saved my life. I think I'll spare you the plan that I had if she didn't. I made sure that I told her that, too. I didn't want to die. I had every reason to live. I could accomplish anything in the world at this rate, and I was well aware of it.

Everybody in my life thought that as soon as I had my hair brushed out, I wouldn't have anything to obsess about, myself included. My biggest obsession was my hair, really just about the only recurring stagnant obsession I had ever had up until that point. I truly wondered what it was that I would have to obsess about going forward. I thought I was done with OCD, and OCD was done with me. I thought maybe my OCD would clear up all of sudden, and I would get a miraculous break at the life I had been tortuously living.

Except doubt began to creep in... *What if* the OCD had been the key factor in what got me through the appointment without shaving my head? I couldn't help but believe my dedication to my compulsions had paid off. I truly believed that by performing all of my compulsions, I had helped the energy and magic in her hands have the ability to brush through my hair. This mentality, of course, made my belief in the power of my compulsions and the energy of OCD that much stronger.

As soon as I walked outside the salon, the obsessions started again, literally in the parking lot. My thoughts told me that the reason that I still had hair was because the compulsions had worked. I was hooked. And almost every ounce of me believed that the reason that all my hair wasn't chopped off was because of my compliance with the energy and my compulsions. I thought there was just NO way that she could have done that on her own. You had to see it to believe it. Over the next few months, my compulsions started revolving around everything and anything that I had even a remote amount of anxiety over: if I stepped here I would get an A on my next exam; if I stepped there, a cute guy would hit on me; if I didn't step here, I would get into a car accident. OCD cut me no breaks. The thoughts just shot in and out of my head, out of nowhere. They were so quick, so strong, so powerful. I was defenseless, still at my worst point, second-guessing my every move in accordance with my OCD.

Author's Note: I have often wished so much that I could go back to that moment when I first finished my hair appointment and felt light as air. No bad thoughts. Just normal brain waves. I hadn't felt that way in so long. I remember thinking that this must be how "normal" people must feel all the time. I realized this was how I must have felt all the time before the OCD set in for the worse. I couldn't remember what that felt like. To just...have thoughts come and go so freely with no heart-stopping moments. If you ever get a moment like that, an overwhelming feeling of satisfaction or hope, bask in it. Roll in that shit, cover yourself with the freeing thoughts, and don't let them stop until you cannot remain on your high anymore. These peaceful moments are few and far between with OCD. Sometimes I wake up in the morning and have just a few blissful seconds before I remember my bad thoughts, current obsessions, and current fears that I will need to face that day. Those few seconds have at times been the best part of my day.

7

"THE BULLIES BROKE ME"

I came back to school with my hair brushed out and all kinds of people came out of the woods to talk to me. I was the talk of the school yet again *because I looked normal?* Girls who I had classes with and never spoke to came up to me to slyly compliment me and try to dig to find out what had caused the sudden change. They didn't know I had OCD. They just thought I was a whack job, but suddenly, they were keenly interested in my newfound appearance. "Kerry, your hair looks so...different...so nice." "Kerry, what did you do to your hair... did you thin it out?" *Thin it out?* I literally cringed when someone asked me that, targeting my worst fear. "No, I did not 'thin it out,' you bitch. I brushed out my hair since I had dreadlocks, which you were clearly aware of, capisce?" was all that went through my head in response.

I do have to say, I looked a lot different, so...normal. My hair wasn't falling out as much, but all I could think about was how badly I wanted thicker hair. The truth is my hair *was* thin compared to the dreadlocks I had. So my obsessions began surrounding around getting thicker hair, and whenever I went through phases where I thought I was losing more hair than normal, the obsessions went back to surrounding around losing less hair. Yes, the knots were gone,

43

but I still wasn't able to thoroughly brush or wash my hair. Losing even one strand would make my heart sink because it was one less hair to help with gaining the desired thickness. Every strand counted. I remember back to the times when I was losing my hair at my worst, I used to comfort myself by thinking that as soon as I stopped losing hair, I could focus on gaining the thickness back. I just needed it to stop falling out first. Now I was at a point where I was losing a normal amount of hair again, and I just needed to grow the desired thickness back. But I was still just as obsessed. If it wasn't one thing it was another. My hair continued to go through periods where it would fall out more than normal, depending on the weather and other factors, and other periods where it wouldn't fall out, and I could just focus on gaining thickness.

The reality was, I was in a downward OCD spiral. Although my main obsessions targeted my hair first and foremost, my OCD continued to revolve around whatever my daily anxieties were. To the world around me, as much as they may have seen a brief improvement in my appearance, it was still very obvious I had problems. No one could pinpoint exactly what that problem was, but everyone wondered. I would mysteriously leave the classroom during every quiz or exam. Anything that I could do in the Disability Services Center, I did. Students saw that I clearly had a disability, and that's putting it lightly.

The truth is, I began to be bullied just like something you would see in the movies, both before and after I had my short-lived life changing hair appointment. I really was that girl that walked by and everybody whispered and stared. I was truly the laughingstock, outcast of my University, and just two years before in high school, I had been the life of any party.

I'll never forget the time when I walked back to my dorm room, and there was a used blonde hairbrush taped to my dorm room door. My oh so caring peers were clearly trying to tell me I should learn how to use a brush. My heart sank, like an elevator that was falling through thin air. I grabbed it and ran inside before anybody else could see this awful moment. But it was too late. All I could do was numb myself. I didn't let myself dwell on any of the details, such as how long it had been there, who must have walked by and seen it, etc. I put on my armor and completely blocked off all the pain I felt in that moment, except for trying to figure out which group of people it must have been. A few weeks later, the same message was obvious yet again when somebody put a picture of a really bushy looking squirrel on my door, showing me what I really looked like to the world. I got the message — thanks. People would write things on my car with ink that I could barely wash off, even after paying for car washes. I would try and wash the obscene words and pictures off myself, but I had to do so in the school parking lot where everyone could see. Mortified, I would jump in my car and rush to the closest hand car wash, only to still need the men to help me use certain solvents to hand scrape and scrub everything off the car wash didn't take off.

Someone coined a nickname for me that I later learned I was strictly known by — "Crazy Kerry." How fitting. The first time I heard someone refer to me as "Crazy Kerry," they said it jokingly as my friend. They thought I knew that was my nickname. I laughed it off and pretended like it was nothing. I didn't know it was an actual "thing." I then realized it was a school wide term used for me and had been since I began college. That's when it began to penetrate into me that I wasn't known as my name, Kerry Osborn, to anyone except my professors. Shoot, maybe even they got word. As much as it hurts in the center of my heart to know that's what they all called me — I get it. To them, I was absolutely crazy. They didn't know about the OCD. Even if they did, I doubt it would have made a difference because everyone has a stigma of OCD, and I was clearly the opposite of it. People would have never believed all that was wrong with me was a severe case of OCD. They knew something wasn't right and that was enough for them to justify me as the school joke. My appearance was so obviously abnormal. Because of the state of my hair, I looked like I didn't take care of myself, no matter how high I held my head or how many pretty clothes I put on to distract them. They saw a screwed-up girl who was constantly walking around doing random, unexplainable behaviors. Once people saw me unknowingly performing these visible compulsions, it was enough for them to think I was possessed, schizophrenic, or just unexplainably crazy. To be honest, I don't know what exactly they all thought was specifically wrong with me, but it was enough for me to go through years of being nothing more than "Crazy Kerry." I could always tell certain people wondered about me. They looked on at me in awe, and I could see behind their eyes they knew there was more to me than what met the eye. Then there were the others who didn't care to know what was wrong with me. I was crazy, and that's all they needed to know. To them, I was some chick that was the exact kind that I probably would have made fun of at one point back when I was so healthy, young, and immature. What goes around finds its way back. I know that now. But it doesn't make things any easier.

Granted, my relationship with my suitemate shortly became about as good as my relationship with Angelina Jolie. When we first started school, she and I got along great. She too had her own dorm room. We made common ground and ate our meals together. Until she and her friends realized something was very wrong with me, and whatever it was, it had no place in their world. We stopped speaking only a few weeks into school. Unfortunately, my OCD affected her as well because we shared a bathroom. I had bought a beautiful new bed quilt before school, and I honestly don't think it was ever once put properly on my bed. It was a compulsion to put it in our common bathroom right on the floor in the pathway. Yep — as in you had to step over it or on it to walk across the bathroom. It absolutely killed me that I did this, but my obsessions with that were very strong. I knew she thought I was a nutcase. I would often-times be in my room, and I would hear her friends go into the bath-room and talk and laugh about the quilt being in there on the floor. What freak would leave their bed comforter on the dirty bathroom floor? Obviously, it was the weirdest thing, and I don't blame them for gawking at it. One day, I came back to my dorm room, and my suitemate had opened my side of the door and put it back in my room. I was mortified, but that just wasn't enough to stop me from continuing to perform whatever compulsions I needed to. I would spend nights just listening to her and all her friends across the bathroom in her room laughing, singing, talking — the sounds of life — of *living* life. Here I was, five feet away on the other side of the door, sitting on the floor crying because it was a compulsion to not sit on my bed, holding my computer but only "allowed" to click a few things on it. I lived in a room full of lasers, and every time I went to move, touch something, play music, *do anything I wanted* — I stopped. My OCD wouldn't allow it. I would try to think of new things I could do to stop the boredom and loneliness of isolation, and every time I got a new idea, I was quickly stopped by my OCD. The constant obsessions overcame my body over anything and everything. "Maybe I'll go get ice cream." Nope, you won't be doing that. "Maybe I'll just work on my essay, since I have nothing better to do." I'd get one word successfully written before my OCD had me stop right there and put the computer down. "Maybe I'll try and clean up some of my room." I would so much as reach for an empty can and have to set it back down. I literally couldn't move to do anything without getting intense obsessions. I was truly and utterly consumed and paralyzed with severe OCD. I was boxed inside of a suffocating world, and I honestly didn't know if I was ever going to get out. I was a self-imposed prisoner in a 100 square foot dorm room. No one knows what I truly went through in that room of isolation and obsession. There aren't words to suffice the true extent.

I would pick up my phone to call my parents only to be stopped in my tracks by obsessive thoughts of what would happen if I called them. I often wouldn't talk to my parents for days, ignoring their calls and not calling them just because of the intrusive thoughts I would get as I picked up the phone. I highly regret the memory of not staying close in contact with my parents that first year of college. It only made me worse. To think of what they must have thought, the worries they must have had. I remember being able to pick up my phone one day and hearing my sweet daddy on the other end say, "Kerry, are you alright? You never call us anymore. You never stay in touch. I miss my baby girl." How was I to even explain? I was allowing my OCD to push me as far away as possible from the only two people who actually cared enough to call me. Heartbreaking.

The pain — just get me away from the pain. I don't know how much more pain I could have felt — the kind that burrows into your soul. Being isolated and feeling like you are the only person on the planet Earth is the most defeating and desolate feeling in the world. At the time, I didn't know any better. I didn't know how to combat my OCD. I thought it was my reality and would be forever. I had no hope, which was the only thing that had ever kept me going in life up until that point.

My schoolwork — the one thing I was actually good at — began to take a toll. Since I couldn't write properly or use certain letters due to the obsessions, I couldn't take notes and therefore didn't remember the material. I had note takers from the Disability Center, but I often couldn't get through reading a paragraph without having a compulsion to stop reading. I couldn't read the chapters of the textbooks because I would get a sentence in and have a compulsion to stop. I couldn't write good essays or fill out paperwork correctly, so my grades just went down. My teachers would make comments in red regarding my grammar on my papers, as if I was writing like a twelve-year-old. I guess I was. It was mortifying, especially because I knew better. I was very smart and full of ideas but couldn't get them across without my OCD stopping my every move. I stopped caring, yet again. As a result, those freshman year grades were affecting my cumulative GPA, which could never be made up no matter how much healthier I became in the years to come before graduation.

One of the most humiliating days I can remember was a day when I was in my Cultural Anthropology class that Freshman year. I was sitting in the far back by myself in a large auditorium. There was one particular group who I knew made fun of me the most, and I was already aware they had field days mimicking my compulsions. I assume they were the group who left the hairbrush and picture of a squirrel on my dorm room door. Most of them happened to be in this same class as me. On this particular day, I distinctly remember how bad I looked. My hair was up in a bun, and it hadn't been washed in days. It sure looked like it. I'm sure I had my resting bitch face on whenever I looked the way of that group because my instincts knew how much they made fun of me. All of sudden one of the guys in the group looked back at me and yelled very loudly, "HEY, WHY DON'T YOU GO AND WASH YOUR HAIR FOR ONCE?" Everyone in the auditorium went dead silent. He just said out loud what everyone was thinking. I honestly can't remember what exactly I said or did to provoke him to yell the statement at me because I actually blacked out from embarrassment. I assume I noticed them all staring and laughing and said something like, "Turn around!" I can see myself saying something to that effect. All I can truly remember is losing any feeling in my body and looking straight down because my face said it all. I was shattered into a million pieces, and not even the finest artist in the world could put me back together.

The truth — that I have only just been able to put into words so many years later — is this: everywhere I walked on that private, Christian University campus, I left a trail of small, shattered pieces of my heart that have left scars I carry with me to this day. Every nasty look or comment, every act of disgrace towards me, every time someone uttered, "Here comes Crazy Kerry," a little piece of shattered glass that used to be heart broke off and fell to the ground. My broken soul still is embedded in that University to this day. And that is where it will stay.

Quite a while into my school career, I walked to my car from my room on campus one evening, and as soon as I walked up to it, I knew something was wrong. Someone had taken a bundle of firewood and jarred it underneath one side of my car. My front end was even slightly lifted. It made absolutely zero sense. Why would anyone take the time to cause damage by shoving firewood under my car so it couldn't move? Was someone trying to get me to stay put? My friend at the time sat on the ground with me and helped me push up the car slightly so we could remove all the firewood. It was a hard job. Afterwards, as I stared down at the scratches, I couldn't figure out why someone would do this. It was beyond just a bully move; there was no sense to it. In fact, it looked like a job that was unfinished. As though mid-procedure, someone had been caught. Little did I know this senseless act was only the beginning of a very serious act soon to come.

Two days later, I was in a very early class and received multiple calls and voicemails from a certain number. As soon as I was out of class, I listened to the voicemail. It was from the campus safety and security department, letting me know all four of my tires and rims had been stolen off my car *in the school parking lot*. I didn't believe it for a second. How could this be possible with how many thousands of dollars in tuition I spent *for* the private campus safety and security department? Security was always on the move, and my school was ridiculously small and private. This couldn't be real. There were gate guards and security everywhere. Besides, I thought they must have my car mixed up with someone else's.

I needed to be sure. I walked down to the parking lot where my car was parked, and the very moment I saw my car hoisted up on cinder blocks with no tires or rims, I collapsed. I collapsed right there on the black pavement. HOW? WHY? ME? Hadn't I been through enough? I panicked. How would I explain this to my parents? How would I figure out who did this?

The police and Crime Scene Investigation shortly arrived on the scene. It was unspoken knowledge this was more than just someone stealing my tires. But on private campus property in Irvine, California with thousands of people to see and security everywhere? Something wasn't right, and everyone knew it.

It soon became evident it had to have been an inside attack, someone who attended the school and knew exactly what they were doing and who they were doing it to. I drove a Toyota Camry with stock rims. No one was after the tires; they were after me. I spent hours talking with police, taking fingerprints, even figuring out how to get my car on a tow truck with no tires or rims to load it with. I looked back once to see a crowd of people gathering behind yellow caution tape and realized I was suddenly not only the talk of the entire school but of the community. Within minutes, pictures of my car were making the rounds on Facebook. The police department said they hadn't seen a crime like that in over twenty years in the city of Irvine — one of the safest cities in all of California.

The school opened up a separate investigation, and I spent weeks giving them names of potential people who could have done this. The truth was I had no idea. There were many people who didn't like me at that point, and I didn't know where to begin. They began questioning all the random people I gave them on their list, which made every single one of them despise me even more. I had just given their name to the police as a suspect in a grand theft incident. But I had to find out who it was, and I was very aware someone around me knew exactly who.

To this day, I've never found out who did this to me. But if I ever do...you'll know.

Author's Note: Being the victim of bullying is nothing short of the worst feeling in the world. The worst part about it is that it can happen in every shape, form, and at any age. If you are a victim of bullying, especially if it had anything to do with the misunderstanding of your OCD, I feel for you. Believe me, I do. At times, we even bully ourselves, yet we can't even help ourselves! I rarely allow myself to go back to this time in my life. The bullying hurt the most. When I do mentally go back there, it hurts like hell. I just wish I could go back and help myself, just like I'm sitting here trying to help you. You are so far from being alone in this. I rest assured of where I am now and where I am going in this life. Rest assured of how healthy I am now, and even though these people who hurt me so badly may never know how much healthier I've become, their small lives are no longer my concern. Although, it would be quite nice to write a book and have it make waves to find some way to get their attention and shove fate right in their sad faces, but I'll just go ahead and keep that one in my head for now...

8

"HUMOR HAS IT"

I'll never forget the state of my dorm room. If you thought my hair was bad — ha — just wait. To this day, it's so hard to think back on it. That Freshman year of college in that dorm will haunt me forever. I don't even recognize myself in what I'm about to share with you. But when I really, mindfully put myself back in that place, I can vividly see myself during those times.

Since I wouldn't allow myself to go the cafeteria alone for meals, I always ate alone in private. I hated going out to eat because all it did was remind me how lonely I was. I was terrified I would run into someone from campus, only to reinforce the notion I had no friends, even off campus. I typically got more depressed when I ate out because I knew I was just facing going back to the hell I had created for myself in my dorm room. I was lonely at the restaurant and then just as lonely back home. I then began taking my food to go from restaurants and eating my meals in my car in the parking lot. Then I could be alone and not worry about being judged for eating alone yet again. When I didn't eat out, I "cooked" meals in my dorm room where the only cooking unit I had was a microwave. Honestly, these weren't even "meals." I'm talking the mini warm up Kraft mac and cheese bowls. I would warm up microwavable dishes, only to find myself not being able to finish them because of my obsessions with odd and even numbered bites. Just looking at the food, I would instantly get bad thoughts. Anything you can think of would get in my way. What's worse, after the few bites I was "allowed," *I couldn't throw it away.* I just couldn't do it. The obsessions morphed into a hoarding phase. My hoarding tendencies came to a point where I could barely throw anything away. I would get bad thought after bad thought every time I went to throw something out. I tried to get around the obsessions with trash, trying to cancel them out, attempt to "trick" my OCD, but it rarely worked. I wasn't strong enough. After a while, I had uneaten, rotten food all over my dorm room. It would just sit there, right on my sink counter as I was doing my makeup every day. Granted, it reeked. The fruit flies began to swarm in and take over. I began to just act like they lived there too.

One night as I was lying down in bed (where, as a compulsion, I couldn't pull my covers over me to sleep, so I wore a robe to bed to keep warm), I heard something moving over on my desk. Mice. I quickly learned I provided their daily meal. I would just lay there with them two feet away from my headboard and listen to them, terri-fied. I couldn't bring myself to do anything about it. *Correction* — I could, but I didn't know that yet.

I would go to bed at 7pm every single night because I was so bored, so confined in my sick world, and I would do anything to take me out of my reality. The sooner I fell asleep, the sooner I was in another world for even just a few hours. Any other world than my own.

I never allowed anyone in my dorm room. I found ways to never allow people to come within a foot of the front door. Granted, it's not like I had any friends who actually wanted to come in, but even the few friends I had made or the guy I had dated were not allowed in the room. He couldn't figure out why I would never let him step a foot inside. We were "dating." He never realized it was just the itty-bitty detail of my hoarded residence that was in the way. He thought I was hiding something in there. I was.

Here comes the good part. One evening I was doing something in my room, and I saw something dash across the room under my heater which was one of those dorm units that are connected outside where the mice came in and out. I LOST IT. Something about me being able to see it in broad daylight threw me spiraling. I couldn't take it another second. I sprinted out of the room and went straight to my Resident Assistant's dorm before even blinking, yelling about how there was a live mouse in my room. Before I knew it, people in surrounding dorms started coming out to see what the entire ruckus was about. I didn't consider the fact that they would have to come inside my dorm room to help me catch the mouse. No! The state of my room! It was too late. There was a group of about five girls that came rushing over, ironically the same group of girls who had been oh so interested in my "thinned hair" when I had gotten it brushed out. They just might get their chance to finally figure out what was so wrong with me if they saw inside my dorm room. And that's exactly what they got that night.

They followed my RA and I into my room, and they all just kind of circled around each other. Other than the fact that there was nowhere to walk or sit, they were just in awe of the state of my dorm room. They finally realized what a hoarding disaster I really was, and how in over my head I had to be. I probably was exactly what they thought I would be behind closed doors. It was very clear why I had a mouse in my dorm room, and they offered to help me clean it. I was so emotionally overwhelmed, I actually agreed. I had given up at that point. I was completely blinded by what my room must look like to a normal person. What's worse, even if I did see it, I didn't care. As skewed as my mind was, continuing to live in my sick world of comfort meant more to me than what they thought. One girl started to clean a counter, and there was nothing but orange soda spilled and sticky all over it. It had been there for days. I ran over to take over and do it myself. Another girl opened a drawer to find some very unsanitary things. I ran over and shut it immediately. One girl looked over and saw a suitcase lying down with clothes laying all over it. She asked why I had a random suitcase laying out like that. Luckily for me, Christmas break was the following week, so she concluded that I just had it out packing. Little did she know it was a compulsion to not move that suitcase, and it was so bad, I hadn't moved it since I moved into my dorm room at the beginning of the August. There were probably thirty half-drunk water bottles spread throughout the small room. I could never finish anything completely, not even water. I honestly worked better in filth, in a mess. The chaos helped me think. My OCD and I were just more comfortable with my room a disaster. I understand this seems opposite of what most classify as OCD, but the fact of the matter is, OCD has no boundaries and is so completely different in each of us. For many people, OCD is about being very sanitary and clean, which is how I am now. OCD takes many different paths, none of which make sense.

After a while, we all realized they couldn't do anything to help me. It was too gross, too much. They knew it, and I knew it within one glance at each other. They helped me as much as they could, and I thanked them and let them leave. At first glance, it was a nice gesture. But in the end, they just left thinking I was more inhuman then when they arrived. Memories like this humiliate me to my core even to this day. They must have died inside and spent hours gossiping, just trying to figure out what was wrong with me. I was broken yet again.

My parents only saw inside my dorm room a few times. My mom would come every couple of months to help me clean it. I would really try to clean up as much as I could before she arrived, but I would leave the half finished water bottles and anything else my OCD stopped me from picking up. I usually was able to get the most unsanitary things out of there before she arrived because there was no explaining any of that to my perfectly groomed mother. As much as I thought I was cleaning it up for my mom, in reality, I was just revisiting and dodging my obsessions and compulsions. Most of the time my compulsions won, and my poor mom had to see most of my reality. My dad only saw the place one time, and I wouldn't let him in all the way. The look on his questioning face the moment he walked in the door said it all. He was so shocked, taken aback that I could live that way. He knew I was very sick, but to see such a disaster after me being away and on my own was so alarming for him. He asked me how I lived like that, and why I didn't just throw the water bottles away. Why I didn't just clean my room that he was paying for? I didn't have answers for him.

Another major compulsion that popped up was leaving my front dorm room door both unlocked and open most of the time. This one really is the most foreign to me looking back on it. Most people with OCD obviously have the opposite problem. So many of us check the door ten times to make sure it's locked. But with me, it was just about obeying whatever miscellaneous thought came through my head in that very moment, no matter how crazy it seemed. I began to have to leave the door cracked open *every night while I slept*. Literally, I would sleep with all of my belongings inside a dark dorm room, and there was my front door, open for anyone who pleased to peer in or enter. I'm sorry to say I'm not even exaggerating. There were two occasions when people just walked right in, and even though I barely knew them, they would ask me if I knew my door was open in the middle of the night. One night a guy who lived in my building walked right in through the open front door, and sat down in my room, uninvited. He was an odd guy, who I'd seen around since we lived a few doors down from each other. I was already in my robe for the night and not expecting company. He looked around and said, "Damn, I'm messy too, but I couldn't take the bugs." He left shortly afterward. I officially died.

My compulsion with not only the unlocked but open door became a much bigger problem when I would go away on the weekends to visit my local extended family. I had to leave my door cracked open *while I was gone. Everything I owned* was inside. My laptop. My personal belongings. Everything. I would spend the entire weekend away just wondering and hoping my laptop would still be there when I got back. I didn't know what I would do if it wasn't. I didn't allow myself to think that far. How would I explain when I called the police over theft? "Yes, officer, I left my door open to the public. I do it all the time?" No.

I had so much relief when my laptop was there when I got back late on Sundays. Somehow it always was there, even with many accounts of theft on campus. Apparently, it wasn't worth stealing from the crazy girl — who knew what was in her room — so they stayed away. Most of the time I would come back and the wind would have swung my door all the way open. It must have stayed like that for days when I was gone. As I write this, I can't even fathom having done that now. How mentally ill can you be to take such as risk with every single one of your belongings? Furthermore, how could I have slept at night? In my mind, the risk was worth it. My compulsions were worth it. This is how strong obsessions are, guys. I don't even remotely relate to this person. That's just an example of how detached I was with reality since I had isolated myself so much due to my compulsions. This all just came down to OCD. It's *that powerful* of a mental disorder, and the world needs to know.

I remember one specific night when I hit a breaking point in that room. I remember the outfit I was wearing, standing in front of my mirror looking back at myself. Who was the girl staring back at me? I couldn't even take one step without a horrific obsession and perform some crazy compulsion. I felt so trapped. I couldn't think. I couldn't breathe. I couldn't take one more night of sleeping in that room at 7pm with no covers in pure, utter isolation and boredom. I wanted to go home. As I stared at myself in the mirror grasping my hair, I decided that I would drive home and skip school the next day. I needed out of there. I never skipped school. This was a huge shift for me because it was so unlike me. Could this be my rock bottom? Could this be the day I hit my final point with OCD?

The truth was I still didn't know there was a way out of the worst of OCD. I don't even think I knew it was all OCD. To me, this was just my world, not my sickness. So I never truly dwelled on how awful my life had become because I was too busy moving from obsession to obsession. My brain didn't have any room for anything else, no ability to think deeply and ponder because there was another compulsion I needed to focus on and make sure it was done right. I wasn't at my breaking point because I didn't know I was broken. I never analyzed it. I just kept moving in my robotic, filthy, sick, and puppet-controlled world, waiting for the next breaking point.

***

Author's Note: OCD comes in all shapes and sizes. It must be unfathomable for someone who has contamination or cleaning and washing obsessions to read about me having the exact opposite problem. This further shows the limitless bounds of OCD, and furthermore, of the brain. We still have OCD, and we have the same disorder. How can two people who have the exact opposite thoughts, obsessions, and fears have the exact same rooted problem? *Because this is all nothing more than a disorder.* Because we are victims of our brain seemingly turning against us. We are victims of a mental disorder where our brains are literally malfunctioning. We are trapped in a malfunctioning, snowballing world because none of this is actually real. It's all an illusion. This is just to show you that although we might have such personally un-relatable obsessions, we are one in the same. Just because we obsess about completely different anxieties in our lives doesn't mean we can't figure this out together. My hand is extended to you and ready to walk through this collapsing world together. I wish I would have known you when I was this sick. I wish we could have held each other accountable, shared a smile, even a laugh if possible. So, from this point forward, here I am, new friend.

9

"THE BEGINNING OF THE BEGINNING"

It could not have been more blatantly clear that I needed more help. Being isolated in my dorm room was only making me sicker, and I needed to be held accountable for my compulsions. The longer I was held unaccountable, the worse I became because I was just not strong enough against my OCD. In fact, I was <u>no</u> match for OCD. At a certain point, even I saw a glimpse of this.

My doctor from home had helped me find a local therapist to see while I was away at school. It was clear that I needed weekly therapy to stay even remotely in touch with what was going on inside my head, since I hindered my very self from it. I wasn't against therapy at all. In reality, it was an hour for me to talk to someone who might just understand and not judge me for anything I said. To be honest, I didn't necessarily go to therapy to combat my OCD head on. I was there to be able to talk about it for an hour. It was a relief to be able to freely discuss the state of my seemingly outer world mind with someone who was genuinely there to find my loopholes and help me fill them. In all honesty, I never thought about going to therapy to "get better." I didn't know it was a possibility, and again, I thought this was just my world. I knew it wasn't normal, but I also didn't think it was that bad...

Unfortunately, I did not have a good bond or experience with my newfound therapist, who just happened to be the one who I saw while at my worst during these previous chapters. How convenient. It was evident as time went on that he had no desire to relate and flat out was confused by me. He made me feel beneath him, like I was there for social hour and attention, and he had better patients with real problems to deal with. In all seriousness, I *was* there for social hour because it gave me time to relieve myself from school and my judged life and time to just talk. But he was not the person to just listen. He thought the best way to deal with me was to just put me on medication. Since I had already had my bout with medication, I had no desire to pick it back up again. In my mind, it just added an element to my already incredibly complicated world. As time went on, he began to realize how sick and stubborn I was, and he just didn't seem to want to work with me anymore. He only ever stared at me and questioned me. There was absolutely no common ground between us, which is so important between a patient and a therapist. The best advice I ever received from him was that literally next door to his office was an Obsessive-Compulsive Disorder institution! I had seen the office as I walked to get to his, but I hadn't given it enough thought to make a specific change. My parents came to town every so often to meet with my therapist, and they too saw the institute next door, prompting them to inquire as well. Within a couple of months, I found myself discontinuing with my current therapist and making an appointment next door, with Jim Sterner at *The Gateway Institute*.

The day of my first appointment with Jim Sterner landed on a day where I was at another breaking point. My anxiety was at an all-time high, and I needed an ear and some serious relief and reassurance. I spent the entire initial appointment rambling on his leather sofa, to a point where he couldn't get a word in edgewise. I just had so much to say. I felt like I needed to fill in three years' worth of information before he would ever be able to understand how and what to work on with me. I was wrong.

Jim didn't need three years of information to understand my OCD and anxiety. All he needed was to assess my case and clearly see that based on my anxiety, I was in need of much more than weekly, basic cognitive behavioral therapy (CBT). CBT can center around talk therapy and probing by a therapist to help reveal and change negative patterns of thought and behavior. I was very comfortable with cognitive behavioral therapy because I could talk all day to a therapist about my OCD. When I talked about OCD with a therapist, I always felt temporary relief, like I was doing what I was supposed to do by discussing my thoughts. I felt like I was doing my weekly "duty" by attending a therapy session. I thought this was the path to getting better, but simply talking just wasn't effective in combatting my very serious OCD. I didn't even know there were other ways of combating OCD other than just talking about it. I never even cared enough to think further ahead than where I was being shuffled to at that very moment. It wasn't like my mind was healthy enough to know I needed more help. I wasn't aware of how sick I truly was. I wasn't looking for ways to manage my OCD or to get healthy. I didn't care or even think to get educated on OCD. I was just literally an obsessive zombie going through the motions, and the next motion was this newfound OCD therapist. All I could see was what was right in front of me because of the intensity of the obsessions. That's when *Gateway* introduced me to Exposure and Responsive Prevention (ERP). ERP is a type of cognitive behavioral therapy which takes a stance of proving by exposing the OCD, rather than talking through it. Since OCD is a doubting disorder that craves reassurance so deeply, one must prove to themselves the illegitimacy of their compulsions by exposing both themselves and their thoughts. Once you've exposed your deepest and darkest obsessions, you have the choice of response prevention. The response prevention is the part where once you've exposed your extremely uncomfortable obsessive thought(s), you can make a decision to prevent your response (not performing your compulsion). By not performing the compulsion you so deeply desire, you have exposed your OCD without the protection of the compulsion, so you can eventually, with time and persistence, see the obsession is irrational and the compulsion is ineffective in reality. All in all, ERP is the most uncomfortable type of therapy to combat OCD, yet it is arguably the most effective. The Gateway Institute leads in practicing ERP, which is a main tool of their OCD Intensive Treatment Program. The program is formatted and tailored around each individual patient, based on the severity of his or her obsessions and compulsions. The determination of severity of the patient is through YBOCS. YBOCS, Yale-Brown Obsessive-Compulsive Scale, is how therapists are able to judge the severity of the patient. After fully understanding the amount of time, distress, and reaction I had towards my OCD, Jim was able to formulate a program specifically for me. There is a rank scale out of forty for severity, forty being the most severe. Initially, I ranked a thirty-six severity. I think you can do the math.

After meeting with Jim during weekly therapy for a few weeks, it was very apparent that I needed to enter the OCD Intensive Treatment Program at Gateway. Weekly talk therapy was no longer my best bet for making progress as severe as I was. I needed the three-week program, where I would be getting intensive and consistent therapy every single day. To be honest, I never really evaluated whether or not the treatment program was the best for me. I was at such a loss of emotion with life; I just didn't care what happened next. If Jim hadn't been persistent that I desperately needed the intensive program to move forward with my life, I would have never done it. I did it because both he and my parents wanted me to, which I soon learned is never the proper outlook while entering a program like this. For effectiveness, you're supposed to *actually want to get better,* which of course, I learned the long and hard way.

Jim called my parents and had them come down for an in-person meeting to discuss the program. The four of us sat there and began to break down why I needed the intensive treatment program vs. the weekly therapy I had been doing for the past couple of years. He took the time to explain the difference for my parents, how ERP works, and why I was a perfect candidate for the program. In all honesty, Jim's explanation was the first time my parents even heard of a way to truly fight the OCD. The reality was my parents were willing to pay anything and go to any length, as they needed me to just "get rid of my OCD." Up until that point, they had wanted me to "turn it off," simply not realizing the extent of this disorder. It was not something I could just stop or turn off. My father even asked Jim if there was a brain surgery that could stop OCD. There were no limits on what they were willing to do. Jim advised the best next step was for me to immediately enter the program, and since the school year was coming to an end, I agreed. I was not willing to miss or fall even more behind in school just to enter the program. In retrospect, I should have never even gone away to school in the state I was in. Better late than never is oh so true.

In order to complete the program, I needed to stay down in Orange County to live. It was decided that I would move in with my grandparents who were about a forty-minute commute from The Gateway Institute. My mom came down to help me move my belongings from school to their home, bless her heart. As my last day of my freshman year approached, it could not have been more evident how awful of a year it had been for me. I had experienced OCD at its fullest extent, been a victim of bullying, and went from being an impressive young woman to not recognizing anything about myself. I had become a different human being. I hated everyone and everyone hated and misunderstood me. My first bout of adulthood away from home, which was supposed to be a freeing experience, ended up leaving me more confined than I have ever been in my entire life. I walked with my final load to my mother's car that last day, never thinking I would set foot back on the campus. I had no idea where my summer was going, and I wasn't prepared to find out. I was just... numb. As I climbed into the car, I threw up my middle finger at nothing in particular to sum up how I felt about everything I was driving away from. And off we went.

***

Author's Note: Does your relationship with your OCD mean more to you than any other relationship in your life? Honestly, think about it. OCD *is* your first and foremost relationship, no? You're always spending time with it, thinking about it constantly, and obsessing around everything about it. It may not be a relationship you agreed to, but you're stuck, aren't you? Whether you realize it or not, you most likely choose your OCD over anything and everyone — and as much as it hurts to see them slip away — your OCD still means more to you. You're addicted, you're obsessed, and you're stuck between a rock and a hard place, unable to move. Every single time I chose my OCD over everything else in my life, I lost something or someone. In fact, I lost everything except my parents, who I did actually lose at one point. Why do we constantly choose the one thing that hurts us the most over everything else in life? It's beyond human nature because we now know we have the choice to make a change and decision with education on OCD and effective therapy treatments, but we don't. When you perform your compulsions, or do something to receive the reassurance you shouldn't be asking for, remember every single time that you are *choosing* your OCD over everything in that very moment. You are. You cannot control the thought that you are receiving, but you CAN control your response to it. We will discuss this further in the second half of the book. Stay with me!

10

"ONE FOOT IN, ONE FOOT OUT"

I began the intensive OCD program having no idea what to expect. I had no expectations. The only thing I knew for certain was that my father was paying a substantial amount of money on my therapy, and *he* needed something to change.

My days seemed to all run together that summer. I would wake up, roll out of bed, and do absolutely nothing to get ready. I then commuted to the institution, dealt with whatever Jim had me face that day, and came right home to get back into bed. I usually wore whatever I wore to bed the night before to therapy. I had no desire to get dressed, and I certainly wasn't going to do anything with my hair. I would come directly home and sleep because I quickly learned when I was sleeping, I wasn't aware of my reality. I would spend around four hours with Jim each day of the week in intensive therapy. My biggest obsession that we set out to target was my obsession with my hair. Although my obsessions ultimately remained the same, it was my compulsions that varied. Jim caught on to all of my compulsions quickly and could read me like a book when I had any anxiety. Every day we focused on the same subject but took different approaches to expose my painful thoughts and obsessions in attempt to change my behavior towards them.

The days were centered on targeting everything that anyone with OCD hates — working directly and consistently head first against your biggest fears and obsessions. Of course, your therapist knows your biggest compulsions, so you can't perform them without getting caught. Therapists trained in OCD know OCD's path — how it works, when it's attacking, and the way in which it wants to hold you hostage. Either therapists are psychic, *or perhaps OCD, when broken down, just isn't that complicated.* My favorite part was the psychotherapy — talking through my obsessions and why I was performing the specific compulsions I was — because it gave me a flicker of reassurance. However, Jim was a professional at knowing when I was seeking the reassurance and consistently held me accountable by not giving it to me.

Early on, Jim told me I needed to bring a brush to therapy. I didn't even own one. Naturally, I bought a brush and brought it with me, hoping I wouldn't have to fully commit to what I knew Jim was onto. Of course, Jim started having me brush my hair in front of him. I would sit on the leather sofa with him across from me, watching my every move, every stroke of the brush. I would very slowly go hair by hair and "brush" or separate each one. I did it very daintily, hoping he would get bored and move on to something else. Needless to say, having me get used to even holding a brush in my hand and touching it to my hair was major progress. Even if I could only brush a very small section, I was still doing something I certainly wasn't going to do at home by myself. Other days, Jim would have me open my notebook and have me write, "My hair is thinning and falling out, and I am going to go bald," or "I'm going to go bald today," as many as up to a hundred times. Sometimes I would have to write, "A thought does not make it the truth," over and over again. Other sentences I repeatedly had written over the course of the program were, "If I eat what I want, I am going to go bald." He was exposing me to the very core of my fears by having me write them out of my darkness into the light, which to me, was about as good as making them come true right then and there.

My notebook from my time in this program is quite a sight to look back on. There are scribbles and doodles everywhere, occasionally the word "no" randomly written throughout the pages, which I know I wrote in response to whatever obsession was going through my head at the moment. There are pages of scattered numbers and letters written over and over again with no rhyme or rhythm. There are various bubble graphs written where I started to write out the compulsions I performed in one and what my attached fear was in the other. None of the bubbles were completed — a compulsion in itself — and none of my writing makes sense because of the grammar compulsions. Mainly, I would have to change the tense from past to present in the same sentences or skip words or letters completely. I have found pages where the word "demon" is written out hundreds of times. I was scared my OCD was somehow related to the dark side, and this was an exposure that I really struggled with, seeing it come out on paper. It was almost too real — until it wasn't.

There are notes that I wrote to myself randomly throughout the pages. As I scan through the stained and battered pages today, I see writings to myself with misspellings and grammar issues such as:

"Hope for you,"

"no hope,"

"cry in bed,"

"Don't go with your gut,"

"much as I don't feel that I have control I have all control, "today I brushed my hair I cannot tell/understood if I'm getting better or not. You all have thought that I am I am the only one who cannot."

"OCD NO NO NO NO no need for you Kerry. Your better than what gone on. Tomorrow will have come. You now have understood that there's no connection. So, why are you doing that, Ker. Your better, & have too much goin for you than what now. So brush and beautiful."

There are pages where I wrote down some of the things OCD wouldn't "allow" me to do. I wrote down things such as:

"say I love you,"

"drive the way I want to,"

"walk,"

"wrote stuff down,"

"eat food and chocolate,"

"talk on the phone,"

"internet,"

"go out,"

"stereo,"

"Mom: Can't say I love you to her, cannot do what she told me to do, hopping around, hidden things, opposite of what she told me to do."

There are areas where I can tell Jim prompted me to write down what my life would look like after the program and if my OCD got better. I wrote things down such as:

"talk to people,"

"look cute,"

"eat food,"

"call people,"

"watch what I need to,"

"get a book,"

"walk,"

"get on Facebook."

"I am walking out of...I come out and have gorgeous hair according to myself. At the end it is thick and full and I have a ton. When I go through my hair there is a ton and I cannot even get my hand down cause it's so thick all the time. I don't worry that any will come out it is beyond/sooooo gorgeous, full. I love my hair."

Wow. This was my idea of walking out of this intensive program with so-called positive results. Notice how I said nothing about OCD and only spoke about my hair? Further proof that shows this wasn't a disorder to me. This was my life magnified, and it was all I could think about or talk about. Looking back on all these little things so many of us take for granted — like getting on Facebook, listening to the stereo, opening a book, simply walking in a straight line — these were things I wasn't "allowed" to do for long periods of time. As you can imagine in my isolation and loneliness, all these little things that could have aided in my emptiness OCD kept as far from my reach as possible.

After a while, it was time to tackle the way I walked. I still hopped around, dodging certain cracks, lines, and pieces of gum on the ground, all in response to what my obsessions told me each step meant. I also still looked down, watching the ground every time I took a step. I rarely looked up to see where I was going. I was watching to see what thoughts and feelings I would get before every single step. Sometimes if I was currently anxious about wanting thicker hair, I would look down at a crack and within a millisecond think if I stepped there, I would have thicker hair. So, I would hurry and step right on the crack. Other times when I was anxious about currently losing too much hair, I would see a certain dark crack and avoid it like a plague. My obsessions and compulsions completely depended on what my current anxieties were, but most of the time, they were between the fear of losing more hair or the desire to get thicker hair. Jim would take me outside to where there were many cracks on the ground in front of the institution headquarters and have me just...walk. He would stand there and watch me in case I hesitated. He would watch the way in which my mind made up whether I was going to prevent my response (not perform the desired compulsion by stepping in a certain place) or whether I was going to give in. When I knew I was going to give in, I would look up at him and say, "I can't step here, Jim. I can't do it." He would immediately respond and say, "Why can't you step there, Kerry?" I would respond by exposing what I thought was or wasn't going to happen if I stepped there. Rather than force me to do one thing or the other, Jim left the decisions of how I was going to respond to my obsessions entirely up to me. His job was simply to help me expose them, but the decision of preventing the response I so deeply desired was mine.

A pattern started to form after a while. Jim started making me *question* the need to perform every single compulsion while I walked. Throughout the repetition of exposure, I actually started to feel stupid if he gave me "the look" when I performed a compulsion. It was almost like they were *losing their power*. Was I was slowly awakening? Instead of feeling the remorse of not performing the compulsion, I started to just feel nothing and feel more humiliated every time he gave me the look of, "you know very well *you don't need to do this*," before I gave in to a compulsion. It was as though he could see the real, older — normal — version of me underneath it all and was just patiently waiting for me to see it once again. It was almost like he saw the logical side of me and knew that if he could just get an ounce of it to play out as a result of the exposures, I would be able to see it for myself.

I struggled most with crediting my OCD as its own entity. I continued to always refer to my OCD as "it." Anytime Jim or anyone talked to me about my OCD, I would talk about and refer to it, as "I don't want 'it' to be mad" or "I feel like 'it' wants me to..." By doing this and giving so much credit by assuming its own identity and name, I was only identifying my OCD as something bigger and scarier than myself. By doing so, I was automatically assigning it more power. My intrusive thoughts were ego-dystonic – thoughts and behaviors that conflicted with my self-perception. I didn't realize I needed to de-personify myself in order to separate and understand the intrusive thoughts were merely being created from my very own imagination. During our talk therapy, Jim would constantly have to question my statements in reference to my OCD as its own entity or being because I would always give it so much credit. He would help remind me that "it" was my OCD created in my mind, not anything greater, more powerful, or really anything at all.

One day, Jim sat me down with markers and a notebook. He told me to draw "it," since I believed in it as its own entity so much. I sat there with the notebook and pens and realized I had no idea what to begin to draw. The truth was I had never envisioned "it" before. I had no idea what "it" looked like, to me it was just something I couldn't put a finger on or see in my brain. I ended up drawing some little monster looking creature, but I knew deep down that I hadn't identified "it" correctly. No matter how much I thought about it, I couldn't draw the perfect personification of "it." **There was no clear vision of "it" because "it" was and is *nothing*. At the top of the page I scribbled, "GO AWAY."**

There were times during the intensive program when I only opened up to a certain extent. I still naturally held back some during the program. I was completely fine discussing and cooperating with most all of my obsessions and compulsions. However, there were certain things I held back on — the deepest and darkest. There was still a side of me that believed I might be blessed in ways others weren't. I thought that at times when I would get thoughts that if I performed a certain compulsion by touching something or stepping in a certain place, I was being given an energy or a gift from the universe. And by not performing the compulsion, I was not accepting it. Although I knew Jim was very in tune with OCD and very understanding, I thought he might not understand this because perhaps he wasn't someone who was chosen by the universe to be presented with these so-called opportunities. Or perhaps he wasn't spiritual in this way of energy that I couldn't wrap my head around. Just as people talk about crystals, rocks, energy, spiritual ceremonies, trusting the universe, the whole "ask, believe, receive," mentality blurred with my OCD to a point where my OCD told me my compulsions were what controlled everything in that realm. I thought that by him telling me this was just OCD, he just might not know it really was energy from the universe because he had never been in tune with it before. I didn't want to lose these "opportunities" once and for all. This was my primary doubt, and the essence of what kept me hanging on to my OCD. This was what sometimes kept me secretly performing the compulsion, or changing it in my favor, or even cancelling the obsession and making up for it later. Ultimately, I tried to stay far away from articulating it because it was what I feared most. I didn't want to give up my OCD completely and just be another normal person if I was able to help encourage things to and from happening through my compulsions. By fighting against my OCD, I thought I was rejecting these so-called opportunities. I realized Jim didn't agree with me on this, and he strongly thought it was OCD. As a result of this, there were times when I tried to half-ass my treatment, so that I wouldn't fully give "it" up. I would find a way around my compulsions at times. Play some mind game, so I didn't piss "it" off too much. This was back when I was still scared of what I was going through. Back when I didn't know I had the fight inside of me...the fight against myself.

The approach I decided to take over the years has been to just combat it as if it were OCD because it has to be. If I challenge it as OCD, it doesn't haunt me because I am pushing the thoughts out of my mind by exposing them. I continued and still continue to push through these thoughts, and do not give into a single one of them because I know what will follow. This has by far been the most difficult side of OCD for me to understand — which has been all the more reason to just fight it.

Author's Note: With anything in life, you have to go in headfirst. Putting up a fight is always an option, regardless of the situation. So many people don't believe that they have it in them to win the fight of a mental disorder, so they don't bother. The fear of the unknown is too great. Many don't know what life would be like once they lose the control, but they rarely consider what they would *gain*. With any real trial or tribulation, I really cannot think of any other answer than to fight. Your only other option is to sit there and accept it. No one who ever achieved anything just sat there, motionless. My life is still a constant battle to always achieve another success, and I tell you, I never have done anything worth talking about by just sitting there. Your fight will always be worth reflecting on, more so than you not doing anything. Do something worth looking back on when dealing with your trials, whatever they may be. You're fighting your inner beast, and no one, absolutely no one, has the power to fight it but you. The catch is you can't put up a fight with *one foot in and one foot out*. I know this because I just explained how I tried this very thing, time and again. You are wasting every bit of your energy by only putting forth half of your effort. Putting up a fight can initially seem terrifying. You understandably want to keep one foot out "just in case." That "just in case" mentality is essentially exactly what will keep you from winning the fight. You're either two feet in or none at all.

11

"MAMA, I SEE THE LIGHT"

Jim seemed to actually get me, which made me trust him and his tools in therapy. He didn't have to speak to me for long to help me understand he knew exactly what I was going through. He identified with me every day and honestly made me feel human. He posed questions that made me question the disorder and fight it. There was no specific "AHA!" moment like one would hope throughout the program, but it was a slow and steady progression as long as I committed. But staying committed is very, very hard when you are faced with hundreds of obsessions a day. Believe me, I wish I had an "AHA!" moment for you, but I don't believe it exists with OCD. You might think in times of reassurance, along with the waves of relief you get, that you might be having that "breakthrough." More often than not, this is just the reassurance talking and everything goes back to doubt within no time. Now that I stand where I am, I believe the quality of life you seek to get your life back truly does come from this serious commitment to fighting this disorder, day in and day out. It became evident very quickly that no matter how hard I worked during the few hours I was with Jim every day, I still had to go back home and face the obsessions and the decision to prevent myself from performing my compulsions for the rest of the hours in the day. This was by far the most difficult aspect because you are the only one to hold yourself accountable.

Jim decided to make a home visit and talk with my grandparents since I was living with them. He planned to discuss with them ways they could help me in the hours I was at home. The only problem was my grandparents were much older, and they didn't have the stamina, the strength, or the ability to understand my manipulating compulsions, let alone comprehend my obsessions. Nevertheless, Jim made a home visit to see in person the main triggers I faced in their home. At the time, I was struggling with the color red. Every time I saw or touched the color red, I associated it with my hair falling out. Therefore, I avoided stepping or getting near the color red at all costs. Of course, my grandparents had the color red all over their home, from towels, to rugs, to pillows. We immediately began the exposures, right then and there — the only way to do it. Jim had me drape myself in red towels and walk over the red rug I avoided so much over and over again. He had me identify what it was in the house that made me so uncomfortable and had me expose myself to these areas and face my fear head on. He had me do all kinds of random things, just in case they were an obsession and I wasn't telling him. The key was that I had to be honest with him. Ironically, when I was more worried about wanting thicker hair versus my hair falling out, I would lean more towards the red colors and white became the color I had to steer clear of. I associated white with thinner hair, so I loved to be around it when I thought I was losing more hair (I thought by touching white it would stop the hair loss), and I hated to be around it when I was obsessed with wanting thicker hair (I then associated red with getting thicker hair). The bottom line? My OCD was far beyond anything my grandparents or anyone other than Jim could help me with, and ultimately my road to recovery came down to the sole responsibility of one person — me.

In the other 20 hours of the day I wasn't in therapy, I truly had to learn to hold myself accountable for my responses to my OCD. Although I could fight the urge to perform the compulsions for the few hours I was with Jim, I was falling right back into my trap the moment I left therapy and went home. I wasn't strong nor committed enough yet to keep up the stamina on my own time. I was essentially erasing any fight I had given during therapy by just coming home and giving into obsessions and compulsions.

I had to learn to take charge of my OCD and to gain confidence that I was stronger than these thoughts, *alone* or with Jim right there. I had to learn to keep myself in check at all times. I didn't want to be in therapy forever. I didn't want all the hours upon hours I spent in therapy to just go to waste, even if I didn't fully understand everything. The initial decision to become my own therapist by forcing half of my brain to hold itself accountable to the other half was obviously extremely difficult. It feels like a 24/7 battle against yourself — your very own brain.

With real dedication, work, true exposure, and response prevention, a more mature side came out after a while and that led to a more logical side of me. Once you continue to fight, question your OCD every single day, battle every bad thought, every obsession, you can't help but begin to think a little more logically. You begin to put things in a different perspective; things start to appear from a different angle. You are weeding out the bullshit. Each day and each talk with my therapist helped me pull ahead. I would see progress through the ERP all the time. I would go against what my gut was begging me to do, and I would realize that bad things were not happening. At least not right then, and that was good enough for me in the moment because I had too many obsessions to follow to ever remember what did or didn't happen from an exposure hours prior.

Slowly, the more that I would fight against the bad thoughts, the more I noticed that my hair wasn't falling out based upon the lack of compulsions I was performing. It was somehow staying in, even when walking completely normal. My movements had no effect on reality — which was the core of my OCD and my strong belief system in it. The way that people fight OCD is by fighting back against their bad thoughts. The longer that you consistently don't give in to the compulsions, the fewer bad thoughts you will receive. It's like smoking, in a sense. Although quitting is painful as can be, if you don't even allow yourself near the smell of smoke or to look at cigarettes, it's less likely to pull so hard against your will and mind. Yet, it's still so prevalent.

And so we went. Day by day, we fought my biggest fears. Halfway through summer, I was able to get my hair cut a few inches. Leaps and bounds had been made. I couldn't get my hair colored yet, but I was able to go in and get it cut and brushed through. The final test would be for me to be able to get my hair colored and cut all at the same time. When I was able to do that, I knew that I would have made unbelievable progress. But I knew that that may take years, and man, at that point, I was okay with that. I was terrified of having somebody go rip through and bleach my strands, which might thin my hair. It was simply still unheard of in my book for anytime in the near future. The real reason I was able to get my hair cut was because my hair loss has slowed down significantly. Whatever was causing the shedding of hair had come to a slow halt for the time being. But my OCD didn't go away just because I was losing less hair. It became even stronger — obsessed with gaining thicker hair. In turn, I was still breaking even by challenging my OCD, and with the help of less hair loss, I got the break I needed to start to see the light and utilize that time to push ahead.

Through it all, testing me in every way, the things Jim taught began to make sense to me. The way that he was able to explain things was like he was inside my head. He already understood what I was thinking, and here I thought that my thoughts were the first time anybody had ever had them. The way that he looked at me after I said something absolutely wild, as if he had *heard it all before*. I thought I was unique and had this lonesome ability and power, like I was sought out. Yet the more I explained it, Jim wasn't fazed. He seemed to have tapped into exactly what I was feeling and thinking. The only possible way for someone to understand what I was going through was for either him to have OCD, which he didn't, or for him to have heard it all before. Bingo. I never thought that somebody who didn't have OCD would be able to understand the mind of somebody who did. To me, this wasn't a disorder. It was reality. So, if he was able to spit at me things that I already knew to be true and exactly what I was already thinking or fearing, if he really could say things that made perfect sense to me amidst the fuzziness in my head, he must know a lot about the disorder. When he began being able to finish my sentences, because he already knew where my OCD was going, I began to realize that this really was *just a disorder*. All along, I thought that I was blessed with these powers, a chosen one, and that I had the power to achieve things at a different rate than others through these magical compulsions. Even though I knew that I was sick, I still thought that it was all part of what it takes to be part of this "gift." It hadn't occurred to me I truly had a medical condition with no cure. It didn't cross my mind that this was a matter of chemicals in my brain off balance, low serotonin, or that this whole thing was nothing beyond malfunctioning of my very own brain.

Once I knew that this was merely a disorder and my compulsions had no effect on reality, I was willing to conquer it. The only reason that I was hesitant to fight it head on was because I didn't want to give up my control. I thought I was special. Like I was the first and only one getting thoughts like these. Sure, sweetie — SURE.

It's all a sick mind game that we, as OCD sufferers, are the victims of. Jim was pulling that logic, deep down in there, out of me slowly, each and every day that I had spent years burying. At this point, I realized that this disorder was really attempting to hurt my quality of life and then I began to put my foot down.

Just because a thought came into my head didn't mean it was reality. It's just a thought! Just because you get a thought the oven is on doesn't mean it is! Just because you get a thought you need to do something specific to prevent you or a loved one from getting a disease doesn't mean anyone will ever get the disease or that anything you do could start or prevent it! These are simply recurring fears that roll through your mind over and over again because you have a disorder that targets what you are most anxious about. None of this is real. These are just fearful thoughts being catastrophized in a make-believe world of our ruminating imaginations. The saddest part about all of this is that you know the oven is off because it is. You know nothing you do in your separate world of compulsions will have any correlation to you or a loved one becoming ill. You truly do know these things, the truth behind your recurring thoughts, but you just can't be sure because "what if." Therefore, you play on the safe side of life every single time, *just to be sure*. Broken down, that little "just to be sure" concept is the very thing that is holding your life back. It's the very reason your disorder continues to run around and around in circles instead of you ever gripping onto any of this.

I had been through enough. That small amount of logic was dangling in front of me, finally. I knew that it wouldn't be a quick process, but it is indeed much faster when you're willing to actually put up a fight. You have to believe in the power of the fight and want to get better. And as much as I was terrified of whatever had all this control over me, I realized that it was all just OCD. Not some devilish power that could really physically hurt me but a disorder that millions of people have. Obviously, we all have different battles with OCD. What happened in my story isn't what is happening in yours. But the key here is that it is a disorder, and you should spend every waking hour fighting for yourself and your deserved quality of life. Some people have cancer, some people have terminally ill cases, some people are already dead, but you are not. You are still living and breathing but in an incredible amount of inner pain. This is the hand you were dealt but that doesn't mean you have to just sit with that. Be an overcomer; be your own hero. Be the example people who know you will look at in awe of your strength.

Once I started working with Jim, it became evident we didn't even need to consider putting me back on medication after my high school bout with it. We came to the conclusion medication wasn't necessary for me to win this fight against my OCD. OCD is a behavioral disorder, and Jim and I concluded the focus should be on my *preventative behaviors*. It is a personal decision for everyone, but I felt I needed to overcome and learn to manage my OCD with no weapons and no gloves. Just using my bare hands; just me versus the OCD. I was going to deal with this for the rest of my life, and I wanted to grab it by the horns. With that attitude, we never even seriously discussed medication. Jim helped provide me with all the behavioral tools I needed and that I learned to in turn provide for myself.

Here's the thing. I am not saying medication is a bad idea. In fact, I think for many cases it is a great idea to lower the anxiety, so you can focus on the fight more clearly. Especially for cases where the OCD sufferer is extremely hyperactive and can't even dream of doing ERP. I totally back trying medication to at least just lower the anxiety before heading into treatment. I do, however, believe if you are taking medication, that there are two parts to it. The medication is performing its duty, so you need to perform yours by in turn fighting and exposing the OCD. You can't expect to take the medication and think the thoughts will just stop and you will be cured. Training your mind through a behavioral transition of not performing any compulsions is how you get better. Medication is a mere crutch, but will do none of the work for you. That is your job. This is a personal decision between you and your therapist. This is truly an area where I believe there is no right or wrong answer specifically. It is a personal decision and entirely dependent upon you, your case, and your trusted therapist's opinion combined with your own.

Fast-forward to years later — today — I am now on medication. Yep. I can say that honestly and proudly because now I know what the role of medication is and what my role is. A couple of years ago, I went through a horrible breakup and can honestly say I was back at an emotional point where I was as low as I ever was when I was at my worst. Except the issue this time was not a question of my belief in OCD. It was a severe case of anxiety in every single detail of life that I was constantly obsessing over. To the point where I could not function in day-to-day life. My breakup triggered a relapse that sent me in a spiraled version of anxiety that I had never experienced before. This type of anxiety I was feeling was not the same kind of anxiety I felt when I needed to give into an obsession. It was even worse. It was a constant wet blanket of question towards everything and anyone who said anything that bothered me. Everything was so fuzzy, and I needed help. I became more and more depressed each day with the state of my life and my loss of place in this world.

My parents demanded I schedule an appointment with Jim to get to the bottom of how to help this newfound paralyzing anxiety. I spoke to Jim and straight out asked him if medication could help me. In reality, it wasn't necessarily the OCD I needed help with. I knew how to expose my OCD. It was purely the anxiety far beyond OCD that I couldn't understand. Jim connected me with a psychiatrist, and I have now been on Zoloft for over two years and have seen incredible improvement on my quality of life. The obsessions haven't changed at all, but my constant ever-looming anxiety has settled down and taken a back seat, which was exactly what I needed.

The point of me being so transparent with you on this is because I want you to see that I went through the entire Intensive Therapy Program at The Gateway Institute with NO medication. I then proceeded to expose my obsessions and painfully not give into my compulsions with NO medication. I was focused on training my behaviors to change when I received the obsessions. I didn't want the influence of any medication, and I succeeded with my own dedication, my own time frame, and strength. I want to make sure you know very well it *is possible* to get to a point where you are living a very functional life amidst severe OCD with absolutely no medication. It wasn't until seven years later, once I had already conquered the worst of OCD, that I decided to resort to medication because my issue was now beyond my OCD.

Sometimes I wonder if the battle would have been easier if I had been on medication all these years, but I have to say I am very proud to be where I am today knowing I went through the very worst of OCD with nothing more than my own perseverance. *And it worked.*

Author's Note: All of us get to a point where we know it's time to put our foot down with OCD. You get that moment after performing your hundreds of compulsions where you don't know if you can perform even one more without collapsing. You are so sick and tired of the control, yet still cannot let go. Yet it's one thing to tell ourselves to stop and another to actually put the foot down. That's how it goes with the preparation to fight OCD. You know something needs to change. You know you're not giving therapy and the tools you are being given your all. Something in you is holding you back. If you're not even going to regular therapy, then you definitely aren't trying to truly put your foot down. If you were, you wouldn't be so hesitant to knock OCD's doors down. I'm not saying the fight cannot be done without therapy — it most definitely can — but you need the initial tools and proper therapy techniques to practice with yourself 24/7. Stop hesitating to make a change. It's getting old for both you and me, and I can only say that because I was exactly where you are whether you believe it or not.

12

"DON'T QUIT WHILE YOU'RE AHEAD"

The bigger perspective of OCD really started to hit me when I joined a weekly support group. Jim thought I could benefit from interaction with like individuals, to have a support system beyond just him. My invitation to the group meant a lot to me because I had absolutely no social interaction that summer. Having six OCD comrades sitting in a circle with me talking about our obsessions sounded simply heavenly to me. I also was not educated on much of OCD and the various types. I was only living in my own obsessed world, so I had no idea what was out there beyond my story. I walked into the group feeling very strong. I longed to feel like I actually belonged somewhere for the first time in a very long time.

The group consisted of about six to eight people every week. I was by far the youngest one there — an amateur at that. These people had been battling OCD for many years. I had been battling for two years and wanted to die. Needless to say, I had so much respect for each individual in the group. To think of the years of torture and personal destruction under their belts, it was beyond me. As I sat there week after week, listening to people talk about every type of OCD you can imagine, I found myself repetitively thinking the same thing. "How can they obsess about all these things that seem so far-fetched, so obviously untrue?" As each person discussed their fears, I realized I didn't identify with their same fears. My OCD was completely different than anyone else's in the room. I had always pictured OCD as the same battle as the next guy, but it wasn't until I heard each individual story that I realized the limitless power of OCD to expand into so many areas and categories of life. It was then I understood OCD really does come in every shape and size imaginable.

One young man was unable to leave his house on a regular basis due to his obsession with germs and compulsive washing. He was stuck inside the confinement of his own walls, day in and day out. Another man in the group mentioned he used to never, ever use the same towels after he showered. He showered up to eight times every day. He would sneak out to Target every night in the middle of the night to buy new towels since he couldn't use the same one twice. He started out with a savings account of twenty thousand dollars and blew through it on towels within one year. A woman thought that her hair stuck straight up in crazy different directions all the time. She would re-shower three times in the mornings before leaving her house to fix her "messed up hair." But her hair was perfectly fine. Here I had an extensive obsession with my hair, yet I looked at her in utter confusion. Of course her hair wasn't sticking up all the time, she had just washed and brushed it! One man had an obsession with brushing his teeth, to the point where he wore down all of the enamel and gums in his mouth. Another man thought he controlled his surroundings through blinking. He would communicate with his obsessions and perform all his compulsions with his eyes. I sat there, listening to each story, watching the suffering evolve on each of their faces as they spoke of their OCD, and realized what I was in for with a future of OCD. Here was this incredible, wise, well-versed, educated group of people of all different races, ethnicities, and cultures, all paralyzed with abstract, varying fears, slowly dying inside just like I was.

At first, these people and their obsessions seemed so eccentric to me, and I say that with all the respect in the world. I identified with them — with their pain — but not with their obsessions. I was nowhere near as odd as them, at least that's what I *thought*. And here, they looked right back at me like I was just as odd. I completely understand how they must have seen me because that was how I was looking back at them. I looked at them like a perfectly logical person would look at them. They looked at me like a perfectly logical person would look at me. We were fighting a different battle, yet the exact same war, each and every day. The battle of pure power and control being held over us and within us — the power of OCD. It was then it began to sink in deep inside me how incredibly powerful the disorder really is. These perfectly amazing people were overtaken with exactly what I was — a measly disorder.

Remember when I said earlier that OCD will target what means the most to you? That's because I believe the OCD *is* one within you. Your obsessions are created in your imagination, and they stem from your greatest fears based on the things you cherish most in life. The thing is, you can have control over all of this once you find out how to execute that control back on your OCD. Please note, I am not saying you are your OCD or that your OCD is you. I am not speaking on an identity level. I am saying this disorder of the brain we have is within us, our brains, but it is not us. It's like this foreign, invisible antibody that exists in our brain but isn't tangible.

I remember arguing with Jim, telling him that my imagination couldn't just randomly come up with these ideas and thoughts. These thoughts didn't define me. They were not who I was, yet they were coming from me! This had to be an outside power, which was speaking to me, or something other than myself. That's what terrified me. He somehow convinced me that the imagination really could be that powerful, no matter how unwelcome these thoughts may be. That's why we can expect our obsessions to target what means the most to us. It's our own imagination getting stopped in its tracks when it comes across something that may go against our morals and values, or something that could sabotage the way in which we intend to live our life, or the person we want to be. These obsessions are truly just thoughts that your brain waves halt over because they register to you as a paralyzing fear. And the common way to respond to a fear is to try to prevent it from happening, which is why we react to obsessions.

Everything in this world that has ever been created by man, labored by man, and conceived by man was from the power of the imagination. Everything man-made in this entire world that exists came from somewhere. And that place is the imagination. When you begin to think about that concept, you can see how powerful the imagination truly is. It makes you believe the power of the imagination is endless. Don't discredit your own self and how you feel, just because you have a wild imagination. Just because you get an intrusive thought that *feels* like an outer body experience or something bigger than you, doesn't mean it is who you are. Whether you want to face it or not, you never act on any thoughts you don't want to. It's your mind, and only you know your thoughts. Many people with OCD have fears they will do something they don't want to do, but you won't. And just because you get a thought doesn't mean that you identity with it, agree, or relate to it at all. It's a negative thought coming from the same place as all your other positive thoughts. They don't mean anything unless you choose to believe them, just like anything else in life. If every human had a visible channel to their brain, and we could all see everyone's actual thoughts, we would see that everyone gets thoughts they consider disturbing or unlike themselves or what they desire in life. Those people choose whether to act on their thoughts or not. Just like you and I can choose. Your thoughts are just more intensified because you have a disorder where certain signals in your brain are not functioning properly. That in no way, shape, or form makes your situation any different. You still have just as much choice to believe in or act on your thoughts as anyone else. OCD may be a disorder, but you alone define who you are. You know deep, deep down in your heart of hearts who you are and that you can choose to believe and identify with whatever YOU want. Intrusive, deeply imaginative thoughts cannot and will never define who you are. They are thoughts in passing, but you will remain.

I fully understand and agree that as stated in the infamous book

Brain Lock, OCD has been classified as a medical condition where the brain is physically dysfunctional in some areas. It's dysfunctional in the sense of how your brain is seemingly getting stuck, caught up on certain specified fears. But your brain is not dysfunctional in regard to forcing you to do anything you don't *choose* to do. The thoughts may be coming from a dysfunctional place, but every compulsion in response to the thought to prevent it or control it is a choice. I really do believe that no matter what type of OCD you have, you can train your brain out of the certain thought patterns crafted in your imagination. It takes work and dedication, but it is absolutely possible, just as *Brain Lock* reveals.

I began to believe Jim. "What if the imagination really is that powerful? What if none of this is real?" This was my constant thought pattern. This wasn't some power simultaneously seeking me out. I had to de-personify myself to create this deeply powerful and life changing realization. This was my subconscious mind digging up my deepest fears and running with them when I was at my weakest. This was my mind taking what I cared about the most in life and tricking me to question my greatest loves into jeopardy. That's exactly why OCD can target what you are most afraid of. It knows everything because it is simply thoughts stemming from the center of your body that know all your greatest insecurities and fears. But that doesn't mean it's welcomed. It doesn't mean that your thoughts are stemming from who you are and what you stand for. Your thoughts can come from a non-realistic world, and it is up to you to de-personify and separate the unwelcome, ridiculous thoughts from who you are and what you believe. My deepest fear in my subconscious mind was losing my looks or not being able to function at the level I wanted to in life. What's yours?

Authors Note: If you were to ask me three items I cannot live without today, one of those three items would undoubtedly be a hairbrush. CRAZY, *right?* No matter how much or how little hair comes out in it, my brush is one of my most valued possessions, one of which is always on standby. I love brushing my long blonde hair these days. I finally see the beauty of my hair at face value and take incredible care of it. My hair is still one of my signature assets, and I still put probably more value on it than I should. However, it is not an unhealthy mindset where I would lose my actual mind if my hair was cut off or destroyed. I can see life beyond my hair these days because I can see beyond my OCD.

13

"DON'T GO WITH YOUR GUT"

The program began to come to an end, and it was time for me to go home for the rest of the summer until school started again. I was no longer going to have to go to therapy every single day! I finished the program rather strong, with a YBOCS rating of 16 out of 40. Remember, I started the program with a severity of 36 of out 40! By no means was I a free spirit, but I had a new outlook, much to which I discovered as time went on.

Jim had me fill out a booklet called, "OCD Relapse Prevention." It addressed many questions about what I had learned in treatment, so when I hit a rough patch, I could read my fresh-out-of-treatment answers and hopefully gain some encouragement and motivation. One of the questions was, "What do you say to yourself to resist an urge to ritualize?" My answer: "Don't go with your gut." This makes me chuckle at myself because this was a term I remember coining while in the intensive program. It just hit me one day that for people with OCD, the saying "go with your gut" was actually detrimental. If we go with our guts, we will perform the compulsions and rituals because it's our gut which seems to be pulling and yanking at us to do something about whatever intrusive thought we just received. The entire point of ERP and getting out of the rut of OCD is to NOT go with your gut. Another pun I love to use along these lines is, "Don't go with your thought."

Throughout the booklet, my answers tell me that it truly was the intensive program that broke the foundation between OCD and me. I definitely didn't even realize this at the time, and who knows if I really believed my own answers at the time, but they are still to this day — eight years later — exactly what I would have said today. My answers on the page tell me, "I have gotten to understand/hope that there is no connection with the outer world and hair loss/bald." Somewhere, somehow, something went right.

Notes from my notebook at the end of the program reveal to me where my head was at when these weeks were coming to an end. I wrote notes to myself like:

"It's all on you,"

"no one will be there every step of the way, you have to make the move,"

"I know how nervous you are, but you have to,"

"OCD can snowball,"

"you can come to therapy and support group as often as you need to but it does nothing for you [unless you do the work yourself],"

"any doctor could tell you all day until you are blue in the face, and as much as you don't know how you will do it, you are able to,"

"stop, hold on and show yourself your stronger than the OCD."

Then I found two letters. One to myself, and one to my parents. These are so eye opening to read. You can tell I was getting better by the time I wrote them because my writing and grammar had improved, but I can still see so many compulsions in these letters. Please excuse the amount of mixed past and present tenses and all the errors. I want you to read how I really wrote them, all mistakes and compulsions included. I want to share these intimate letters with you in hope that you resonate with my most vulnerable self at my worst. You see where I am today, but you deserve to know what it took every step of the way.

Letter I found addressed to me:

"Lover-

*You need to have understood that all you have gone through is better than you will prob know in your world. You have to work each and everyday more than the day before. **What you do and how you reach/act towards to the world will be what will make you go on.** (*Goosebumps). You are a fun, gorgeous human and your letting all OCD in your way. Why. Your better — no connection make now fun and perfect. If what you need is to be comfort then damn, be comfortable any, you are beyond capable. **If you would love to have the world, go for the world.** No joke. So nothing is more than you could control.*

Love, one."

Whoa. I couldn't call myself by my own name, even in a letter to myself. As much as I see grammatical errors and awkward sentences, I see foresight. I see that even back then, I knew somehow, someday, I would make a difference.

Letter I found addressed to my parents:

"Dear Mom and Dad,

You both know and understand that I have problems. Until now, I knew I could make it through all of them. My problems involved good therapy, and being able to overcome psychological things. After all, therapy helped me that much. I have become much normal afterwards. Thanks so much for being there, paying, and understanding. Now, as always, nada [I couldn't write the word "nothing"] unusual, new problems have came towards me. You both understand that we are much stronger now and are much better able to have talked in matured ways. That being true, I am going to have shared some personal thing/problems with my mom and dad. Maybe, hopefully, when you read and have read what is really happened, you may better understand what's happened. Yes, the best thing ever — in my entire life has appeared — being one of three/two fashion girls. Best thing that's happened to me in a very long while. Now, I understand that you can't understand what your daughter, Kerry, has to go through every day. I am still very much taken under by mutilating thoughts. I take every day and try harder to make it to the next day. Yes, that gets hard each and each days. When I came away two months before now, I was feeling much more normal. And knew that I can come back nowadays and do exactly what I wanted. But, when I'm depressed, I cannot even think the problems with being depressed are that, you can't even start to tell somebody who isn't depressed how that feels. It's the worst thing I can even think of humans are faced on every basis. That being talked, I really wanted to share what's happened to me today.

*Understandable that you both have feelings of remorse towards your daughter, and you both don't know what to do, or how you can help me right now. Maybe if I go into further details, you can, maybe, maybe you both can help. We already have known and established the reasons I get depressed are when "my hair falls out." But since my last two years mainly, we have learned that because/based on what I have gone through. For a while, it went away. The days that I never say anything — that's a good day. I can't have held in my problems, I really will have exploded. That's how come we always talked of my many problems. Every one of my problems has been relayed to you both, maybe so you could/can help me. I've ran out of options. That's how come I get so depressed — when I can't see a future. When I have talked about things such as no future, **I mean that**. That shows you how bad I am. Therapy cannot help me now, except to stay sane, not from going insane. When that has come to what we can do in the future, I'm really scared. I'm asked you both to stay with me, to take each day for each day. Right now, normally I get depressed for a couple days (3-4)* *maybe and always come up. It has been a few days and I haven't come up. I wanted no more than to have lived a fulfilled lives and I'm scared I won't be able to. Please understand I wanted you both to understand more where I came from. You both mean the entire world to me, and I can't live another second with no support. Thanks so much for always being there, I am really focused on how to get healthy. Been going to double therapy, trying harder to find solutions. There have been so many days when I wanted to fall back into your arms, ma. Every day I work harder to get more healthy."*

This is really how I wrote. These grammatical and wrong tense phrases were intentional compulsions, although I knew better. I went along with each compulsion and wrote it however my mind told me to, just to be able to keep writing.

FYI — *I never gave the letter to my parents.*

The intrusive thoughts still came to me all the time, but I began to give less and less authority and credit to them. They were there, taunting me, but not consuming me quite as much, little by little. I still had to continue with weekly therapy to continue my fight, but I was able to go back to my home town for the rest of the days in the week. If I had just quit the therapy altogether then right after the program, I would have relapsed. Having to fight a disorder like this is just like an addiction. People with addictions go to rehab, and people with disorders go to intensive therapy. No matter how long you go through treatment, every day is another day to re-double your efforts, just like it's another day to fall behind yet again. Just like one drink can send someone back into the alcoholic stage, even performing one compulsion can make someone re-gain all the beliefs and give back all the credit in the world to OCD. The key for me was being intentional in capitalizing on the times I was able to mentally detach from the OCD. The more I was able to take those moments in strength and mentally detach myself from the OCD, the stronger I became and the weaker the OCD became.

The idea that I might never fully comprehend this disorder is a fact of life. The idea that you may never completely overcome your trials is very much a possibility. It's just something that we need to accept in this life. Once you accept it, you can push forward without that preconceived standard or notion and just do the best you can. Accepting your OCD and overcoming your OCD are two completely different things. You can't just accept your OCD and never try to overcome it. And you can't overcome your OCD if you haven't truly accepted it for what it truly is. You must first accept your OCD, try to understand how the disorder works, and then seek the proper treatment to overcome the worst of it.

Remember, you still have a life to live. You can still live a fully functioning life amidst OCD. You can. You just need the proper tools. Although you may not be able to completely reject the cards that you are dealt, you can learn how to play them better than anybody else at the table. Now take a look at those cards and think about your next move. Or just listen to mine.

Author's Note: There's that saying, "Quit while you're ahead." This couldn't be farther from the truth with OCD. If you quit while you're ahead, you'll never know how far you could have gone. You will have stopped. If you just keep going, and don't quit while you're ahead, you will continue to break your mental boundaries down and *keep* them that way. You will be shocked what you are capable of when you continue to push through these mental boundaries with OCD. This is a dedicated risk that you have to be willing to take in life, especially in situations with trials such as OCD. OCD is never ending. It can get much lighter and much more manageable, but it is a constant fight. If you ever quit, if you ever stop putting up the fight because you feel like you have "enough" control over your OCD, you will lose to the fight and fall behind. You must keep at it. You are the tortoise and OCD is the rabbit. You must never quit because you think the work you've done on your OCD is enough. It will never be enough. OCD will always find a way back in. You must never quit. Accept the life style. That's just the point. Your job is to realize that quitting is never an option, because at any point that you quit, you have become subject to weaken against your disorder once again. Weakening myself to fall back into the depths of belief in my OCD after so many years and constant effort to control it is not an option in my book, and it sure as hell shouldn't be one in yours.

14

"SHE FOUND HER GOLD-TIPPED WINGS"

I returned back to Concordia the following semester. It made the most sense. Dealing with a transfer, finding a new school, moving my life just because I had managed to humiliate myself for my entire freshman year was still far over my head given my current state. The school was just as small, the people were just as secretive, and the memories were still very prevalent the moment I stepped back on that campus. I was facing the brink of my life after battling OCD all summer long. At least I looked like a normal person when I went back. I remember that very day and how I actually felt attractive. My hair was still healthy from the cut over the summer and was brushed, and I had a semi-new outlook, just hoping for a new chance at my reputation. But I was carrying a lot of hurt and baggage with me (I swear an invisible chain was attached to me at all times, lugging the world's heaviest suitcase of emotional baggage known to man), and it stung every time I looked into the eyes of someone who I knew questioned me or remembered me at my worst state.

My OCD was still with me every single day. At the beginning of the semester, although the OCD was prevalent, it didn't completely consume me as it had when I was at my worst. I still battled with desperately wanting thicker hair, but my OCD began to branch further into other random anxiety provoking obsessions. If I had a speech coming up, I was always terrified and would sometimes give in to last minute random compulsions right before the speech. I did this because I knew I would stop dead in my tracks mid-speech, anxious with fear of forgetting my words if I hadn't "kept it safe" by doing the compulsions. Although my compulsions had no effect on reality, they sometimes gave me momentary confidence before I had a highly anxious task in front of me. I performed them "just in case." By this point in time, I knew very well I shouldn't be giving into them, but sometimes I just needed the temporary confidence in my false belief system to get through a part of my day. If I had a test the next week, I would have to perform all my compulsions so that I would do well. Or if I had to present in front of my class, I would have to perform a ton of compulsions just so that I wouldn't mess up and go blank with fear as OCD would taunt me. What I was really doing was mentally convincing myself that because I had kept up with all my compulsions, I had the ability to perform whatever it was that I needed to perform at confidently. Even though the actual compulsions weren't doing anything in reality, I was just giving myself that confidence, *just in case*. What I didn't realize at that moment was that confidence could stem from non-compulsory acts! I just needed to test myself by not performing any of the compulsions before my anxiously awaiting tasks. I couldn't seem to commit and just do it, even though I knew better.

Performing my compulsions "just in case" was one of the most dangerous things I could have done after the intensive therapy program once I was back at school. Granted, I was performing them as a last resort unlike before, rather than viewing the situation as though there was no way to get through it without my OCD. But l was still hurting my recovery progress, feeding and strengthening the belief system in OCD. Fighting your OCD has to be somewhat cold turkey dedication, in my opinion, to actually see results. Me allowing certain compulsions in my highly anxious circumstances was a safety blanket for me, not allowing myself to completely let go. Each time I quickly performed a compulsion before an anxious task was yet another instance of regression. It was yet another time I pulled that safety blanket out and over my head. I knew at the time I wasn't supposed to be doing them, but I did them regardless. I wasn't holding myself accountable like I should have amidst all of the progress I had made. But I also *could admit that.* I could separate my OCD from what I should and shouldn't be doing instead of it all mushing together as it used to. The difference between before and after the intensive therapy program was that I now knew exactly when and how I shouldn't be giving into my obsessions. Therefore, every single time I gave in and reacted to my thoughts by performing the compulsions, I knew exactly what I was doing. I tried to push the immediate guilt I felt of performing the compulsions out of my head, but that guilt was a good sign. It meant I knew what I was doing was wrong.

Although my new dorm room was a million times better than the state of my old room, I still had certain tendencies in the room. I was light-years better with being sanitary, but I still was rooted in having certain things in certain places, not touching certain items, and having the room help lower my anxiety by maintaining certain routines. It was more of a sanctuary that year, a place where I could just be me, where I wasn't afraid of my every move like the previous year. There was definitely room for improvement with my personal sanitation, but I was much better than I had been in a long time.

The worst part of returning to school was remembering how to act in social situations. I had been out of a real social life and any real social interaction with people my age for so long, I had truly forgotten how to act at times in regards to what to say in certain circumstances, social timing, and just how to be the fun loving social butterfly I had once been. But I was at a point where I could return to school and hope for the best. I had just come out of the most intense summer of my life. A big part of me also wanted to return to that place, hair brushed, standing tall, and show them how wrong they had all been about me. *Yes, even little, battered me still had things to prove!* I wanted to graduate from a university with all four years completed in one place and not be run off by bullies because of my fear of fitting in from my own doing.

A few weeks into the school year, I met a baseball player that took a liking to me. People started to look at me again with a double take, but this time for all the right reasons instead of the wrong ones. I was able to put my head, well, a portion of my head, back into the real world. He took me home to his father's house after dinner one night, in retrospective because he wanted to show me how wealthy his estranged father, who he had recently re-connected with, was. Needless to say, I went along for his little ego-seeking game. I walked my new, little, improved self inside the monstrous home and ended up having an extensive conversation with his father. He was a very wealthy real estate mogul who had little to no time for a young girl waltzing into his house from his son's college. He actually seemed to have little time for anyone for that matter. Yet we ended up discussing everything from real estate, to ranches, to investing, and private planes. We had a lot in common since I was raised in a similar way, but it was obvious this man had never heard a nineteen-year-old girl remotely propose the things we discussed.

Fast forward through the evening — his father and I spoke the entire night. Matt, my coy little wannabe millionaire, just watched his father talk to me in pure awe. He couldn't believe that his father was speaking so much, let alone to some blonde girl he brought home with grown-out roots. The changing moment in time for me was when his father asked what it was that I wanted to do for my career. Funny thing was, I hadn't really put this on the forefront of my radar in the past year. I had just been focusing on trying to make it to the next day. I spit out that I wanted to be in the fashion industry. I mean, I loved fashion. It was one of the few real interests that I continued to have while I was so sick. His response? His daughter had a full-blown, high-end fashion label for women's casual wear. He mentioned she had been in Vogue, and her office was stationed in Newport Beach, right down the road from me. Did he say *VOGUE*? Although he didn't know all the details, he did give me one favor. An interview.

All I had on my résumé was secretary skills. But underneath all of my OCD and mental captivity, I knew I had a work ethic that was rare. I was willing to get a job done, no matter what it took, how long it took, or what extent I had to go to in order to do so. The only problem was that my OCD often got in the way of proving all of these things. That dedicated work ethic was all I was able to provide, and either this lady was going to accept me or deny me. If she really sat me down for a meeting, I would be able to show her the real me. I mean I could hide my compulsions for an interview, couldn't I? The problem was, I knew that the moment I left this bigwig's house, he would forget entirely about me and possibly never get me an interview.

Think again, darling! After Matt brought me home that night, he walked me to my door, and we said our goodbyes. I was still daydreaming about my future non-existent meeting with, well, his estranged stepsister. Two minutes after shutting the door, I heard a banging. I opened the door to Matt's phone being pushed to my face, with a text message from his father that said, "Whoever that girl was that you brought home tonight, feel free to bring her around anytime." Matt looked at me like I was just crowned the princess of Sweden. He had no words. His father never texted him, *let alone* about some girl he brought home. He said, "You're getting that interview." I shut my door, having no idea what was ahead of me.

A couple of days later, I got a call from the designer herself. Her father had put in the good word about me, and we had an interview scheduled for the following Friday. I was exactly where I wanted to be for the first time in three years. Mind you, at this point, I hadn't made anything happen. Once you get an "in" like this, you realize you can either recognize it and grab it, or ever so slightly overlook it. And I grabbed it by *the you know what.*

Author's Note: When I am drained from life, my mom and I have this thing where I go to hug her, and I fall into her and go limp. She then tells me to "tuck in my wings," meaning my arms. I do so, and she holds my arms and back tight as if she is recharging my wings. She has always told me that I have wings — specifically gold-tipped wings — and only she and God can see them. Our family spends an enormous time in our second home, Colorado. She knows how much I love the fall in Colorado, when everything turns pure gold. She tells me with each fall season that comes, I ruffle my wings and the gold dust sprinkles onto all of the Aspen trees, and that's why they are gold. If you're laughing, I feel you. If you're crying — I *feel* you. I tell you this in confidence because it was right about this time in my life when I started to believe her.

15

"THE CHOSEN ONE"

Leading up to the interview, I had the anxiety of a raging lunatic attempting to break out of an asylum. I had never had a real interview with a stranger before. Since my anxiety was so high, I had compulsions up the you know what. That was the last thing that I needed — for my potential Vogue ranked boss to see me touch objects multiple times, stare at a specific place and count the seconds to an even number until I could look away, wait a certain number of seconds before I answered her — any unusual or abnormal behavior like that could cost me the job. My OCD could be somewhat under control, but as soon as my anxiety heightened, so did my obsessions, and therefore, my compulsions. But what's so funny about OCD is that distraction is oftentimes an outlet. This interview and potential internship was my distraction, so I couldn't dwell as much. If anything, worst-case scenario, I would just make up for all the compulsions later, I thought. *"You can't screw this up, Ker!"* I kept telling myself. At one point, I would have completely chosen my compulsions over my interview. I would have performed all of them because it was more important for me to perform and protect myself from the potential repercussions than to get a job. But I was no longer at that point, where I was willing to sacrifice an opportunity like this for my OCD. Watch where that new mentality landed me.

"Let's just pretend that I get the job. Let's just say that I was able to handle my compulsions enough for the fifteen-minute interview with her. How could I hold a job with constant, still noticeable compulsions?" The questions rang in-between my ears. I was at least able to walk in a straight line, which I couldn't have done a year ago, but I still performed notable compulsions. It's not like I walked out of the intensive program at the institute as if it was the fountain of freedom and I was cured. I couldn't have my compulsions interfering with her company. I couldn't really enter numbers correctly or stick with a synchronized system. I couldn't write sufficiently, still often skipping certain letters in words. I was a smart young lady, mind you, with an incredible vocabulary. But every time I wanted to speak my mind, some intrusive thought would enter my head, not allowing me to use my vocabulary and knowledge to sound as smart as I actually was. Nevertheless, I knew I could pass with a few small compulsions and thought that I could hide the rest. I had become so good at hiding my compulsions when I first met someone, and the more I got to know somebody, the more I would allow my compulsions to come out. So, in a case like this, all was well until, that is, I got hired...

I showed up for my interview, prepared for the worst but also for the best. I knocked on the office door only to find no answer. Again and again, I knocked. All of a sudden, right outside the side door, I could hear a frantic woman gathering all her stuff from an overly waxed black and silver Bentley and making a run towards the office I was standing in front of. She entered the door to greet me, apologizing profusely. She looked like she had just walked off the set of "The Hills," the popular reality TV show at the time. She looked like a mix of Paris Hilton and Whitney Port. Easily could be a sister of either. She's that girl who looks better without any makeup than with it. She swayed through her office door, her long, ombre, still damp curls swinging, revealing the cutest office of all white and clear furniture I had ever seen. After complaining about what a "mess" the place was, even though it was totally fitting with the décor, she sat me down for my interview.

Mind you, all I had on my résumé was having worked at my father's oral surgery office for a summer in high school. Why she would even consider me for an intern position in the high-end fashion world beat me. I finally realized why I was sitting there. It was because of the work of her father. She said that her father had called her and said that she must meet *this girl*. That "girl" was now sitting in front of a golden ticket as far as I was concerned. This was my break to try and get out of my head and force myself into reality. This was my break to begin building a resume and create the start of a normal, balanced life. In that instance, I realized one of two things could happen. I could either push aside my OCD and focus completely on what she was asking me, thereby portraying myself in the best possible way, or I could give up this opportunity of a lifetime and sit with my OCD misery for who knows how much longer. Guess which option I chose? Bingo. Slowly but surely, I stuck to my guns.

She stared right into my eyes, as if she was waiting to see if I would do anything abnormal. She spoke to me about life, and after making a real effort by simply being myself, she mentioned that I reminded her so much of herself. Ha! That compliment! If she only knew...

I went as far as telling her that I would be happy to just take the trash out because I was so honored to represent her company. I just needed an in. As we spoke, more and more intertwined connections and similarities surfaced. We connected on family affairs, properties, and the business itself. We had so many similarities, yet she was unaware of all of our differences. She was unaware of my little secret, which I was trying so hard to hide. She concluded our session having mentioned that many, many girls had applied from Fashion Institute of Design & Merchandising (FIDM) — the largest fashion merchandising school in Los Angeles. These girls had actual fashion experience...and she chose me.

My secret in the few moments of my interview was pretending that I didn't have OCD. I simply enjoyed the moments as a "normal" girl... A normal girl who would cut off her leg for the opportunity she was literally sitting in front of. We finished our discussion with the intention of following up the next day regarding scheduling. I waltzed out the door making sure to tap a chair three times (my obsessive number at the time) just before exiting the building. A girl has to be on the safe side you know.

Author's Note: Notice how I said my secret was pretending that I didn't have OCD for a few moments. So now I'm asking you to take a moment and picture where your life would be without your OCD. Would you have a different job? Would you be able to get out the door faster without all your rituals? Enjoy the bliss of a calm state of mind, no matter what life threw at you? Date freely? Breathe? *Enjoy this instant.* Close your eyes, and let whatever you picture sink in. Allow yourself to be mentally free, right now, even for just a moment. Mentally walk through the steps of a day in that new life for your own entertainment. Can you even imagine? Yes, there would still be other trials, but if this huge one wasn't there, that subtle voice torturing you, if there was something you could do about it to stop it in its tracks... Ahhhh, how life would be. Now open your eyes. Whatever you pictured should be your goal. In fact, your life was meant to be that very goal because we are given the gift of free will. As human beings, we are able to practice that free will, if we can overcome the trials that stand in our way.

What's stopping you again? That S.O.B — OCD. Think of it this way, nobody just walks right into a brick wall; they find ways to walk around it. Even if it takes longer to walk around, they choose to do that rather than keep pounding their head against the brick. So think of that brick wall as your OCD, and think of ways around it. Make a move and schedule an appointment with your therapist. If you don't have a therapist who you know is an OCD specialist — find one. Go to the International OCD Foundation website or the Psychology Today website and search your state and area. Find potential therapists, call them and ask what areas they specialize in. If they say OCD, ask them how they approach treatment. If they don't mention ERP, you need to move on down the list. I will explain this in much more detail in the second part of this book. Research and read books on OCD to educate yourself, reach out to others you see online (like me!) who have OCD and seem to be living what you would consider true quality life. Persevere through the fight against OCD, just get the hell around it. Make a move in the opposite direction of your OCD. Think about every possible option for getting out of whatever situation you're in, no matter how ridiculous or impossible it may sound right now. Write them all down: all the solutions that may or may not be possible to help you fight your OCD, resources, and people to touch base with to lead you in the right direction. At least train your mind to start thinking about the options you have to work on knocking OCD off its endless tracks. Train your mind to believe there is life after the worst of OCD, even while still living with OCD. Train your mind to think about the possibility of living a fully functional life with OCD. Dealing with actually making that step happen can come later. At this moment, just entertaining the hopeful idea of being without the extreme weight of OCD is key to prepare yourself for what's to come. Give yourself this gift of imagining something good and well deserved for once.

16

"TWO STEPS FORWARD, TEN STEPS BACK"

My sophomore year turned out to be far from smooth sailing after my time in the intensive program that summer. I got the incredible internship, was giving all my classes my best efforts, but I started to sink back into the power of OCD worse and worse as my hair started to fall out at a fast pace again. Most of all, my hair was providing an immense distraction from being able to perform at my utmost ability on all fronts. I would go through periods when I would get breaks from the hair shedding, and my heart was always a teensy bit lighter and brighter during those times. Then, my spirit would be crushed when I noticed it started happening again, and my heart would return to black. As my hair started shedding yet again, my compulsions became my safety blanket once more. They interfered with me being able to really think outside the box, contribute something worthwhile to my new internship, and they even interfered with me being able to do the most basic tasks asked of me. My head was once again consumed with everything except the task in front of me. I eventually told Lacey, my boss and the designer, about my OCD. My pain was too consuming and too obvious to avoid discussing it any longer. She was very understanding of my situation even though she didn't understand OCD. She must have been able to tell I was suffering deeply inside because she would take the time out of our days when I was so unfocused to help me think of ways and products to stop hair loss. I ended up investing in everything she told me about, from hair pills, to a hard water filter for my shower, to certain expensive hair products. I wanted to have an outlet to depend on other than my OCD. I wanted to make sure I was giving every single thing I could a try so that I didn't have to only rely on my OCD.

My internship with Lacey proved to be the greatest experience of my life at that point. It set a foundation for me to take on a new level of life I hadn't known existed outside of my isolated world. Although I struggled immensely with my OCD, being around a normal environment and watching how Lacey worked and lived her life was so encouraging to me. I wanted to live a life that...effortlessly. I was able to force myself to work against my obsessions at times and proved to be of actual help to the company, though I knew I was capable of more. I grew in so many ways through the internship, mostly because my world had expanded so much. I felt so far from where Lacey was, yet no matter how far off I felt from living a normal life, I was still experiencing life outside of my dorm room. I was experiencing a reality that made me realize the importance of fighting my OCD, so I, too, could live in that same reality.

More than anything that year, I felt defeated. I had already been to through intensive outpatient therapy — that ship had sailed. I knew the basis of OCD and how to fight it, but I just lost my strength yet again. It would take one look down at my arms and see fallen, long, blonde hairs that would send me into countless, paralyzing traps of nothingness. I started to give up on everything because I realized I didn't even have OCD to rely on anymore since I had learned there was no correlation between my obsessions and compulsions. It was my only sense of control in the world. A part of me, of course, still believed in the correlation, but a larger part of me knew deep down my compulsions were nothing but fluff and a waste of time. I started to lose interest in life again. Now that I didn't have OCD as my power to ease the paralyzing fear of my obsessions, what control did I have over anything in life? I still performed compulsions, because I so desperately wanted something to lean on, but my belief in the OCD was faltering, which left me with just my reality. There were nights in my dorm room that I will never forget — nights where I would cry so hard, I would lose the strength in my body and fall to the ground. I would practically scream out to God, praying for nothing more in the world than just relief from it all, which I hoped would provide relief from my OCD. I needed relief from my hair. I needed peace — just a moment of peace. My mind was overtaken and every direction in which I thought, there was another roadblock stopping me from my mental happiness. My mind was so intertwined, I couldn't see through the fuzz anymore. I didn't see how I could continue living in such captivation. I wasn't living life the way it was supposed to be lived; I was instead living day by day, just trying to get by.

Whenever I would come home for a weekend or for school breaks, oftentimes my dad would take me for a drive. It went unspoken really, but he knew I needed to be driven in order to relax. Many times, I would climb up in his truck, and he would just drive. I would stare out the window and no words were ever spoken. Much of the time I would fall asleep and actually be peaceful for an hour of my life, as long as my daddy was driving me. I'll never forget the first time my song came on, "Angels On The Moon," by Thriving Ivory. My dad was driving me, and I remember him turning up this song because it was just a great rock song. But I was listening to the lyrics. Word by word, it began to crack right through my core, my soul, my mind. I would turn my head so far, my neck would hurt so he couldn't see the tears pouring down my face and ask why. Music has never really spoken to me like it does for some people. But this song...this song spoke to my deepest pits of darkness. It goes a little something like this:

> Do you dream, that the world would know your name
> *So tell me your name,*
> Do you care, about all the little things or
> *anything at all?*
> I wanna to feel, all the chemicals inside *I wanna feel*

I wanna a sunburn, just to know that I'm alive
To know I'm alive.
Don't tell me if I'm dying, 'cause *I don't wanna know*
If I can't see the sun, *maybe I should go*
Don't wake me cause I'm dreaming,
of angels on the moon
Where everyone you know, never leaves too soon.
And do you believe in the day that you were born
Tell me do you believe?
Do you know that
every day's the first of the rest of your life?

I've always been able to control my outward emotions, but not once to this day have I heard this song and not found sheets of tears falling down my expressionless face when I hear these lyrics.

The difference between my sophomore and the year before the institution was that underneath it all, I was much more in tune with my OCD that year. I was much more educated on the power it had over me. I was more mature to make better decisions, and I actually started to care about developing a social life. I so desperately wanted all of these things, but I couldn't touch them. My mental barrier became a physical barrier. Here I was, doing much better socially, not such an obvious outcast, yet I was so far from being emotionally stable. The truth was, deep down, I knew how to handle and get a grip on my OCD even without therapy, but I deliberately made decisions not to because my anxiety was always so high. That was the problem. Instead of staying on a solid track after therapy, I let my fears surpass the small strength I had gained.

I still longed every single day to have the relief I felt the day I left the salon a year prior when my hair had been brushed out. I felt like I lived among the clouds that day. I had no idea how sunken into the wallows of life I had become. You know how whenever you leave the salon after getting your hair blown out, it looks a hundred times better, no matter how hard you try to do it yourself? I remembered that feeling. I desperately needed to feel that again, even just for a moment. I made an appointment with the same lady who had separated me from my dreadlocks the year before to just get my hair shampooed and blown out. It didn't go as planned.

After she washed my hair, and I was sitting back in the chair while she brushed it out, I saw all the hair that was coming out. My plan had backfired. I began to sink in the chair, wishing with every fiber in me I had never stepped back into the salon. I began to cry uncontrollably and caused a scene. I couldn't help it, no one could calm me down. I was emotionally draining out anything I had left in me. My hairdresser began to get frustrated, retreated off, and came back with something in her hand. It was a small silver dollar with an angel engraved in it. She put it inside my palm and closed my fingers. She told me to hold it close and pray every time I felt the way I was feeling in that moment. Unfortunately, I couldn't have cared less about anything other than my hair right then. I eventually calmed down as best I could and was able to drive home. Let's just say the next time I went to make an appointment with her — a year after this incident — she declined me as a client because of her previous experiences with me. Do we blame her?

I went on throughout the year succeeding further in some ways, such as not letting my OCD interfere as much with my schoolwork and social life, but I suffered in other internal ways. I began to devote myself entirely to my schoolwork as my outlet. I stopped letting my OCD prevent me from being able to dictate the things I needed to do, and really used school as a channel to execute my best. As a result, I became an excellent student again. It provided me with such confidence. I was able to give almost all of myself to something and was slowly proving my worth to myself. I had always taken school very seriously, but the year before, I had allowed my OCD to overtake the one thing I was best at. Once I got myself focused on my schoolwork, something other than myself, I started to progress in other ways. I wasn't going to continue to let my OCD interfere with something I was so good at, my only outlet, or the very few things that brought me relief and joy. No — never again.

Author's Note: Regression after such significant progress has to be one of the most defeating feelings in the world. How can you still feel empowered when you are watching a battle of you defeating yourself? You're climbing a ladder only to have someone tugging your leg back down. You can't control when OCD flames and flares up out of nowhere when you are working so hard on yourself. But you can control your reaction to the flares, regardless of your anxiety level at the time. Once my hair started shedding again, I didn't care enough to keep fighting. I had just enjoyed a break, a little time to focus on defeating my OCD, only to revert back once again. I needed to quickly learn that this would happen my entire life. This was a life with OCD. Right when I thought I could catch a break from OCD, it always found a loophole to spark. It's a fire that never completely goes out. It simply simmers and sizzles down until it lights you up again. However, the harder and more consistently I fought my OCD with ERP, the stronger I became over time. How you react in these regressing circumstances will be the most critical times in your life to use your inner strength and train your brain that you are stronger than your OCD. Once you begin to prove how in control you can be amidst these regressing times by stopping the compulsions, you start to gain confidence in your character. You can't help but smile at yourself, and your progress, to which you can only ascertain and credit to yourself. Allow yourself to receive that credit. No matter how lost you may find yourself, if you're still reading this, you are one badass human being. You deserve credit for being wherever you are. You deserve credit for even reading this book on OCD Recovery, even if nothing comes of it for you.

17

"A LIFE TO BE LIVED"

I pressed onward towards my junior year at Concordia University. My hair had stopped shedding again at some point going into the new school year, and I was able to use that time frame to become healthier. I seemed to be on an upward slope again, becoming healthier every day. My anxiety stole from me and gave me the constant living fear that any day I would fall back into my black hole again. Every time I got that thought or pictured myself back in that place, I took myself back to the present moment, not allowing the fear to get ahead of me but rather stay close behind me. I just remember always pressing forward. Once I had a few good days in a row, I would do everything I could to stay on track and continue to have those days. After a while, the good days became a month. Then two months. I was becoming healthier very slowly but steadily. I was regaining my social appeal towards others and wanted to pursue a normal college life more than ever. I couldn't shake some of my OCD tendencies, but at first glance and first conversation, I could control it to a point where you might not be able to tell there was even anything wrong with me.

One day I received a message on my social media account from none other than my freshman year suitemate. This was the same girl who completely gave up on me within only a few weeks and who was a leader of those who doubted me. She messaged me to tell me we had somehow been assigned as suitemates — again! How could this happen? What were the chances? Her message was sweet, and instead of telling me she was filing for a repeal, she let me know she was willing to live together again if I was. *I was dumbfounded.* First of all, she had no idea about the institution or how much healthier I had become, so I couldn't imagine why she would take a stab at living within the same vicinity, let alone the same school as me again. She said in her note she knew we had a "misunderstanding," and my first thought was, 'That little misunderstanding is something called OCD, which is actually a BIG misunderstanding...but O.K." It was truly a sign and gift from God. I was faced with a second chance to re-build what I had destroyed and become part of a world I so desperately sought. I wrote her back explaining my situation, my OCD, the institution — everything. I assured her I was much healthier, and she would not face what she had previously had to live with. Ironically, I recently went back and read my responses to her on social media and could not get over the amount of compulsions in my responses. I couldn't use proper grammar and still couldn't use certain letters. So if I were her, I would have still been put off. Regardless, she couldn't have been more understanding, and we ended up working it out and moving in together.

My junior year was the year I started to really get my head about me. I applied for an internship to a local music management company because I wanted to expand my résumé beyond just fashion. The logical side of my brain was slowly crowding in on the illogical side. Between my dedication, distraction of school, and my new internship, I was well on my way to staying busy and productive. The busier and more productive I was, the more back down to earth I came. I was submersed into new worlds and was interested in parts of life again. I was so busy focusing my time on my various projects, I didn't allow my OCD to surround every single, solitary thought. I was still faced with many obsessions, but they seemed to somewhat decrease the busier I became. There were many new occasions when

I would get intrusive thoughts where I strongly felt I needed to perform a compulsion, but I just pushed through the thoughts and ignored them simply because of time. *My time was becoming more valuable than my obsessive and intrusive thoughts!* I was pushing myself back into reality, and because of this, I was forced to live within the boundaries of reality. On top of everything, I started making real friends. As my incredible friendships elevated, so did my life. I developed actual lifetime friendships with people who had once used me as their daily laughingstock. One of my newfound friendships was my suitemate's best friend — a girl from one of the groups my freshman year that had treated me awfully. She had never been horrible directly to me — but her friends had been — and she had borne witness to it all with her nose seemingly in the air. But something in her heart always went out to me, as if she saw behind my broken heart that I was just misunderstood. Ironically, we became incredibly close after those two in-between years, even though she was still friends with all the same people. I began to find my true personality again and could truly be myself. I started to think outside the box, organize school related functions, get out and meet people, and actually become a human being again. The more I saw the effortless way my friends lived their lives, the more it began to sink in that I could do the same. At times, I found myself wondering, why I was still allowing my disorder to complicate my life when I knew how to control it? When I knew I just needed to push through it? There was no reason to keep treading water when I had the education and knowledge of how to control my OCD right back. It became so much easier to push through my obsessions and not dwell on them. I thought there would be this looming, horrific anxiety that would hover over me when I pushed through my obsessions, but that shortly passed. The more I began to push past my obsessions and took the risk of uncertainty, the easier it became to keep pushing past them. There were times when I knew I needed to expose something using ERP because it was a recurring thought. So I did, and then I moved forward. There were also times I still gave into strong obsessions. However, I maintained a more constant control and began to feel less of a pull to perform my compulsions so often. My world was just so much bigger than it had been in years, and I was so full of life. That's really what it eventually came down to for me; I had a life to live beyond OCD.

I'm telling you, immersing myself further and further into the real world is what led to less and less time for my OCD to interfere in my life. There were times when I would get a moment to just breathe and realized I hadn't been performing as many compulsions as usual. That's when it began to register how unnecessary they were! My life was moving on, and the compulsions began to make less and less sense. What purpose did they serve? None! They were simply for comfort that I no longer needed because I was in complete control while at the same time knowing there are things I simply cannot control. And I was finally okay with that. Compulsions were simply distractions from the life waiting to be lived right in front of me. I learned this only by testing it, by not giving in to the OCD.

Many people were still skeptical of me. Others constantly grilled my new friends as to why they were friends with me. It broke me a little more each time I heard this had happened, but my heart was instantly fused back together when I heard my friends' responses back to them. People started to realize I was just misunderstood, and I was an incredibly funny, kind, caring person underneath my OCD. After a while, my life began to make sense again, and above all else, I had purpose. I had come so far in so little time because I wasn't just dwelling on each and every thought. Instead, I was living life. I was just another girl within the world instead of just creating it inside of my head. I never knew how isolated I had been until I was back inside the real world. It all came down to the realization and commitment that I could choose to make my quality of life a higher priority than to choose and rely on my OCD, the one thing that took me away from actual reality. It all came down to a choice; a choice I had never known was mine to make.

Author's Note: Second chances are not for everyone. And not everyone finds second chances. I didn't get the years I feel I wasted back, but I got the chance to finish what I started. I am so glad I was able to have a second chance at a healthy, young adult life before I finished college. I never had a true college experience because I was sick for most of it. By the time that I was better, I had ruined my reputation and was known as the girl who had something seriously wrong with her. However, there were a select few who gave me a second chance. I'm not saying these friendships were easy; in fact, my OCD affected each and every friendship. But I still had better friendships than I had previously. Overall, observing my friends helped me *so much* in my recovery. I wanted to live the same effortless life they did, and I knew that in order to do that, I would need to fight my OCD even harder. At first glance, it doesn't seem fair that I always had to play catch up with the rest of the world, but in actuality, being sick and playing catch up saved me from a lot of potential issues my friends went through. I never got involved in anything very bad because I was too busy trying to straighten my mind out. Sometimes I wonder if God allowed my OCD at the adolescent stage in my life to help me stay out of trouble and not get involved with the wrong crowds at such a crucial time in life. Regardless, I was somehow always in the right place at the right time, which is something I never question.

18

"AND SHE MOVED ON"

The faster my world moved, the faster my OCD was getting put on the backburner. I was still tested throughout my days but not in every single move I made. If I wanted a salad for lunch, I ordered a salad. If I wanted to wear red, I damn sure wore red. If I wanted to go somewhere, I went! My obsessions no longer made my decisions for me. But I certainly wasn't 100% better. The thoughts were still present but didn't sting as hard when I didn't give into them. Every day, amongst all of my OCD thoughts, I would get at least a few strong obsessions that I found it very hard not to give into. For these, I would actually still stop in my tracks and would sometimes perform the compulsion. I was much better at hiding the visible compulsions at this point. People knew I was better, and I couldn't allow myself to disappoint them, and myself, by giving them more reasons to think I was no better than before. I would be doing so well, then my anxiety would heighten about something, and one intrusive thought could throw off my entire day. I knew that I needed to stay very strong during these times because I was so much better, and it only took a few compulsions to reinstate the question of my belief in OCD yet again. When my head was in a good place and I was doing well for the most part, the absolute last thing I was going to allow was my mind to drift off and analyze the "what if's" because I knew where that would take me. So, I would mentally stop my mind and focus on something else before it could speed up and spin out of control. It wasn't just about doing exposures at that point, since I knew the effect of the exposures and what the results would be. It came down to me *just pushing through these thoughts.* I was aware of the strength between my mind and OCD, but I was also aware of my ability to make conscious decisions against it. The truth was, I still gave into many more compulsions than I should have. I had come leaps and bounds, but I still had leaps and bounds to make.

I kept my head in the game. I could feel my determined self still fighting, a side of myself I hadn't seen in years. I didn't feel so constricted — so close-minded. We are resilient human beings who have lived through mental torture and beyond. There is always something better on the other side, but we have to stay in the fight against the OCD and not give up because of the temporary anxiety we don't initially believe is temporary. But it is. You just have to do the work and persevere to prove this to yourself.

I got a job as a trend representative and sales associate at Nordstrom, which elevated my life in so many ways. I spent my days using my creative side, using my outlet to dress how I wanted, and most of all, help others dress how they wanted. I developed so many incredible customer service relationships and quickly became on the radar of the Nordstrom management. The biggest thing that I took away from my time at Nordstrom that summer was a confidence level I had never known before. One that even surpassed what it was pre-OCD. I was slowly finding myself, a little more every single day. My confidence gave me a new outlook on life, which helped me keep trucking ahead of my OCD. I was social. I was thriving. I was dating, and I was flourishing. A new life was developing before my eyes, and I knew I had to keep ahead of my OCD in order to keep this life from falling back. I had to keep this life from falling back to feeling like I had been buried alive but couldn't die.

The next summer, I got an internship with an LA based dress and gown designer, Tadashi Shoji. I commuted three days a week to Los

Angeles from Orange County for this new internship in the fashion public relations department. I was introduced into an entirely new and sophisticated world, worked with astounding people, and gained an immense amount of newfound knowledge.

I slowly started to make mistakes at the internship because of my self-doubt in a new and confusing world. Change can be very triggering, as we all well know. Once I made one mistake, I began to make more and more. I had two prestigious women that I worked under, and I felt like I was under a microscope, as kind as they were. After a while, it became a mindset where I would be constantly fearful of the next mistake I knew I was going to make. I spent so much time just trying to prevent these mistakes. I often zeroed in on them so much, that I kept making them. I became obsessed with not making a mistake. Unbeknownst to me, it became obvious that amidst any small mistakes I was making, my work ethic and dedication to be the best version of myself for the company was clear to the management around me. I was a blessing to them because I was working harder than any intern typically would with my obsessively dedicated mindset to each task. I recognized my OCD mindset vividly during this time and knew I needed to rise above it and see a wider scope than my tunnel vision of obsessiveness, or I would never get off this endless spinning wheel. I was slowly able to channel my OCD to help hold me accountable and stay organized, but at times I knew it was acting up over potential fear. I needed to slow down, reevaluate, and intentionally change my mindset. And that's okay!

As time went on, I ensured my OCD and self-doubt interfered less and less in my work. As I received obsessive thoughts that I was going to make a mistake, I intentionally shifted my mindset literally out and above the negative thought in that very moment. I then focused on performing to the best of my ability and scanned every detail to avoid mistakes. I began to see improvement and was able to shift my negative, obsessive mentality to a lighter, more efficient mindset. I developed confidence through this and realized how powerful a certain mindset can be. It can take you over and manipulate you just like you can let your OCD control you. I realized then the importance of keeping my mindset positive to avoid going down any rabbit holes, keeping my faith in myself, consistently remembering how far I had come, and how little of a chance it was that I was going to allow myself to go back the place I once was.

I was my very healthiest and happiest my last year of college. I believe my experiences with my internships and jobs leading up to that point are what gave me a sense of normalcy. When you are working for someone else, there comes a point where you just can't let your OCD win. You need to pay the bills. The more often I powered through my obsessive thoughts and didn't do anything about them, the more efficient and happier I became.

It truly couldn't have been more opposite from my first year. I had the most beautiful, organized, and neat apartment with a friend of mine, and for the most part, it was a very positive and uplifting environment. I was self-sufficient, healthy, and working towards a better me every single day. I was submerged in my schoolwork, and gave everything I had to every single task in front of me. I became a notable speaker in my advanced public speaking class, graduated with honors, and had a bright future ahead of me, as long as I didn't allow my OCD to completely overtake me again. I found ways for my OCD to actually enhance my work ethic rather than take away from it. I used it to be better detail oriented and efficient. I became so busy that I powered through every task, as though there was no time for OCD to come into play. I ended up securing yet another internship after I graduated, which was necessary for the industry I was going into — being a fashion publicist for celebrity red carpet dressing. I moved to Los Angeles, worked forty hours a week as an intern for free, and eventually landed a full-time job at another firm.

By that time, I wasn't at all worried about my OCD interfering with my new job. Consistently over these periods of time, I had the ability to control it whenever I needed to, and give into it if I really wanted to for comfort, without having my original diehard belief system in it. My OCD did, however, end up being a large factor in my new job, just not in a way I was accustomed to.

The company was one of Beverly Hills' top fashion public relations firms. It was a cutthroat, extremely fast paced, ruthless business dealing with high profile clientele daily. At first, I was one of the company's biggest assets because I didn't miss a single beat because of my OCD. It was a detail-oriented job, where the more small things you remembered, the better off you were. I noticed and caught little things no one else did. My OCD sees everything. Nothing goes unnoticed — that overstimulation is what had clouded my mind for years. I was very efficient, could do multiple tasks at once, and made sure everything was running according to how it should. But as time went on, I began to realize how obsessive I was becoming in the company. I became obsessed with maintaining constant control, making zero mistakes, and achieving perfection. In alignment with my OCD, I only saw things in black and white, but the company thought in grey. I was excellent at memorizing things, and whenever I was shown how to do something, I was able to closely follow the directions exactly every time after that. Because of my OCD, I stayed inside the lines at all times and never ventured outside of them. I became more and more confined to my black and white box. This may work for someone who is in a black and white work environment, but as I've said, this was not that place. The problem was my creative side was slowly getting left behind, and my black and white, rigid, obsessed side began to surface more and more. My boss was dedicated to perfection and had no time to hear or see anything but. This began to instill a deep-rooted fear in my already obsessive mindset. I took that very seriously and only became more obsessed with making no mistakes and certainly not being affiliated with any mistakes. I took every single thing I did extremely seriously, mostly because I was terrified of getting in trouble for the most mundane things, as everyone did. I felt an absurd amount of pressure to avoid getting a nasty, uncalled for email or an undeserved lecture. I became so obsessed with not getting into trouble and making sure everything was perfect, I began to cause issues with my coworkers. If I noticed they were doing something that wasn't in the best interest of the company, were plain lazy, or weren't following every step the exact way they should, I would get visibly upset. They didn't get my deep care and uptight obsession, which led them to purposely exclude me from company communication that was applicable to my position. Oftentimes because of the programming and tracking system we all used, their mistakes would affect my assistant position. As much as we all had our own lanes and clients, there was an overcrossing infrastructure that was hard to obsess over. I was working so hard to impress my boss — which I often did — and I couldn't let anything, or anyone, get in the way of that, especially mistakes that weren't mine. Fear drove my OCD.

My boss noticed that I was giving every fiber of my being to the job. It was so obvious. What she and I didn't realize at the time was my obsession with having everything "just so" was beyond just my character; it was my OCD. It became a problem; I became a problem. I only became more obsessive, more rigid, and treated everything as though it were my company because I cared *too* much. I remember the day my own boss told me I needed to almost care a little bit less. Can you imagine? As phenomenal at the job as I was, it wasn't the job itself I was really good at. It was my obsessive dedication to be perfect and make sure everyone and everything else was as well. That is when I realized OCD goes much further beyond intrusive thoughts and physical compulsions. It can also be a natural, constant state of obsession towards any certain thing or everything in life. My mindset was being filtered through an OCD lens, in a disguised way. All of a sudden, years later, I see now so clearly how my OCD was no longer just distinct obsessions followed by distinct compulsions. It was a mind frame in its entirety. OCD seemed to be a part of me that was all too natural, to the point I didn't even know it was OCD for a very long time. I realized how big of a problem I was contributing at times; although in retrospect, I was a blessing in disguise for the company because I didn't miss a thing and caught everything. I cannot take all of the blame because my work environment was far from anything that was positive or well structured. There was no healthy management. It was the type of work environment that OCD feeds off of and festers in — extremely fast paced, nothing is ever good enough, instilled real fear, and obsession to not let the same bad mistake or instance happen twice. The more toxic my environment and coworkers became, the more toxic and obsessed I became. A couple of years and many, many confused tears later, I decided to leave the company.

Throughout the unfolding of everything just mentioned, there were still days when I would forget I had OCD. I was so incredibly busy, so focused, even happy at times when things were going well. I didn't think about it. Obviously, it was my entire mindset, but again, I wasn't often receiving distinct obsessions and performing compulsions. Then there were days when my OCD was in full effect. Something would trigger it from work, and I would have to battle off unwelcome thoughts all day. I lived in constant fear of my boss calling my name. No matter how stressful things became, no matter how far off the edge I was pushed, and no matter how mean they became, one thing was very prevalent. I was living an incredible life, with many opportunities any girl my age would have killed for, and I still had OCD. I had managed to learn to control it to the fullest extent that I could. Yes, my OCD continued to develop into other themes of OCD — from symmetry, to sexual OCD, to perfection and beyond. But no matter the direction it went, I still knew deep down how to control it. At the end of the day, I had still exposed myself to the root of OCD. Neither obsessions or compulsions have ANY merit whatsoever and are complete illusions. Amidst all of the issues I was facing in the real world, I found ways to cope with them other than my reliance in OCD. At the time, I had only ever met one person, other than myself, with severe OCD who was in active recovery. The bottom line was I knew my case was rare — a case that went from a dire, life-threatening belief in OCD, to a case within a few years that knew exactly how to manipulate OCD right back on itself. When I was at my healthiest place in my senior year, I had a brilliant and life altering idea. I was going to document my story because the truth was, I had a story of all stories to tell. Over time, I had developed many tools, reasoning, and solid advice that I credit to overcoming my severe OCD. I had gone from a person who looked and acted possessed, homeless, and crazy, to a high fashion junior publicist working at a top agency in Los Angeles with the world at her finger-tips. I felt compelled to share my story and all of the incredible tools and mantras I used to begin to live a fully functioning life amidst severe Obsessive-Compulsive Disorder. The decision was made. I was going to write a book.

Author's Note: It hit me during the summer of 2013. I had to get my story out there. How could I never share with my fellow obsessive outsiders my 180° circle with OCD? Many people cannot even get to 90°. The bottom line is that my story is one of stripped bare, pure, no nonsense, *real* hope. The fact that I couldn't even write a full sentence five years ago to being able to write an entire book today blows my mind. I figure if I get a second chance at living life with OCD, you should too. Or you should at least have someone to look to and know it *IS* possible to leap off the seemingly endless spinning wheel if you truly want to. That is why I created the premise of this book. I wanted you to hear an OCD success story solely from the sufferer herself, not a therapist or doctor who studies OCD. This is me talking to straight to you — patient to patient — to get on your level, look you right in the face, grab your hand, and help take you above it all. The saying goes, "and to all a good night," but I say, "and to all a good life."

PART II

19

"THE TABLES ARE TURNING"

S o now you know. I am one of you, yet another obsessive outsider. Now we move on from my story...to yours. I am not writing this book just to tell my story. I needed to tell you my story to gain your trust so that you will listen to my advice on fighting OCD and know it's coming from a place of personal history. After all of my personal disclosure and experience, I felt compelled to leave you with concrete advice, tips on how to even begin this process of returning back to a life worth living. I am living proof this mindful transition is doable and so extremely worth it.

Because of how far I've come with overcoming severe OCD, I am so passionate about sharing the tools that worked for me with other fellow OCD sufferers. I am most passionate about putting just about everything you need to know in one place so that you can read the last page of this book, throw it down, and make some serious moves in your own life. I want you to walk away from reading this book and have a solid wrap around what it is you need to do to take the next step towards living a normal and fully functional life with OCD. But this process can only truly begin with you. I really do mean that. It's not a cliché statement. Let me be even more specific — no matter how many therapists, doctors, and specialists you've seen or spoken to, no matter how much you think you've learned about conquering OCD, none of this is part of the actual process to you getting better. That is all the preliminary work — the duty of your research — but it is not the work itself. The process of you truly working towards living a more normal life with the worst of OCD behind you does not begin until you begin doing the work *intentionally and internally.*

This is the part where I break down for you what I believe are the essential tools for making leaps and bounds in your progress. Before I do so, I need you to fully understand something. You may have read my story and not related to my OCD at all because you could have a completely different theme of OCD, such as cleanliness OCD, sexual OCD, or harm OCD. You may not at all believe or relate to my magical thinking with miscellaneous compulsions. But I guarantee you one thing, if you have hit the worst of your OCD, you related to the struggle and the pain of my story. It's hard to understand a type of OCD you don't have, just like I struggled to relate to my peers in my support group. At first, I didn't understand why or how they could believe some of the things they did. But it didn't matter if I understood, it mattered that I related. It mattered that I supported them and identified with them in the same struggle I was going through. This brings me to my next point. As you continue reading, remember that although you and I may have completely different types of obsessions, *the way to combat and conquer OCD remains the same.* That is my focus and intent for the rest of this book — to show you that although we are different in our obsessions, we are woven from the same cloth and can share the same thread count to get where we are going. So far this has just been my story. Let's incorporate yours now since we all have the same desired outcome — to live a life free from the constant binding chains of OCD. The name of the game is the same for all of us.

Before you can truly begin your attack on OCD, you must first find sustainable guidance in doing so. By that I mean a therapist trained in anxiety disorders, specifically someone who specializes in Obsessive-Compulsive Disorder. I went through countless therapists and psychiatrists who could not help me in the long term because they were not practiced in how to effectively treat OCD. They were talk therapists who only use psychotherapy week after week, without honing in and taking action on the behavioral part, which is the core of OCD. You know the drill. You attend weekly therapy to do your part, attempt to disclose your current obsessions to your therapist, leave feeling slightly encouraged, and then get home only to realize the therapy was only momentarily satisfying because you are yet again, trapped in your own mind. Countless patients go through this same system for years and years, wasting thousands of dollars and sleepless nights wondering what will give. And I don't blame them. Most people don't even know about the need for Exposure and Response Prevention (ERP) to combat OCD because their therapists don't regularly practice it in an intensive manner, as they are not OCD Specialists with primarily OCD patients. A lot of people don't even realize there are very specific, sound ways to combat OCD, rather than just live in torture. You don't talk your way out of OCD; you *prove* your way out of OCD. ERP is the most effective therapy to combat OCD, and I can tell you that firsthand, not because I am getting it out of a textbook. Since ERP can practice physically, mentally, and orally exposing your thoughts, you are taking them from inside your head and putting them out into the open. I will never be able to say it enough. Talk therapy will rarely get you far in your progression of battling OCD. You must PROVE to yourself that your compulsions in response to your obsessions — no matter what they are or what your OCD tells you — have no effect on reality. You must prove to yourself that you are not going to actually do what your violent thought is telling you. You must prove to yourself that nothing bad will happen if you don't check the door lock for the eight time, check that the stove is off for the ninth time, or remain filthy and diseased because you didn't wash for the tenth time. You will get nowhere if you only talk with a therapist about these thoughts! Well, technically you will get worse because you are honing in and picking apart your thoughts, analyzing any truth in them which will only intensify your obsession. The cycle continues to go around and around and around. You must prove to yourself what you fear deep down *will not happen* by doing the *opposite of what your OCD is telling you to do.* That's all any of this really comes down to — a grueling fear, a mere thought. Air. It's not real. But I understand why you are terrified it is real, because it *feels so real.*

I can't express the seriousness of finding the therapist that fits best for you and your OCD. This therapist will be the one to initially guide you on this incredible fight. They are your most useful resource. Finding the perfect therapist can be a daunting task, but it is essential that you find a therapist you can trust with everything in you before you even approach the beginning of your fight against OCD. If you don't trust your therapist, you will not trust him/her to help you truly overcome the worst of this disorder. You will rather continue doubting everything they say, which you will do enough of already. Furthermore, you have to go beyond just trusting your therapist; you have to be utterly and completely honest with them. Be an open book when it comes to your OCD, or you will never fully get over the depths of your OCD. Don't hide anything. For a long time, I thought to myself, "How can I ever expect someone who does not have OCD to fully wrap him or herself around what I am going through? How was I going to explain to another doctor, who I knew was just another human being that didn't have OCD, everything that I was truly thinking?" I felt I was subjecting myself to somebody that didn't understand what my obsessions were and how they worked. "What if he is insensitive to my darkest feelings? What if this isn't OCD, and they call someone on me because I really am what I'm thinking? What is the point of trying to even remotely explain what is happening in my head, when I don't even know what's happening?" The thoughts pass through so quickly — yet so slowly — at times even we lose them before we can catch them to expose. You must develop unwavering trust in your therapist. That will be the only thing that keeps you coming back.

If you need a recommendation of a therapist, mine would be my very own — The Gateway Institute. The primary office is based in Orange County, California, and they have recently opened a practicing branch in Scottsdale, AZ and San Francisco, CA. Further recommendations can be found in the OCD Resources section in the back of the book. To be clear, I'm not being compensated for any of my recommendations. I cannot stress the importance of having the right backbone of the right therapist to help jumpstart your very personal fight. I am giving it to you straight. Finding a trustworthy and appropriately trained therapist who has confirmed they practice Exposure and Response Prevention (ERP) will be the best decision you've ever made in your life. And *that* is where you start.

Author's Note: Chances are, if you've purchased this book, you are aware of your OCD and have sought some type of therapy for it at one point. Perhaps you've already found a fantastic therapist, one you've built trust with over a period of time. Perhaps you do not honestly feel you have found a therapist like mine, one who will take on your individual journey and truly guide you in the right direction. Perhaps you don't feel the need for a therapist at all at this point, or you just don't know where to begin. My advice for you is to shop around. Do your own thorough research, ask for recommendations, schedule consultations with a few different therapists, and see how well they can identify with you. Look into the therapists that your insurance will cover and find out if they practice ERP. If not, move on, as many of us who have incorporated personal ERP often say. Make a list of those in your insurance plan who confirm they do practice ERP and are OCD Specialists. Then move on to a few highly recommended doctors outside of your insurance and do the same thing. Skype therapy has taken off as well. I have a friend who lives in California, and since there are no OCD Specialists around her who practice ERP, she found an incredible therapist in New York (who is also licensed in CA) she Skypes with regularly. I also know people with OCD who cannot drive and Skype with therapists in their very own state. Don't cut yourself short in your research or give up, thinking you can't find anyone who will take your insurance or that you would have to re-locate to another state for therapy for a few weeks. This process is so much bigger than any of these issues. This is the rest of your damn life, a life that you don't deserve living in its current state. There will be a "downfall" or an "excuse" or feeling of hopelessness around every corner. But you are resilient, dammit, and *you will not give up*. Once you've got both lists of potential OCD Specialists, schedule a few consultations and feel it out. This research is a reflection on the rest of your life because this therapist could *change* your life. If you have a current therapist, and you don't feel the therapy they are using is effective, and you have not been trained in ERP, my advice would be to find a new therapist. It sounds harsh at first, but you don't have the time or the money to waste when you could be having breakthroughs in OCD recovery as you read these very words. Finding the therapist for you is a really big deal. Do not underestimate it. This is solely and completely your journey, and no matter how strong you think you are, knowledgeable guidance of OCD is pivotal in your recovery from the worst stages OCD uses.

20

"STEPS TO OVERCOMING OBSESSING"

If you are serious about overcoming the worst of your OCD, you must personally take action, oftentimes through a series of steps. Sometimes the distance between these steps or the amount of time we spend on a certain step varies from person to person. However, the essence of the concrete steps that I am about to break down is what I would summarize as applicable and effective to everyone with OCD, no matter how minimal and no matter how severe. OCD is OCD. You now understand the importance of the search to find a truly helpful therapist. Now, we must build upon that. Each of these steps leads into the next step, and they build upon one another. In my experience, these are most effective if they are completed in the following order: *Mental Preparation for The Fight to Free Will*, *The Fight to Free Will*, and the transitional and continuous recovery stage, *Become Your Own Full-Time Therapist*. Essentially, this is an equation, with each piece connecting and equating to the next piece. When this equation is used part by part to its fullest efficiency, you will absolutely see proven results that lead to a more functional life no matter where you are in your battle with OCD.

I recently read the book, *Brain Lock* by Jeffrey M. Schwartz. I was directed to read it when I was in intensive therapy, but of course because it probably would have helped me, it was a compulsion to not read it. I also couldn't have cared less about reading a book written by yet another doctor or therapist who attempted to tell me what was going on inside *my* brain. I truly didn't think anyone could relate to what was going on inside my exact head and words were never sufficient to articulate it. Looking back, I wish I had been able to push through the compulsion and read the damn book.

I had finished all of the content of this book before I read *Brain Lock*. As I turned each page, I could not believe how much of *Brain Lock* aligned with my point of view and advice on OCD in this book. Not only did the read give me even more confidence in my upcoming tools and advice, most of which I gained out of my own experience, reading the book further proved to me why you needed a book straight from someone *with* severe OCD. What I've done with the next section of this book is put into words through inspiration how you can begin taking actual steps moving forward and past the worst of your OCD today. These steps have concepts and terms you may already be familiar with, but I have decided to put them in a concise, detailed order, all in one place for you. They are rooted in inspiration for you to gain your own courage. That is all I am trying to accomplish in this book. I want to bring you inspiration to know there is a very real and effective fight against OCD out there waiting for you, and I want you to once and for all shovel up the courage you so desperately deserve to face the fight and take back your life.

My advice as you read the following chapters on the "Steps to Overcoming Obsessing" is to read them slowly and steadily. As you read them slowly, I advise you to constantly reflect on your own battle and how you can apply each step to *your* OCD. If you search deep enough, these chapters will resonate with you. I will say that if you just breeze through the next few chapters, they likely will have hardly any effect on you. This will become just another self-help book that you set down, and you'll climb back on the hamster wheel of OCD and keep the small life you've been living for far too long. Even if you think you might have OCD, you've already been dealing with this torture for too long. These steps are the core of this book, and what you can actually take away from my story and from me. Permission granted to use them to your advantage completely. *This is for you.*

Author's Note: I desperately want you to see what life can be after hell on Earth. I so badly want to pull you into the moments when I realized I no longer had room for OCD in my brain or in my life. Some of you may be in your hell on Earth right now, and I want you to know that the only way to get out is to see a light through the fire. Allow me to shine a light for you. It will take energy, a therapist to hold you accountable, your spiritual faith for strength (this is my opinion, but it helped me — period), and most of all, perseverance. Nothing about this battle is impossible or too hard to face, but you *must* have a dedicated and devoted, "I'm-not-playing-around-this-time," mindset in order to see the results. Now, it's your turn. I already took mine. And if I hadn't taken that leap of faith to just see if there really was a way to live life without constant obsessions, my life may very well have been obsession free — because my life would currently be non-existent.

21

"MENTAL PREPARATION - THE FIGHT TO FREE WILL"

The first step that you must take before surmounting one of the greatest ascensions of your life is **Mental Preparation for The Fight to Free Will.** Just as before one goes into battle, you must be fully prepared and ready for what you are about to endure. By that I mean, no man walks away from a battle successful unless he is willing to commit every fiber in his body to that battle. Unless he is willing to give up his world as he knows it. Unless he is willing to submerge himself in the utmost uncomfortable situations, but stick with them, until he has defeated the enemy and won. Because the reward at the end of it all is worth every uncomfortable moment.

You have no choice but to go straight into battle with your OCD. You can beat around different types of therapy, invest 50% of yourself, or dip your toe in. But as far as I'm concerned, you're treading water in a lake full of excuses, and you don't even know it. I would know. That *was* me. I understand you're tired. Tired of fighting within yourself and within your mind. You would give anything to know life without OCD, but you are also terrified to know life without OCD. Who are you without OCD, really? I certainly didn't know, and I wasn't ready to find out for a long period of now wasted time. I was scared, scared of letting go of the one thing that I felt actually defined me. I didn't think I had the proper tools to face this world without my OCD. Everyone around me wanted me to "lose my OCD," but I couldn't. I couldn't handle the thought of living in a world where I didn't have the control. When I was approached by my therapist about the Intensive Therapy Program, I was skeptical. I had gone years without seeing any progress, and I didn't think it would ever happen, especially not in a three-week program. But I was missing the point. The entire point of the program, which is specifically formatted to you and your obsessions, is to conquer them head on, so blatantly, so boldly, that you are no longer fearful because you see the light. At first the light may be dim, but the flame grows. And grows. And grows. *Until you can see again.* That is the beauty of fighting to find and take back your free will! Unfortunately, we don't get to see the beauty until we've earned it. You might be thinking to yourself, "I didn't ask for my OCD nor deserve it, so I shouldn't have to 'earn' my way out of it." I completely understand where you're coming from. But understand this, each and every human who walks this Earth has their "thing" or "things" in life they didn't ask for. Life has never been and never will be fair for anyone — no matter what it seems like on the outside. No one asked for cancer. No one asked for autism. No one asked for abandonment. No one asked for failure. No one asked to be cheated on. No one asks for any of his or her worst nightmares. Yet, here we are. Ours is OCD. So instead of weighing ourselves down any further with questioning "why," let's focus more on "how," because you will never understand why. But you can control the how.

The reason that the mental preparation for the fight to free will is an entire step on its own is because you cannot enter the fight stage until you have become submissive to yourself and your willingness to fight your OCD. At some point, you must stop scarring yourself on the shackles on your wrists and ankles and BE STILL. BE MINDFUL. BE COURAGEOUS. BE BRAVE. You have every right to take this back into your own hands.

Accept that you can't live this life anymore. The fight will never work long term if you hold onto any part of your OCD. The truth is that many people won't actually fight their OCD until they have hit rock bottom. Many people have to be so fed up with how they are living, they cannot go on another day. Other times, family members or significant others threaten the relationship, or even worse, something bad happens in life to wake you up to realize you can't keep living like this. It is usually then, when you submit yourself to be defenseless, giving up all the power and control, that you will be able to truly fight. You have to truly tell yourself you cannot live like this anymore and know with every fiber in your being that you will not hold onto your OCD any longer. It is only then you will be effective in your fight for the long term. Put all your guards down. This is not a normal fight or battle. Put aside everything you have been told or keep telling yourself. Put aside every bit of your reassurance. Stop reaching for anything other than yourself. Put aside that power deep down inside that you cannot imagine letting go of. You have to let go of it, of what you are holding onto, the small amount of power you feel you control. What you don't realize is the *full extent* of control you will have once you have conquered the worst of your OCD. You think you have some control through your compulsions now? Wait until you slow down your intrusive thoughts by putting up this fight and see what life is like when you don't have constant obsessions. That is when you will feel true control over your actions and life again. You are so used to being controlled by these intrusive thoughts that you seek your very own compulsions to maintain as much control as you can. That is what you need to be ok letting go of. You have to take the risk of not responding to these controlling, dictating thoughts. You have to know within yourself that you will fight until you show your OCD who is in control of your mind without stopping, full speed ahead. You cannot half ass the fight because you have the "doubting disease." Putting in anything less than 100% effort will just leave you doubting everything and anything at any down moment. You have to be at a point where you don't even know if you can continue to live this life in the state you are in because you are so desperate to stop suffering. None of this is possible unless you not only *want* to stop performing the compulsions, but if you are finally willing to *take* the measures to do so.

I didn't fully want to get better going into The Intensive Program. That's what was originally missing from my case. You have to *want* to overcome this period of your life, to overcome this thing controlling your every move. First of all, I didn't originally understand the fight or how important it really was for me to want it so badly instead of everyone around me wanting it for me. I was just going with the flow, doing what everyone around me thought was the most logical next step. Everyone around me could be as fed up with me as they wanted, tell me all the changes I needed to make, threaten me all they wanted — but if I wasn't ready, I wasn't going to get anywhere at all. Because of my somewhat laissez faire approach, I didn't get effective results as soon as I could have because I wasn't fully open to letting go of my OCD. It wasn't until hard repetition of ERP that I saw any changes in my belief system in OCD, and even then, I was skeptical. The truth is, I wasn't ready to fully give up my OCD. I *needed* it, or so I thought. It was only once I saw progress and reflect back on it now that I fully understand that *no one but you is in this fight.* Which means your therapist can't be ready to fight, your parents can't be ready to fight, your friends can't be ready to fight, and your partner can't be ready to fight. It has to be you and you alone. I used to rely on the people around me significantly for reassurance and support. But it was never their battle, and they had absolutely nothing to offer me over what I needed to offer myself. This is no one's battle but yours. This may sound harsh, but I am your friend (whether you want me to be or not), and I am going to give it to you straight. If you are not completely and utterly ready to give up and let go of your OCD, you are not ready for the fight ahead of you. I'm very serious when I say that. If you are someone who is unsure if you are ready for the initially uncomfortable commitment, you will likely start the process of the fight, revert back to your compulsions at the first sight of discomfort, and never get above the OCD to see it for what it really is. You have to stay in the game.

I know it seems like you will never be ready, but there will come a point at which you will be ready. You will hit a point when you are *done*. Don't wait until you hit your rock bottom, and if you already have, I'm asking you to get up. If you do not want this, to get control of your OCD and take your life back with everything in you, you are simply not ready, meaning that you will not get the results you deserve and expect from the fight. If you can't fully commit to the fight, you will not see progress and everything you have read in this book will seem like rubbish to you. Nothing I say or have said will make any sense to you if you are not ready and fully committed. Trust me.

But if you are — all of a sudden there you will be. If you are willing to <u>temporarily</u> subject yourself to being uncomfortable so that you can have results that last a lifetime, you are ready. Ready for battle, for the unknown, as uncomfortable yet as slightly optimistic as ever. If you stick with it, truly stick with it, it can only go up from here. Period.

Author's Note: Do NOT underestimate this step. You may wonder why I've devoted one of my entire three steps to simple "preparation." It's because I am that serious about it. There is nothing the following two steps, or anything else in this book for that matter, can do for you unless you have committed to this first step. No one understands better than me that you have to be ready for what you are about to go through in order to overcome the worst of this disorder. The core of being ready is unequivocally wanting this more than anything else in your whole world. As much as I want everyone to drop everything right here and right now and begin the journey of fighting OCD, I do realize everyone needs to be ready on their own time. That is why this book's purpose is to mainly serve as inspiration. That inspiration represents me giving the reins over to you. Stop handing the reins over to something or someone else. A lot of people hear about ways to fight OCD and think they can just jump right into it, but I truly believe with everything in me — because that *was* me — that you have to step back and evaluate how bad you want to get rid of your OCD and what measures you are willing to take to do so. The effectiveness of your treatment will almost entirely depend on this step — your mindset preparation and dedication to *yourself.*

22

"THE FIGHT TO FREE WILL"

Once you have reached a point when you know you are ready to give your OCD the middle finger, you are ready for the second step: **The Fight to Free Will.** *THE* fight. This is a fight you will become to know all too well.

The crazy reality is that the core of OCD only gets so complicated. Before you judge that statement and say, "Are you kidding? OCD is the most complicated and twisted area of my life!" think about this for a second. The solution for OCD, which I believe that there is one, is this: The Fight. I didn't say "cure," I said, "solution." There is only one solution: to put up an honest to goodness, grueling fight against your OCD. It may be the most abstract fight that you have ever had because it has no boundaries. For the first time in your life, you have the chance to set the boundaries of a fight.

This fight can save your life.

Because it saved mine.

It's the scariest part of OCD. The absolute last thing that you want to do with OCD is put up a fight. In my case, I was scared — literally scared. I was terrified of losing something that, even though I knew was hurting me, was almost...protecting me. OCD was my blanket, and I didn't remember life without it. And as much as I knew that I couldn't live like this for the rest of my life, I knew that I wasn't ready to give up this "gift" I thought I had to help control things around me.

Until all of a sudden — *I was.*

My fight didn't happen in one day. It has taken a period of time to even believe in the fight, to get the encouragement to keep going, and to honestly continue to put up the fight each and every day. I can even feel my desire to give into my obsessions as I write these very words. But I won't. I have been here before; I know this temptation all too well. It's not worth it.

I started my fight when I was in the institution but wasn't ready to fully commit. I wasn't willing to commit until I saw proof. You may feel great momentarily after receiving reassurance, and then all of a sudden, you begin doubting a conversation that happened ten minutes ago. You can literally have an hour conversation of break-throughs and within minutes of being on your own again, you will begin to doubt everything and anything you talked about. You have to stop the reassurance seeking right now. You have to physically prove to yourself time and time again what is real before you will ever truly believe. I didn't see proof until I put up the fight, a real fight, by pushing through all of my obsessions and intrusive thoughts.

My therapist designed the program so that I would not rely on anything except physical proof (through Exposure and Response Prevention) that bad things were not going to happen when I didn't perform a compulsion. His intention was helping me realize I didn't have control over everything I assumed that I did. He dug deep into my biggest obsessions — what exactly they were, and where they were leading to — exposing the basis of my fear. We spent an enormous amount of time figuring out how to fight these very obsessions and provoking thoughts. As I previously mentioned, for my fight he would have me not give into all my miscellaneous compulsions that I so desperately wanted to give into. These included everything from stepping on specific cracks when I was determined not to, to walking in certain areas outside of the strict path I always took. He even had me ask myself why I was doing or not doing something in the very moment I was getting the obsession, before I made the decision to give in or not give into the compulsion, so I would have to verbalize it. Somehow, when you talk through the compulsion you are about to perform and why, it begins to take on a senseless reality. You hear yourself literally saying out loud the ridiculousness of what you about to do, and at times a logical piece of you might laugh a little. This means you are actually putting things into perspective. Before I believed in the fight, I knew that I was going to face whatever bad thoughts I had, and I was going to deal with the repercussions later on. You know, that feeling you get in the pit of your stomach very briefly because you didn't perform the compulsion? Yes, that one — until eventually I didn't face any repercussions.

After enough repetition of anything, the edge begins to wear off. The meaning and effect behind it begins to fade. That is exactly how it works with OCD, just like anything else. The more you persist, tear the blankets off the person in bed, and really see it for the dummy it is, the more the OCD shrivels up and dies. You're not watering the bastard anymore.

What "The Fight" really is at its core is going against every single thing your OCD wants you to do. It's extracting every intrusive thought that comes into your head, articulating it (exposing it, calling out the ridiculousness of it), and then deliberately choosing your response (not giving into the desired compulsion). It's exposing each and every intrusive and unwelcome thought that comes into your brain through ERP and going against your mind telling you to perform the reassuring compulsion. It's all about doing the opposite of what your gut is telling you to do, what the OCD is telling you is going to happen if you don't obey it in a sense. It's THE FIGHT TO FREE WILL OVER YOUR OWN LIFE. If you take every single obsession and ignore it completely, call it out, or just move past it instead of giving into it, you are exposing it. Once you have exposed it, you can begin to prevent your response by not giving into the compulsion.

This applies whether you have physical compulsions like I do or mental ones. Any time you are doing something physically or in your mind to avoid or stop a thought or react to these intrusive thoughts to keep them from happening, you are performing a compulsion.

If your OCD's compulsion of choice is asking questions from others to get reassurance, take a stand within yourself and don't ask the question. I know it will feel like you aren't strong enough to do this in the very moment, but I promise with all of my being that you are. Your mindful and intentional decisions are bigger than your OCD. Rely on yourself and mindfully CHOOSE the "what if" path.

This is your battle. It's no one else's problem or concern, so don't bring them in and make them part of your reliance. If your OCD is telling you to wash yet another time — with everything in you — you don't do it. Expose the thought and don't give into it. Don't feed your beast. Starve it. If your harm OCD is telling you that have the potential to violently kill a family member while they are sleeping, sit in a room by yourself and out loud create an entire story about what your OCD is telling you about how you are going to kill them. Write it all down. You can rip it up, or you can use this to read over and over again until it loses its effect on you because you made OCD finish these ridiculous thoughts. Get into details; get it out in the air and out of your mind. Everything is better when it is light out, not inside the darkness of your lurking mind. I guarantee you, once all of this scary paranoia is out in the open, it will seem less likely, even ridiculous, especially with time. If you love children, but you intentionally avoid them because you are getting thoughts you *could* be a child molester or pedophile, push through the thought and mindfully surround yourself with children, such as your nieces and nephews. How do I know you won't do anything, you ask? Because the very thought of this terrifies you. If you really were this person OCD tries to convince you of, you wouldn't be scared at all. Put yourself in that position you are so afraid of, so you can prove to yourself that it truly is just another meaningless thought. **The point is to take the ridiculous thought a step further than just the initial jeering thought that shot through your head.** That intrusive thought will keep coming over and over again until you break it down and expose it for what it really is. If your harm OCD is telling you that you are hitting pedestrians as you drive, hit the gas, keep driving, and decide how many bodies you hit and mentally plan their funeral and write their obituaries. You don't let the OCD win by never getting behind a wheel to LIVE YOUR LIFE because "what if." If your OCD is telling you to check something *again* to prevent something bad from potentially happening, don't you dare let yourself check. Take the risk this time. Instead sit there and tell yourself, it's just too late and whatever intrusive bad thought you had is going to happen, and it will all be your fault. The door is unlocked, and you're going to have an intruder. The curling iron was left on, and your house will burn down while you're at work. You left the car unlocked, and it could be broken into at any given moment. You ate that ice cream today that could have been contaminated, and you could become extremely ill, or even worse, your loved ones. People will die because of you, people will be sexually abused because of you, and the world will turn against you. Whatever your ridiculous thoughts are, such as these, let them wash over you and *just take it*. If your OCD is telling you that you need to read a certain number of Bible verses every day in a certain way to get into heaven, don't read them in the way OCD is telling you to. Change it up and study the Word on your own terms. God doesn't work the way your OCD will try to convince you of. He is a *just God*, you are His child, and *OCD itself is the enemy*. If your OCD is telling you the Devil is going to come into your room while you sleep if you don't touch the bedpost six times in a row, don't touch it. See what happens. Nothing will happen. If your OCD is telling you that you *need* to have everything in a perfect order, slightly mess up the areas you feel strongest about. Don't allow yourself to give into that perfection. It will never be perfect enough; the urge for perfection will only get stronger to a point **in which it can't be met.** For once, lower your standards in order to train yourself out of your rigidness.

Do you get where I am going with this? For each and every obsession you are putting up a serious fight, going against your OCD. It truly comes down to *pushing through the heightened anxiety* each moment after you get an obsessive thought. That's all this is — anxiety. You literally just have to push through it without requesting the reassurance through any compulsions. If you do this for every single intrusive thought you get, your intrusive thoughts will slow down greatly, especially with persistence over time. The less credit you give the obsessions, the less compulsions you will have to perform. The thoughts really stop coming or slow down immensely! It all eventually begins to make sense. After so many repeated times of going against your OCD, something triggers that there is no connection between your thoughts and reality because you've physically proven it time and time again. Sorry, but you are just not that powerful.

It's almost as though there is this little creature inside of your head that is in charge of feeding you all of your bad thoughts. He puts them in a chute, and they fire into your thought process. Once you stop paying him any attention, he has no business being there. He's bored. He would rather go and bother somebody else than stay with somebody who doesn't acknowledge him. That little shit. He begins to pack his bag of tricks and find his way to the door. This always reminds me of that mucous commercial that has been on TV for quite some time. The one where it shows a person taking Mucinex, and as soon as it hits, it zeros in on those little creatures who pack up their belongings and move out. They know they don't belong there anymore. That's EXACTLY what it is like with OCD for me. As soon as you consistently stop paying "it" mind, "it" gets so bored. It's done with you. You're done with each other. That side of your imagination is losing patience with you and you with it. You're starving the creativity of your imagination to come up with these absurd thoughts. Pretty soon, you will notice a slight improvement. You will realize you went an hour without any serious intrusive thoughts because you took the time to expose your biggest triggers and obsessions head on. You'll realize that certain triggers are played out, and you question them in a way you never have before. The longer you go forgetting about "it," the more it stays away from you. For the first time in forever, _you_ will be in control. And you may have forgotten how beautiful that feeling really is.

The ultimate goal of The Fight to Free Will is to get to a point where you never at any time, on any level, give into even one compulsion. I know this sounds impossible right now. That is okay. Stay with me. Don't let your OCD convince you to stop reading and give up hope if you've made it this far.

As I have mentioned, one little compulsion will bring twenty more with it. You have to go all in, and I promise you, if you truly do not give into any of your intrusive thoughts for a certain period of time (this period can vary for different people, but can be as short as a couple of weeks), your obsessive and intrusive thoughts will decrease immensely. I will go as far as saying the fight against OCD is very similar to rehab. If you don't stay sober the entire time, you won't see the light on the other side. If you take just one drink, even just one smoke, your recovery is history until you start completely over again. The exact same mentality applies to not giving into one intrusive thought. By giving in, you are re-igniting a part of your brain you have been working very hard to *shut up*. You must keep it quiet for a certain period of time, so it shrivels up and goes away. It comes down to the mentality — the mindfulness, the mindful intention — to fight your OCD with everything inside of your being, as if your life depends on it.

Yes, you will experience much more heightened anxiety during this fight. For the first time, you are sticking up for yourself. What do you expect? No one wants to put him or herself in a position where they are going to experience high anxiety. Isn't that what we are running from? Yes, but you have to remember this anxiety is only temporary and will soon pass. It absolutely will. Will the process of ERP make you feel naked in public? Possibly, at first. I mean, you are allowing yourself to sit with the uncertainty of your worst fear. ALL YOU HAVE TO DO IS SIT WITH IT! At times when I am in the midst of the worst of my anxiety, I ask myself in that very moment, "What is the worst thing sitting with this anxiety can do to me? Nothing." It can't *do* anything. It can't hurt you. It can't kill you. It's just uncomfortable. Temporarily. Once I started to realize there was honestly no harm in just sitting with the discomfort, I was much more likely to do it. Why not? **The long-term effect of sitting with this temporary discomfort is more worth it than any amount of anxiety.**

I had nothing left to lose. Little progress is so big with OCD because as soon as you start rebelling against it, something, somewhere clicks. In order to see results, it takes immense dedication and progression soon follows. Believe it or not, the thoughts really will decrease if you devote yourself to this fight.

The more credit you give your OCD, the more intense your thoughts become because it's a DISORDER. OCD lives and feeds from you giving into it. I began with fighting little compulsions, ones that weren't life and death for me. Nothing bad happened. I didn't feel like my world was going to end...because it didn't. Then I would just try this with bigger compulsions. I simply wouldn't do them. I would let the thought come over me and then go, just like a wave. Wave after wave. It wasn't until I started performing the compulsions much more infrequently that I realized how unnecessary they really were. You start to reflect on how much valued time you spend on these very compulsions and how they really and truly are a complete waste of time. But you can't know this until you have gone without performing the compulsions for a certain period of time — until you have faced the heightened anxiety of not performing them many times. **It's a monumental realization when you realize your dire devotion to the compulsions becomes irrelevant.**

Part of me sometimes believes that I was just tired. I was so sick of surrounding my every move and steps around this OCD. I even had OCD and performed regular compulsions in my dreams. I couldn't even use sleep to get away anymore. It seemed like there was no escape. But I continued. I continued to combat every thought I was strong enough to handle.

Little by little, they begin to fade. You are training your mind and your OCD, as you are simultaneously gaining your control back. Eventually, the same thoughts will become meaningless because you have proven time and time again there is no correlation with what you are doing and reality. The reality is unavoidable. *Your life has already been planned by God.* You can't control life itself, and your mental or physical compulsions have no effect on it. You can only control *your* free will. You performing any certain compulsion has absolutely no effect on anything. You are wasting precious time. I promise you the discomfort of battling your OCD will only be temporary, but the results will last for the rest of your life.

I get it. Trust me, I have had these intrusive thoughts for years. But the day that you say, "screw this," is that day that your life begins again. I don't care what rebuttal you are thinking right now. I know what's going on inside of your head! Don't believe me? What do you have to lose by putting up this fight against yourself? Your *sanity*? That's been gone for quite some time, hasn't it? You just don't want to deal with the fight right now because you are so busy with work and everything life is throwing your way? No. Your sanity comes before everything, and you owe it to your family, your loved ones, but above all else, you owe it to yourself. Don't want to pay for therapy to jump-start your battle? They don't take your insurance? This is your life we are talking about. Your literal sanity. Your wellbeing. *It only gets worse, and you only become more dependent on your OCD. This is your drug. This is your addiction. It needs to be addressed now.* I guarantee that deserves more attention than most of the meaningless things you buy, no? This battle marks a new beginning for the rest of your LIFE.

If I wasn't going to die on my own account, I at least wanted to live a life that was somewhat separated from OCD. That was my decision, same as it is *yours*. After putting up the fight consistently over time, I faced life with less obsessive thoughts, and I was practically turning into a new woman. You may as well try it because there is only one life that you were given to live. Since not every person on the Earth is walking around with OCD, you have the power to overcome it. Just like me. If someone like me can walk around after everything that I have been through, and still function in areas of life I never thought possible, then maybe I'm onto something. You can keep living the way that you are. Go ahead. But you may as well stop reading right now. You're wasting so much money on un-targeted therapy, even money on buying books like this one to help you if you're not willing to change. *If you don't want to change.* Be willing to put up that fight. If you're still not ready, I get it. I feel for you, desperately I do, but I don't agree with you. At one point I did. But seeing where I am now and where you are right now, I'd choose where I am any day. Do I sound harsh? That's okay. Your life is already harsh. I am that friend that you don't have right now without a filter, and I'm spitting you some serious truth. It's because I have nothing but the best intentions for your future self, who I pray will thank me later.

The truth is, you can go to weekly therapy for years, but you will never accomplish what you can in a short amount of time if you put up the intense fight that is essential to overcoming your OCD. You simply cannot rely on regular, routine therapy sessions to battle OCD to the extent it needs to be fought. I am not saying that you aren't strong enough, but I am saying that you need a therapist there with you for the initial battle. This is precisely why I feel so strongly about the Intensive Therapy Program with trained OCD Specialists. The one I attended at The Gateway Institute was the jumpstart that I needed. It forced me to stop everything and face my OCD head on, but on my own terms. It was ultimately all my decision to get better, but I had every resource and tool in front of me, which left my excuses seldom any room. I was tried day in and day out for three weeks, being given different tips and tricks that helped me use the more logical side of my brain. I do believe that if you have the opportunity to look into an institute that provides treatment programs specifically for OCD, you absolutely should. Starting this journey with the proper guidance and direction is key. The only way to do it is to fight head on, horns out thrust, and no excuses. You have to show the OCD who is boss in a very intense way, or it will find gaps. You leave weekly therapy happy and relieved that you just talked through all your issues, but as you already know, the relief will be temporary. You will start obsessing immediately. That's why you need to go back the very next day. And the next. And the next after that. You have to battle it hard, every day, like I did. You can't let enough time go by where you are *forgetting that nothing bad is actually happening.* Nobody is getting hurt. No harm, no foul. You are not only holding yourself accountable, but you have a therapist right there to see your weaknesses, your failures, and your doubts. You must give yourself entirely to your therapist, because if you hold back your deepest thoughts and obsessions, you are wasting everyone's time. I did that for way too long, trying to put *almost* everything on the table to battle, but I had a really hard time putting every literal thing out there. I wanted to feel secure and hold my worst and biggest doubts and fears to myself. But then again, those were never addressed, and I still battle with them today. A therapist will also see your breakthroughs that you may not even see. They can document your progress, and day in and day out, you are going to make leaps and bounds. You will look the beast in the eye, and you will turn weak into strong. Eventually, **the intensity drives out the beast. OCD is the most powerful sense that I have ever known, but I do know that I am stronger.** And so are you. I proved that to myself and to it. OCD is a coward. It will persist and persist until it realizes it can't win. Then it starts to give up. And you begin to get your life back.

Don't get me wrong — I think anyone can start the fight at any given moment on his or her own. You could literally start today, by beginning to shift your mindset to actively wanting to get better. You can begin to squash your excuses and make the change before something drastic in your life happens that *forces* you to get help. Once you get yourself geared into mental preparation for the fight, you can begin to fight by not giving into every obsession and by not performing the compulsion, whether it's mental or physical. You can begin to fight back by allowing the intrusive thought to sink into you, and right as it starts to get painful to think about, *sit with it.* Do not do anything to get the thought to leave. Sit there with it and articulate every part of the thought in your head or out loud. Do not perform a compulsion or wave the thought away. And then...go about your day. Go about your life. Let the intrusive thought blow over without participating in its sick and twisted game. Then as soon as the next thought comes, try it again. Don't give in. Don't go with your gut. FIGHT IT. Fight every damn thought you can by not giving in. You will slowly get stronger, and your OCD will slowly get weaker.

Through the fight, you are breaking the literal bond of OCD itself. You are separating it and pulling it apart in front of your very eyes. You are **breaking the seal** of OCD that has been stamped on you.

At the end of the day, you OWE it to yourself to prove that none of this is real. You owe it to yourself to prove that this is all for nothing and that you really are wasting hundreds and thousands of hours of your precious, short life. You owe it to yourself to see if going all the way back to your house to see if the oven was on was worth it, if washing for the ninth time was honestly necessary, or if creating distance from those you are closest to because you are scared you might hurt them was truly imperative. You deserve to get down to the bottom of this mental disorder and realize you are giving into a complete falsehood. You deserve to realize by proving to yourself time and again that none of this is real, was never real, and will never be real.

Author's Note: Sometimes I wish we had the same persistence in life OCD has. It's relentless. It's a beast within. But then I realized *we do* have the same persistence as OCD inside of us. We have to face the realities of everyday life along with OCD every step of the way, and THAT is persistence at its finest. We obsessive outsiders underestimate our inner strength due to our fears. We are so overcome by each and every fear of ours, we don't ever get to see how strong we are in actuality. We are SO STRONG. Not a lot of people around you could go through what we do every day. You have this disorder because *you* can handle it. Don't underestimate your strength through this fight. This is the best damn thing you will ever do for yourself in your entire life. And the longer you've dealt with OCD, the stronger you are within to fight it. Give it back a taste of its own painful sting. *Fight so hard your OCD cowers in your presence. You are the master now. Take back what's yours.*

23

"BECOME YOUR OWN THERAPIST"

The third step stands by far just as important, if not more so, as the previous two steps — **Become Your Own Therapist.** And I mean just exactly that. Becoming my own therapist was by far the best tool I ever learned from The Gateway Institute to combat my OCD. I use this mentality every single moment of every single day. If I didn't employ this, I would still be quite possibly in the thick fog of severe OCD.

There will come a point after you have been working on the fight for some time when you realize your therapist will not always be there. You will also no longer rely on your therapist as much as you once did because you will have unknowingly taken the reins into your own hands. That's what happens when you pursue the fight. You are taking every tool your therapist has given you and slowly taking over for yourself. That is when you know you are making major changes and are on the exact path you should be on to overcome the worst of the power of OCD. Your therapist is your support system, and they are going to likely be the only person who remotely under-stands what you are going through. They don't need OCD to know exactly how to deal with it. Remember, they have done this all before — many times, with many clients. Your therapist should help guide and ease you into the fight and be right by your side for much of the initial exposure. It's about *accountability*. There will come a point when you will realize that is the real reason you need the therapist initially in the fight. You will need to be held accountable for not giving into your OCD and have the incredible support system you didn't even realize how much you needed. You need to feel the empowering courage that you are in it alone but that right on the sideline is your coach, there for you at any moment you need them. It's the same concept as when you are learning to swim with a swim instructor. You have to learn to go underwater by yourself, but in the event anything bad were to happen, your instructor is right above you, ready to grab you. But nothing bad will happen.

Once you have pursued the fight, and you have dedicated your entire self to combating your OCD for a certain period of time, you will get to a point when you realize your therapist is just a crutch, not your lifeline. You will come to a solid realization that everything you are doing is completely on your own, which is why you needed the initial preparation mindset and motivation. It's not your therapist putting up the fight; *it is only you at the end of the day.*

The main reason becoming your own therapist is so incredibly important is because although therapy stops after an hour or so, *your OCD doesn't stop.* OCD is still living within you as soon as you leave his/her office, as you go on to live your life for the rest of the 23 hours in the day. *This is why you need to learn to hold yourself accountable and not rely on a therapist.* The point of the intensive program was to hit my OCD as hard as possible, from every angle with every single obsession I had, and make sure to battle and fight giving into any compulsion. But I want you to really think about this. If I was in the institute for four or five intensive, hard hours a day working on myself but then leave and go home, the obsessions are not going to stop. They don't care. OCD doesn't care. If I were to just continue giving into my compulsions the rest of that day, I will have just erased all the work I did that morning. It has to be consistent. Someone has to hold you responsible 24/7 because you have to put up the fight 24/7 and make sure you are staying strong with every obsession. Giving into one obsession is failing what you owe to yourself. The fight will only work if you hit it hard; not one obsession gets what it wants. Your life might initially feel uncomfortable 24/7, but aren't you already uncomfortable?

By this point, you should have all the tools. You **can** put up the fight by yourself because you know exactly what it is you should or shouldn't be doing. You innately know more about how to fight OCD than you realize. Your therapist can only say so much. The fight is not that complicated. It's abstract and awkward to wrap your head around at first, but the fight itself is not what is complicated. It's the commitment and self-accountability. Yes, your obsessions and your mind are complicated and intricate, but the OCD itself is not, which is why it can be fought using the same techniques for so many of us. At the end of the day, they are just thoughts circulating in YOUR head. My therapist was my safety blanket when I no longer fed my obsessions. He was there for me to use when I got too uncomfortable. But all the while, he was just waiting for me to find the logic on my own. He wasn't going to "cure" me. He was going to push me to help myself because that is truly the only way to get through life with OCD.

You have to become your own therapist because you are the only one who is with you 24/7.

When you leave and go home, only you can look out for yourself. Your therapist can make a home visit and help your family understand how they can help hold you accountable. But at times this didn't work for me because the second they caught on to my compulsions, I changed them. At the same time, having them know my compulsions was an immense help (even though I hated it at the same time) when I was losing the momentum because they would call me out, which was helping hold me accountable. But then I found ways to work around and lie about what I was performing and not performing. No one is inside of your head, so they don't truly know the obsession or the compulsion. By finding ways to get around the obsessions, you are literally only hurting yourself. You are cheating nothing and no one other than yourself by hiding your compulsions to avoid awkwardness or being called out. No one knows your thoughts but you, so you are the only person who can truly hold yourself accountable. This is a blessing in disguise because you don't have to rely on anyone but yourself. The sooner you embrace yourself as your only reliance, the better off you will be in many walks of life.

You must learn how to be completely independent when you receive any intrusive thought. You need to be able to be alone and fight off the thought by exposing it and not performing the compulsion you so desperately feel the need to perform. You need to be the one in charge of running your Exposure and Response Prevention at any and every given moment. This is completely achievable in less time than you think, if you are dedicated to the fight.

It's important to note when I say to become your own therapist, that you are not confusing *holding yourself accountable* and *reassuring yourself*. The point of holding yourself accountable is to not allow you to be comfortable (by using reassurance) but to allow yourself to be uncomfortable, initially. This discomfort is the time in which you will grow the most. The less reassurance and more targeted exposure, the more comfortable you will be in the long run.

Face it — therapists are an incredible source. But they make a lot of money seeing people like us every single day. We go around and around in circles, and they are still getting paid to tell us essentially the same thing after a while. We avoid taking action and continue to come up with the excuses. We keep *thinking* it's so complicated. We will keep seeing them as long as possible because it is our only shot at reassurance or to feel like we are doing *something* about our OCD. Therapists don't give up on us like everyone else in our life does, and we subconsciously hold onto that. If you and I clued in to how we can help ourselves, we would be able to see a therapist less often. Checking in regularly with a therapist is fantastic, and I encourage it greatly, but weekly visits may not be necessary if you can truly hold yourself accountable. You will be able to finally back off on so much therapy and get a grip on it yourself. It's terrifying to know you are the one who is holding yourself accountable. It's hard to trust yourself. You clearly feel like you can't trust yourself because you rely on your OCD! It's like you're having a war within your own body — half of you is dying for relief from your intrusive thought by having a compulsion always there to fall back on, and half of you is trying to stop and convince you in the moment to not perform that very compulsion. **It's a battle of the better half** — *make sure the half that wins is the permanent kind of relief.*

Author's Note: Do not be scared to hold yourself accountable. Once you have been through the intensity of the fight, you will not be as intimated by being your own therapist as you might be at this moment. Something comes over you when you regain that control over your life, and you will be almost eager to be the one holding yourself accountable. Once you gain control over your OCD, you will begin to gain control in so many other areas of your life. A shift will set in of less dependence on your therapist and more dependence on yourself. That shift creates a feeling of empowerment that in turn helps bring you the courage to keep going.

24

"THE BREAKUP"

I often reflect back and try to figure out when exactly it was that I became healthy again. Of course, the Intensive Therapy Program at the Gateway Institute was my jumpstart to lessening the intensity of my OCD, but it took about another two years after that until I felt like I had control over my life again. I wish I could pinpoint my growth to a healthy me to one certain thing, but I can't. I want to bottle up my breakthrough and give you an equation of exactly what you need to do to get better. I so desperately want to be able to pinpoint and summarize quickly what works and what doesn't. I want all this grey area of OCD — what it is, the recovery of how to get there, even prove that OCD recovery is a very real thing — to be summed up and put into one place. I may not have the ability to do that for us, but I am hopeful that someday, someone will. Most of all, I want people to fully believe recovery from severe OCD is possible. It's not a phase or an exaggeration few people blissfully experience — it's a lifestyle. And in order to style your life, you have to do something about it. You have to believe; you have to wholeheartedly believe that you can recover from the worst of this and that it is just time and effort that it takes for you to get there. You'll still have OCD, but I promise you, it won't hound you like it used to. The urges become so faint, so distant. Other times of high anxiety, they are right on your back waiting for you to give in, and you straight up have to check yourself before you wreck yourself. By then, you will know immediately how to rip the bastard off your back and keep walking. It shouldn't even faze you.

I believe that I came to live a fully functioning life again because of a series of tools. The largest tool I credit to overcoming the worst of OCD is undoubtedly incorporating Exposure and Response Prevention into my *everyday life*. The first task was to prove to myself that the connection between my obsessions and compulsions was a falsehood and a complete waste of my time. Instead of my OCD making me question everything, *I began to question the OCD*. Oh, how the tables have turned.

But at the end of the day, it was much more than just ERP that shifted my mindset. It was a change of lifestyle. It wasn't until I began to change the life of isolation I was living in that I began to get better all around. Once I started to even slightly question the OCD altogether, because of the constant ERP, I was more in tune with life in general. I was able to lightly let go of the death grip I had on the reins of OCD and look up — ha, literally. I started to invest myself back into life again. I focused on outlets such as my schoolwork, developing and interacting with people to gain friendships, strengthening my talents, and getting out of my room to do anything, really. The more people I interacted with, the more positive distractions I invested myself in, the better my mental health became. Once I had a glimpse of the life I had been missing out on, I only wanted to get out more. I truly believe that this was the true climax for me — forcing myself out of my head and *into life around me, not inside me.*

Once I started enjoying friends, parties, events, school functions, and small successes in school and at work, I only wanted more enjoyment. The enjoyment of life became more important than my OCD, and the deep desires to give into my OCD seemed meaningless as time went on. Once I had broken the seemingly inseparable bond between the obsessions and compulsions, I eased my way back into life. I believe that keeping this uphill momentum going was what helped me stay above water and helped transition me into a fully functioning life amidst severe OCD. I just needed to get to a point where I was able to **break up** the obsessions from the compulsions. They didn't need to go together; they didn't have to be a pair. I initially couldn't control the obsessions because you can't control what intrusive thoughts come into your head. But through controlling my reaction to the compulsions, I was able to seemingly control the obsessions from coming around so often.

I had initiated the breakup by cutting the cord between the obsessions and the compulsions, and from that point on, it was just about keeping the breakup intact.

I began to learn how to "rise above" my thoughts. To this day when I get obsessive, intrusive thoughts, I do what I call "rise above." I let the thought keep going, and I mentally put myself above it, like a wave rolling over my head. I don't feed it. I don't give into it, and I try to not pay it any mind. It's just a thought, so I keep it just a thought.

Another tool I taught myself was to laugh — at myself. I began to make fun of my compulsions in front of my friends, and we would laugh about how ridiculous they were. Pretty soon, this transitioned to when I was alone. My compulsions were comical! Incorporating my sense of humor into my OCD made such a daunting area of my life a little lighter and was yet another thing that helped me slowly realize OCD was not what I had always thought it was.

I obviously did much better at times with less anxiety in my life. The times in which I wasn't shedding as much hair gave me periods of time when I wasn't as anxious and constantly looking for an outlet. As I've mentioned, my OCD always found other things to be anxious about, but my hair was by far my biggest trigger and always has been. My OCD took my hair and stretched the fear of my reality, slowly burying my logic. The reality was, I was losing more hair than normal for the first time in my life. It exaggerated this reality, helping me find ways to try and maintain some control over the situation by performing compulsions. But it wasn't the hair loss that was exaggerated; it was the connection and false belief in my magical control over it. The more I obsessed about my hair, the more I grew into a deep belief on the effect of my compulsions. In my magical thinking OCD theme, OCD just made a real-life problem become my falsehood. The fine line of doubt is what OCD targets. OCD targets the "what if," parts of your brain; the parts where you are most vulnerable. OCD snagged my deepest fear, got caught up on my hair, and it became the center of my life. OCD will never target the black and white parts about you. It likes to get caught up in the wrinkles and tangles of what you love and fear the most. It was a telling truth when my hormones calmed down, my hair loss slowed down, and yet the obsessions were still there. The obsessions just shifted onto the next fear of mine based on my momentary anxiety, whether it be an exam I had coming up, a speech I needed to give, or an argument I had just had. You name it, my OCD was right there. My OCD seems to always be in alignment with the real-life anxieties I am struggling with in the current moment. If you have a different type of OCD than I do, such as sexual or violent OCD, you should already know within you that OCD isn't based in any reality at all. It's simply OCD coming after what you care about and/or fear most. There is no reality there for you. Don't take what I said about OCD "exaggerating my reality" the wrong way. I am not saying that your reality is that you are a murderer or rapist and OCD just exaggerated it. My reality was something that was physically happening to me in my life, but the OCD was still coming after what I feared most. There was no "what if" about it. The only "what if" was the one I was creating myself, through the magical thinking I could have an effect on controlling it rather than just live with the uncertainty.

Jim summarized all of this best for me when I was struggling with understanding why OCD targets what it targets. Why does OCD pick out to destroy the things in your life that means the most to you? Is OCD truly all bullshit? How do we know OCD isn't just revealing the core of who we are and what we believe deep down? Why does my

OCD seem to attack the things I am anxious about, the things that have no definitive answer? Jim's response couldn't have nailed it on the head any better. "OCD doesn't necessarily attack what you're unsure about. It attacks what you love that makes you unsure about it. *It causes you to be unsure about it.*" THAT'S the bottom line, and the one thing to take away from all of this. OCD isn't revealing "the real you" or what you believe. It's just taking the things you love the most or fear the most in life and making you unsure about them. Any thoughts revolving around these topics that mean the most to you, the ones you are most sensitive towards, sets our OCD off, thereby making our brains go into a heightened anxiety flight mode. All of a sudden, the things we love and care deepest about in life are put in a state of question and uncertainty — the fear of the "what if." You must suffocate the "what ifs." Don't give them any air, any room to expand to convince you the "what if" could actually be a reality.

Let's look at this from a new perspective for a moment. Since OCD is likely the first and foremost relationship you have in your life, take a moment to examine how harmful that relationship has been. Has this relationship been suffocating, debilitating, confining, and emotionally exhausting? When people step back and examine their relationships, if they feel all these negative emotions from it, their first instinct is to move on. They want to find a new relationship that doesn't come with all this daily baggage that affects their whole world. This is the same concept as how you should step back and evaluate your relationship with your OCD. It's only causing you harm. There aren't any positives to the relationship. *You need to break up with it.* But it just doesn't seem that easy to let it go after all you have been through with it. How do you even break up with OCD? By fighting, just like a relationship. After enough fighting, you realize it's time to let go and move on.

Granted, when you've been hurt by a relationship, you will always live with those memories. That's inevitable. But a certain amount of time without that harmful person or thing, and you will most likely see how positive your life is without the toxicity any longer. You either found someone new, or you just realized how much better off you are now without it. But you didn't know that at the time. Just like right now, as you are desperately struggling with letting go of your OCD, you can't see through the other side of the tunnel. It's too dark. It might not be worth the risk. It could take too long. You'll feel naked. You literally don't want to live to see the other side if it doesn't go as planned. Like a relationship, the breakup is necessary to know if you are or aren't meant to be with someone. But the only glimpse of hope to know that you are making the right decision is knowing that if your world really does end after the breakup, you can go back to them. You did the breaking up, so you have a good chance of them taking you back. If you quite literally can't handle just throwing your hands up and being done with OCD, then try breaking up with it by putting up the fight I have laid out. But just like in a relationship, you have to give it time. Give it a week, then two weeks, and then finally, a month. But you can't cheat. You can't perform one compulsion, or it won't work. The thoughts WILL slow down if you stick with it. But if you half ass it, you may as well not even try. It won't work. You owe it to yourself to try this. If you truly stick with this, your thoughts will start to lessen and eventually go away. If done right, you will never ever go back to this relationship. Your life will elevate, and you won't look back.

OCD will never break up with you. It will only gain years more of control over you and your life. You have to be the bigger one here and do the breaking up with your beast.

Author's Note: OCD thrives in an environment in which it is allowed to blossom. If you are allowing your OCD to blossom by giving into it, it will continue to thrive and flourish into bigger and more valuable areas of your life. You have to shut those doors in the face of OCD before it gets there. It's like OCD scours your brain to see what loopholes it can find, and then once it finds one, it unpacks its bags and makes a cup of tea while it plots its attack on you. OCD is trying to get you to take an average fear and create your own rearing falsehood out of it. The more blurred the line is, the harder it will be to fight it. With our OCD, things need to be black and white, spelled out, and blatantly clear for us to be able to wrap our heads around it. Since your OCD will never step into the light for you to make sense of anything, you have to be the one to step in the light. Typically to do so, you have to start by moving one foot in front of the other, and in this case, that begins with the breakup. The longer you sit and wallow throughout a relationship, the more wasted time you will be investing. Every day is another wasted day, spent contributing yourself and your time to *something that doesn't exist.*

25

"YES, YOU."

I think back to countless conversations I've had over the past few years about this book with OCD sufferers. I have explained time and time again that I had come so far with my trials and tribulations with OCD, that dammit, I was going to give my book of reason to others going through everything that I had. I was creating a rulebook for patients just like us. So many of these sufferers were going through the immense amount of torture and pain I was in the middle of overcoming so well. I saw myself in each and every one of them. I realized people who are suffering from OCD, whether they have or have not been diagnosed, are completely confused by what OCD is and what OCD is not. Even people who know what they need to do, but just can't seem to muster up the courage to truly use ERP, these people are my ideal readers. No matter what stage of suffering you are in, you represent the entire reason as to why I wrote this book. So many of my conversations have been with *good* people who have this terror of OCD inside them that seems so much bigger than what it really is — a quintessential case of OCD. I knew they needed someone like me, an obsessive outsider, who had had many revelations to pave the way. I needed to be an example. I needed to find a way to inspire you to get better. I didn't suffer all these years to not continue to kick OCD's ass by giving back what I have learned that actually works.

So many of us have had enough therapy to know what we need to do, how to challenge OCD, but just don't seem to have the accountability to take action and become our own therapist after learning the proper tools. Many aren't ready for the leap. It might not be worth the risk. The thought of using ERP terrifies you. You don't feel strong enough by yourself to incorporate the ERP, so you stay in your dungeon. You have no idea how little ERP it would actually take to start seeing improvement in the intrusive thoughts. You just need to get the courage to sit with the anxiety of exposing your thoughts and stick with it. You need to prove to yourself the anxiety is only temporary by continuing to expose the next thought and then the next. You need to prove to yourself that you can overcome the momentary anxiety. You don't have to rely on the reassurance of the compulsions.

Right now, your obsessions are likely all jumbled up in your mind, sometimes multiple shooting thoughts at the same time, and you wince because it's just too much. It's so fuzzy, it makes our heads spin. This is when we have to stop and articulate our obsessions, rather than letting them stay wound up in a rubber band ball. I don't mean dwell on them and pick each of them apart. I simply mean slowing down and picking one consistent thought out of the rubber band ball and facing it head on. Just stop what you're doing and sit with it. Focus on your breathing. Let's bring that anxiety level down right before your very eyes. The longer you sit with this, the more your anxiety will physically lessen. That fight or flight mode will slowly come to a halt, and you will be left with the thought. Now, without that sense of "siren like" anxiety, you can truly sit with and look at the thought for what it is — a thought. *It doesn't have to be an obsession.* This is where you control your reaction. Let the thought roll again and again. Let it come at you hundreds of times a day. But let the thoughts naturally become weaker and more faint by not giving into this snowball effect anxiety and prevent these stupid, meaningless thoughts from becoming serious obsessions.

When I speak in person to OCD sufferers at conferences and

events, I almost always see myself only a couple years prior. I want to pull you all into my world to get a glimpse of the freedom you could feel, *even just for a moment*. I desperately want to reach out and shake you to stop everything you are doing and expose your OCD. I want you to stick with it long enough to see a change, not just expose one thought and wonder why it isn't working. That is exactly how I feel when I talk to each and every one of you. I want you to feel what life is like when you take control and never look back. It's the same freedom you feel when you walk on a beach, feeling the cool air brush past on your face. In that moment, you feel so pure, so free, even for just a second. *That is the feeling you can have every single day, once you take your life back.*

Author's Note: A lot of people rely on reassurance to get them through life with OCD. Instead of fighting the OCD, they find temporary reassurance to be able to go on with their day, anything to just quiet the OCD and keep going. Except typically, one bout of reassurance isn't enough. They need to keep coming back to check the stove, the door, the curling iron. They need to touch something a certain number of times for relief. They need to probe and pry to get their therapist, family, or friend to say something that will reassure them. I certainly used to do this. I used to pose questions in different lights in hopes of receiving an answer I was looking for. We are brilliant at this! I would instantly feel relief for a few minutes and then the doubting process would begin again. The reasoning? Although reassurance is simply temporary relief, it also is forming a crutch that we begin to rely on due to the addictiveness of needing that relief. So we keep coming back, again and again for reassurance. At some point, the reassurance needs to stop, and the fight needs to begin. **The fight is the knife that cuts the lifeline of the reassurance between the OCD and you.** *And it is absolutely necessary.* The sooner the knife cuts this link, the healthier you will become.

26

"IT"

My therapist always described my giving into the OCD as giving it "credit." The more credit you give your OCD, the more plausible and realistic it seems. It is then you are making a non-tangible thing become tangible. But OCD is not tangible. It is just air. Just thoughts in passing — simply brain waves. OCD locks onto your imagination, taking your subconscious loves and fears in life to an unhealthy level. As you know, I always have referred to my OCD as "it." I did so because it didn't feel like it could be my own thoughts or from within me. It felt like an alternate controlling force that had crept its way into my brain. But by always describing and crediting "it," I only made "it" seem more real to myself. I gave it (OCD) *its own credit, its own identity, but "it" is nothing.* I just knew it *felt* like a being or something other than myself. Isn't that what all of this is? **What you feel, rather than what it actually is?**

A lot of people find comfort in the phrase coined in *Brain Lock* — "It's Not Me, It's My OCD." This is an ingenious phrase that helps many, many OCD sufferers separate their identity from their OCD, so they realize their obsessions are not who they are. The irony about this phrase is that the opposite happened to work for me with certain obsessions. Once I became in touch with the fact that my OCD wasn't an "it," an invading force into my brain that I needed to fear, and that it was simply my exaggerated imagination, I felt comfort. I felt comfort that my OCD *was* just my brain and not a law of attraction, or spiritual entity I needed to be afraid of — one where I would suffer consequences if I didn't perform the compulsion I so desired. In due time, I have figured out my OCD is simply that — OCD, a mere disorder that I needed to overcome. **There is a fine line where OCD is not who I am, but it is what I suffer from.** Since I have read *Brain Lock*, I have started to incorporate the phrase at times when I get intrusive thoughts. As I have been doing this, I understand the catch. There have been many times when it brings me comfort to know that my recurring fears that roll over and over again in my head are just my OCD talking, not connecting to anything at all. And it needs to be shut up. I have begun to verbally say the phrase out loud, and I find that it creates good separation between the OCD and me in my mind. I can finally compartmentalize that my OCD is a disorder extorting my imagination, but under no circumstances do I need to allow it to get away with consuming me.

It has always bothered me so much that my OCD knew everything seemingly before I did. Every anxiety of mine, it targeted. My deepest, darkest fear, my latest drama, my subconscious thoughts. It was a while before I realized it knew everything because it *was* coming from me in a sense. I needed to know OCD is not an alternate being, creeping inside of you to attack you. It is a sick and twisted disorder that creeps into your brain waves. But broken down, it is really just series of thoughts. I've just been battling with myself this entire time, not the universe or an alternate power sending me thoughts that I needed to respond to. It's my brilliant and toxic imagination. I thought "it" could get into my head, control my thoughts, and had a greater power that would punish me if I didn't obey. I thought something was being sent out in the universe to this power if I didn't obey by performing a compulsion. That thought alone scared me out of my own damn head. Well, I guess I was already out of my head, wasn't I?

For so long, I couldn't crack that just because a thought came across my mind didn't mean it would come to fruition or had any merit. Just because insane thoughts enter your mind, doesn't mean you have welcomed them or agree with them in any way, shape, or form. It doesn't mean that subconsciously you are the person your crazy thoughts are telling you that you are. You are not always what you think. The brain is an incredible part of the body, but you should never underestimate its power... all of its power. It's *your* brain. It's *your* body. Your brain can have a mind of its own, but it is still you. Nothing is attacking you or can get to you because nothing can tap into your thoughts and control your reactions but you.

It is very important to identify that although these thoughts are coming from your brain, and your brain is in you, it doesn't mean you deeply feel and believe in the thoughts you receive. Everyone gets wild, out of body thoughts once in a while. People with OCD just unintentionally take them and handle them differently, often running away with the thought. Although you can't control what thoughts enter your brain, you can control how you handle them *once they have entered*. This is the key to getting better and getting OCD under control. It brings me back to the saying, "You can't control the cards you were dealt, but how you play the hand." The same applies to OCD recovery. You didn't choose this. You didn't sign an application for this suffering. Who does? But it has overtaken you, and now it's time for you to play the hand, *your* way. When the unwelcomed thoughts enter your mind, you know what to do. You push through them; you fight to not give in to whatever it is telling you. Start by focusing your brainpower on other areas, little by little. All of your brainpower is currently focused on OCD. How can you expect to ever perform at your full potential in life when the only 10% of your brain you are physically able to use is being overtaken with obsessive thoughts?

Imagine if you had the ability to clear out the mind games, the pain, and the real struggle of obsessing. Chances are, you wouldn't know what to do with yourself. What would you do with all of that newfound time? Imagine the things in life you could accomplish if your brain allowed you the time to focus that incredible energy and devotion elsewhere? *To real life?* Everything somehow falls into place when you begin the battle. You aren't meant to be at battle with your brain your entire life. Everyone does have something though, don't they?

OCD can't kill you. It, alone, can't. Even if you have thoughts that make you almost end your life, don't you dare blame the OCD alone for it. If it gets to that point, that is you making a conscious decision. You are responsible for your responses to these thoughts because whether you want to face it or not, you have the ability to control and retrain your mind. You just need to figure out how — which is where I come in with inspiration and your therapist comes in with direction and the how to. Keep in mind, your OCD targets your deepest fears, not *who you are* as a person. OCD can only target who you are as a person if you allow it to.

Granted, you may not be aware that you are allowing it to target you as a person, but by now, you should be able to make more of that inference. Let's say for example, you have harm OCD and are getting repetitive thoughts that you are a murderer and that you are potentially going to kill someone. You would be going out of your mind. What if who you are is a true murderer? What if you kill someone in your sleep? If there is a sharp object near you, will you use it against someone? It would be normal to be wary and initially terrified of these thoughts if they kept circling in your brain. Here's the separation — **just because you are getting these thoughts doesn't mean you actually believe any of this deep down.** They are coming from your brain, but that doesn't mean the thoughts reflect who you are. I understand that you may be reading this with contradictory views. You are not getting these thoughts because you are actually a murderer but because being a true murderer is *one of your deepest fears.* Your fears are completely separate from both who you are and reality. That's what makes it a fear.

You may think I have no real grasp on your particular OCD or other kinds of OCD and its power over you. But I don't need to know every detail because the concepts of OCD remain the same, only the elements change. All I know is that no matter how serious or how sick a human being is with Obsessive-Compulsive Disorder, or any like disorder, you have the ability to fight it. It may take a really long time to believe in your fight, to believe that you can actually even win the fight. I understand that. As much as the levels of serotonin and other chemicals in your brain may be unbalanced, as much as you may think you need your medication, as much as you may not see what I am trying to get across to you, I still believe there is no excuse in the world to not fight your OCD. You should still give it everything you've got in you. I certainly did. I was able to see past the sickness. I only saw past it because I fought by not giving my brain or my gut what it wanted, over and over again. Millions of us go through life every single day, accepting our OCD, giving into it, truly believing that these are just the cards we've been dealt. It is **you** who I am talking to. It is **you** who I am showing that no matter how serious your case may or may not be, the fight is always waiting for you.

Author's Note: Sorry, but your OCD is no exception. No matter what type of OCD you have, it can be fought, and the intrusive thoughts will immensely slow down to the point where OCD is no longer number one in your life. OCD cannot attack you. It can only attack your fears, and your fears are not who you are. You can stand up against your fears at any time. These fears are just surrounded by a dark cloud called OCD. OCD is just like one of those blackout back-drops where you put something behind it, and it looks larger than life. But when that something walks out of the backdrop in front of the crowd, it is a measly little thing that attempted to disguise how pathetic and small it really is. It was an illusion. This measly little thing is what is controlling your every move, your happiness in life? No. It shouldn't be allowed to today. It shouldn't be allowed to for even one more day.

27

"OCD -VS- LOGIC"

This is my belief. There is nothing, absolutely nothing logical about OCD. Essentially, this is what OCD does — transfer us into a world that becomes more illogical with every intrusive thought and reassuring compulsion. Therefore, you can see the importance of understanding how to get back to somewhat of a logical state in order to start to see what OCD is actually doing to your mind. In OCD therapy, we are taught there is no logic in OCD. But I thoroughly believe you as a human being, no matter how far gone you may feel, have logic instilled in you. You begin to inadvertently get in touch with this more logical state the more you put up a fight against the OCD. The more dependent you are upon your OCD, the less logical you are allowing yourself to be. You don't want to constantly reassure and feed the illogical side of your brain. We now know we can train our brains behaviorally through exposing obsessive thoughts and seeing first-hand that the illogical, unwelcome thought you just had has no effect on reality. The intrusive thought isn't true. Nothing happens because you took the step to logically prove to yourself nothing bad happened, rather than rely on a compulsion to avoid seeing the logic — just in case. The more often you do this, essentially the ERP of exposing the illogicalness of this disorder, the more your mindset will begin to shift to thinking logically more often. You are training your mind out of a certain thinking pattern and shifting it into a healthier one.

We believe that we have a way to control the air around us and spend our lives performing certain compulsions to avoid that particular feeling we get in the pit of our stomach. We believe in a connection that isn't there. We believe we have influence on causation and reality. You triple checking something and continuing to doubt yourself only makes your logic bury deeper and deeper, thereby digressing any work you have put in to begin to train your brain.

You know you turned off the lights. You *do*. You know you locked the door. You *do*. You know you are as clean as physically possible and quite possibly cleaner than any human you've ever met. You *do*. You know you aren't a murderer. You *do*. You just aren't sure that you really *can* trust your mind, even though it seems to be constantly turning against you. So, I am telling you. You absolutely do have the logic inside of your very being to know the honest to God truth. That is why finding and bringing out your logic is a key element in recovery. I look at logic in the sense of getting back in touch with your authentic self, outside of your OCD. The best way you can get better is to get in touch with your logic and continue to separate real from unreal, or you will continue living in your hell. You get in touch with your logic by taking that control back and allowing the logic to resurface. In regard to OCD, the only way to bring out that logic is through proving to yourself your compulsions have no effect on reality. The only way is by putting up a constant and consistent fight. If you give into one, only one intrusive and obsessive thought, you will get the relief you *need* to be running from. And this very thing sets you back in progress significantly. I know you might be thinking, "She's crazy. There's no way I can eliminate ALL my compulsions." My answer to that is perhaps you can't at the moment, but that doesn't mean you don't need to hear this. I cannot tell you how detrimental it is to have these setbacks. In the end, you've only provided temporary relief, and you've made your logic go right back down where it was buried. Remember, the only thing you are battling with is yourself, but YOU can remain in control, always, regardless of what your imagination might be telling you.

Eventually, the further down the OCD hole we go, we seem to lose touch with what is real and what is not real, and it's to the point where we lose hope. Everyone around us seems to live life so simply — so easily and effortlessly. Their logic seems to just flow so naturally, yet here we are, just struggling through each hour to figure out what effect we have and what effect we don't or who we are and who we are not. We are second-guessing every single thing we think and do because we don't feel like we have logic to *trust* ourselves, as most people seem to have. Trust me — you will only become less and less logical the more you decide it's not worth the fight. I became in touch with my logical side *only* once I consistently put up a fight because I was consistently proving something to myself, not relying on my imagination to tell me what is and isn't real. Within every human being with this disorder, there is *still* at least an ounce of logic, no matter how deeply it's buried. I thoroughly believe that. It is simply covered up by this horrendous disorder.

As soon as you can grab that small amount of logic — don't second-guess it — run with it. You have a fighting chance. Usually that little piece of logic sliiiighly surfaces once you have exposed a good amount of obsessional thoughts. You may hardly notice. But in time, you will get a free moment when you will actually question your OCD, even just a little bit. THAT is the tiny piece of your logic, desperately trying to get to the surface for air. It wants to serve you and help you, but by continuing this downward cycle, you are in fact allowing the OCD to trump your logic. Even if you aren't sure if you have any logic left, like you don't know real from fake, I assure you, you do. You have to think logically in order to survive. You wouldn't be alive without your logic. It's part of your human nature. It's just about finding the separation of what is real and what is simply not. That is the core of this disorder. Finding your logic and bringing it back to life through confidence gained in the fight is the real issue and can be immensely difficult. It really helps to have a therapist probe and bring up the right questions to spark your mind and spark your logic. You can sit there alone for hours, and you will just confuse yourself even more. You have to be able to spark your mind in order for it to stand up for itself. Oftentimes, it takes another person at first, specifically someone who understands this disorder, to help get you out of that spiraling daze. The more probing my therapist did, the more he helped me think logically. The more he got me to put myself to the test, the more my inner self started to realize that the big, tough bear I was up against was just a cub. A cub that had a mother waiting for it close by, to keep going. You just have to find a way to get out of being between the mother bear and baby cub, so you can get to safety and see the rest of the forest for the beauty that it really has without that insistent fear. If you were to judge the entire forest by the intimidation of the bear, you wouldn't venture out and see everything else the forest offers. The same mindset can be applied to OCD. If you just look at life through your OCD scope, you are missing out on so much that life has to offer.

I am **not** trying to say OCD is *just* a matter of finding your logic. I don't need the OCD police coming for me. I am saying that OCD can cause you to sink further and further into a world that only becomes more illogical. Becoming more in touch with my logic, after proving my compulsions were a total waste of time, helped me immensely. It was like I was able to see above the clouds once in a while, and I was able to use those times to see the illogical state I was in when I was back down under the clouds.

Just because I would get quick, intrusive thoughts and images that my hair was falling out, didn't mean it actually would because I didn't perform the compulsion. Just because I saw my hair falling out inside my brain didn't mean it actually was in that moment. Even though my skin and scalp were crawling and there was no convincing me out of it. That is the power of anxiety, which keeps us gripping the OCD so hard. All of my random, miscellaneous compulsions had literally no effect or correlation to the intrusive thoughts. I had to learn to separate my deep inner mind and thoughts from reality.

I am the queen of hearing something and planning out every single worst-case scenario that could soon happen. The problem is I create all of these worst-case scenarios within just a couple of minutes, before I even get all the facts. Then I panic, my palms usually sweat, and I lose a little bit more touch with reality in my anxious state. But I have to take a step back and realize that everything I just pictured hasn't even happened! They haven't even come to fruition because I literally created them in my mind. My mind is so vivid, and what I picture always seems so real, but I sometimes still forget they are just mere thoughts. I tell myself I just like to be prepared for the worst-case scenario, but in actuality what it's doing is getting in the way of the reality! You prove this to yourself again and again, and after a long while, you will actually get to a point where you have a slight question about the connection between your compulsions and reality. You will begin cracking the foundation of OCD's hold over you. THIS is the true first breaking point where you will know you are on the right path to battling your OCD. Then you keep going. All in. Headfirst. Let the cracks get bigger and bigger.

Author's Note: Above all else, I *cannot wait* for you to get to the point where you begin to question your OCD after you have begun the fight. It is one of the most groundbreaking feelings in the world. You begin to question the biggest element of your life for the very first time. Except it's not one of those feelings where you feel like everything in your life was a big lie. It's a feeling where you knew deep down that was the case all along, and you are just sealing its fate. You can only go up from this point forward.

28

"THE DEATH TRAP OF ISOLATION AND EMOTION"

To this day, the biggest scar my OCD has ingrained in me is through my emotions. Well, technically, the lack there of. At one point in college when I was so left out, so gossiped about and bullied, so turned upon, and so alone, I couldn't be in touch with my feelings because they just hurt too much. I couldn't allow myself to actually swallow the pain I felt. It hurt far into the core of my being. I could feel the pain panging in my heart when I really thought about how emotionally hurt I was. So, I learned to train myself so my brain wouldn't go there. As soon as I would feel the pang of pain, I stopped myself and thought about something else immediately. I avoided any emotion.

And I have never been the same.

Essentially, I developed a system where I rarely let myself think deeply about anything that could bother me — a system that a part of me unfortunately still abides by. I don't reflect on much of anything just in case it hurts. At some point I stopped letting anything close to me. I didn't let my emotions come out to play any longer. To this day, I still don't get nearly as excited over anything as I used to. I don't get very angry much; I usually manipulate it into sadness. I guess I don't feel "excitement." Anything that is considered exciting to everyone else has morphed into anxiety for me. I'm not excited; I'm anxious. The twinge in my stomach of what should be butterflies is anxiety. "What if I can't? What if I fail? What if they don't like my work? What if I hate it?" The closer whatever "exciting" thing is coming up in my life, whether it be the plane I'm on somehow getting off the ground, or walking onstage to speak, you can bet your last dollar my obsessions are swirling. My palms, nose, and upper lip are covered in droplets of sweet sweat.

At times I hear a song or inhale a smell that brings me back to a single moment in time before my OCD, and in those moments, I briefly feel the original emotion I felt the first time around. That feeling is usually so blissful — yet so distant —and it is then when I realize I feel nothing of that sort anymore. I've noticed such a lacking in my care, my motivation. All my life I have been the most dedicated, eager, motivated, and hardest working human being that I have ever met. I've now lost so much care and concern. You know what keeps me going and does give me motivation? This book. Getting my thoughts on paper to send to you. I may not be able to help myself at times, but I do care about helping *you*.

OCD has put limitations on my brain. I can't wrap my head fully around anything. Oftentimes, my fear of something makes me not try at all. I won't even let my brain think deeply because I'm scared of where it will go. What's worse? *I'm scared that it won't go anywhere at all.* After so many years of my brain constantly racing, constantly thinking thoughts that controlled my life, I have to say, I fear my brain going nowhere. It's actually...quiet. I remember when I used to wonder what my brain would do with itself without OCD. I thought I would be incredibly bored with life. What would I do with all of my time? But I wasn't considering the entire concept of *living life* that I was missing out on. There are countless subtle joys every day I now feel since I'm not being controlled by something — something I feel the need to stand up to.

I have a natural tendency to focus so hard on things that I don't see the bigger picture. I'm so zeroed in that I can't seem to step back and assess a situation and then present my thoughts clearly. My head is so fuzzy, and I can't articulate what my brain is thinking. I get so wrapped up in my thoughts, I often can't find the words to say what I need to; it's too much stimulation all at once. It gets more and more restricted, almost like I had a long, hard day, but all the time. I don't sound professional and intelligent because my brain is so lost in fearing that very thing. In fact, because I am having one of those days, I can't actually explain it to you the way that I would like to. Why am I so focused that my brain goes fuzzy? Because I'm *obsessing about obsessing*. I may not have to perform hundreds of compulsions a day, but I still obsess on certain things to a point where I let it interfere with my life. In times such as this, I have to step back and review my situation, write down everything that is happening that could remotely be affecting me, and assess the best solution. That's an example of how OCD can really change and alter; it's always morphing into anything it can to get to you. I do believe that with proper learned exercises, continuing to live life, and plunging myself into it, I will overcome the restraints in my brain. I will fight through the black and white restrictions of my brain just like I fought to be free from the ultimate beast. And I hope to never look back.

At times, I still fear I have lost the ability to think so critically, along with the ability to challenge myself to be better. I believe the reason for all of this is because I just don't care. My true motivation is gone because my emotions are gone. My brain obsesses with this — the constant fear of not being able to face reality and what's ahead of me in this world. It is too difficult for me to set long term goals, picture myself fulfilling them, and watching them as they may or may not come into fruition. Somehow, I feel that if I don't let myself think deeply, *I won't be deeply affected by anything.* Just like the obsessions wash over me like waves, it seems I've allowed life to wash over me as well. I went through so much emotional turmoil in my past that I just have trouble facing the realities of the world since I've had relief. I didn't face reality for so long. I was so far off in my mind. I never faced real life battles of how to fend for myself and how to think with true common sense. My parents handled many things for me while I was sick because I was too detached to make appropriate decisions. Now I just feel late to the game. I am still learning how to put up healthy walls against the world and deal with real life situations without OCD as my barrier. I don't use OCD as my excuse or as my defense now. I use *myself*.

The one emotion that I typically go straight to and is the most comfortable for me is sadness. I am far more comfortable embracing sadness than happiness because it is literally all I felt for years. There are genuinely times when I have momentarily felt happy, and I am almost uncomfortable because I am so unused to the feeling of being happy. I subconsciously find ways to revert back to my comfort zone, sadness. How can one live like that? Is that even considered living?

The truth is, it is very hard to pull yourself out of true emotional numbness. Once you've trained yourself to turn off your emotions, to not allow pain in, you can hardly turn them back on. For a long time, I missed the feelings I felt before the OCD sunk in, where I would feel a rush of emotions, allow myself to be truly excited, truly happy, and truly energetic before stopping myself in my tracks with one single passing thought. At times, it still feels like I am the walking dead because I feel nothing. That's what scares me the most out of everything — feeling nothing. I would rather feel anything than nothing, but nothing has become a comfort zone which I am afraid to leave. I miss the feeling of actually living life. For the majority of my life, I have *lived to simply exist*, not *existed to simply live*.

All of this changed when I got into my first real relationship almost three years ago at the age of 25. Within three months, I went from feeling virtually nothing to falling in blissful love for the first time and shortly after, heartbreak that ran deeper than any emotion I've ever felt. All of a sudden, after years of training my mind and heart to shut off to emotion, out of nowhere I felt every single emotion known to man. After the breakup, my anxiety began to attack my emotions on a daily basis. It was as though my anxiety was directly linked to my emotions, and I had no control over either. Everything and anything began to give me anxiety, and I was on a constant rollercoaster of unnecessary emotion towards anything I truly cared about. At times, my emotions ran so high, I could hardly wrap my head around them, and I drove my loved ones crazy because I would do anything and everything to calm down my emotions. This anxiety, although I always based everything on real facts, often led my mind down routes that created assumptions, and I convinced myself that they were facts. Sometimes I was dead on with my assumptions, and other times I couldn't be farther from the truth. Ironically, I found myself at a point wishing I could go back to being emotionally numb rather than getting so much more worked up than the average person. But I knew that wasn't the right answer.

Just as with training the OCD, I've needed to train my emotions and anxiety, so I don't have to continue living in emotional hell. I still struggle in the area of emotion. I feel everything so *deeply* now, but my passion for connecting with fellow obsessive outsiders keeps me going. I constantly seek purpose and fulfillment, and with those two things, I pray to fall upon steady happiness. Although I am a much happier and healthier person than I ever was when I was at my worst with OCD, I know I have a long way to go. When I do stumble on my happiness, I plan to fully embrace it. I've noticed as each year comes and goes since my time on the battlefield with my OCD, I feel more accomplished and much lighter. I know I am on the right path, but I have to keep pushing to expose my emotions and really let my mind go there, just like I had to keep pushing to expose myself to my OCD and anxiety.

My advice to all of you would be to watch your emotions carefully. Get in touch with them rather than shove them underneath a rug. If you can articulate your emotions, you will be much more likely to identify with yourself and in turn, your OCD. If you are truly in sync with your obsessions and compulsions, you will be much more likely to control them rather than be submissive or shun them. For so long, I was submissive to my OCD and emotions, fearful of what I would feel if I was actually in touch with them. The takeaway? Don't take a page out of my book (HA!) in that regard.

You can only imagine how my struggle with emotional numbness coincided with depression. When you feel bondage by something or someone, the first reaction is to find a way out. You search up and down and side to side, just searching for a loophole. There were too many times when I couldn't find a way out. OCD was the best outlet I could find where I was able to grasp some sort of control in my life. I just couldn't see life as just *me* again. I was so dependent upon my OCD that I couldn't imagine life without it. That's why therapy is such a struggle. The attempt to maintain any relationship is such as struggle. It's so much easier to just be alone all the time. You don't have to explain to people; you can just be in your own little world where no one bothers you. But it gets old doesn't it? It gets to a point when you find your loneliness no longer lonely. To the point where you have convinced yourself you would rather be by yourself than around anyone else. That's where I find myself time and time again — and that's a huge problem.

When you stop and actually take a moment and look at the world around you, you finally realize that *you're not a part of it*. You've created your own world. You've literally taken away the one thing that God gave you. **The gift of *living this life*.** You are not meant to create your own world. "For freedom, Christ set us free. Stand firm then and don't submit again to the yoke of slavery." Galatians 5:1. We are slaves to OCD, and it holds a whip in hand. We cannot continue to be at the mercy of OCD; we must be at the mercy of Christ alone. We are human, and humans are supposed to coexist. Isolation will make you more and more sick. Doesn't it make sense? Whenever I see homeless people talking to themselves, I think about how deeply lonely they must be. You hardly ever see homeless people just all sitting around, sharing whatever food they find and telling stories. It's "to each his own" — survival of the fittest. It's no wonder they talk with themselves. They just got stuck in that life, a life of isolation. Just like you have the ability to get stuck in the life you are living now with OCD. DON'T get stuck. That's why I'm here, to help you realize how close you might be to getting stuck. If you already are stuck, we are still in this together; I'm no different than you. I'm stretching out a hand for that sinking sand you're in right now. Humans are only so strong. Not to mention that the strongest thing about us is our minds, which appears to be *our* entire problem. It's okay to need someone to give you a lifeline. People get lifelines all the time, just in different senses. Maybe this book can be yours. Separating yourself from the people around you can be deadly with this disorder. You must be surrounded by "normal" people in order to stay afloat. There were many times when I so deeply isolated myself that I would be in a casual social setting, and it was like I was looking in through a glass window. I would listen to their conversations, observe how normally they moved, how beautiful they were, how effortless life was for them. I looked in on their lives like I lived in an alternate universe, an alien just wishing I could be part of their world. Yet, it really hadn't been that long ago that I *was* part of that world. It doesn't take long in isolation to further lose touch with reality. With loss of reality comes a blur in logic. The farther isolated you are, the farther detached you will become and the harder it will be for you to ever get back.

A really solid piece of advice that I can give you is to surround yourself with a support group with like individuals. Do anything to get yourself out of isolation, even if it is just a support group once a week. I'm very serious when I say what really helped me was surrounding myself with normal people, because I felt so abnormal. Don't take the word normal the wrong way. I just mean people who don't necessarily suffer from the same or related disorders. I was able to see what I was missing out on. I would step out of my comfort zone to make small talk. I would start to do things like go to dinner with someone, and I would force myself to live somewhat normally. I found myself just realizing at the end of the night how much I was really missing out on. My logical side would just want to crumble by the end of a social encounter or outing. I was back in my horrific world. Once you take yourself out of your own mind for a second, you start to realize how effortlessly they move about. They don't stop in the middle of something because of heart pounding thoughts.

They don't have to stop everything to tap things multiple times. Nothing slows them down. What took everyone else five minutes took me ten minutes because of all the extra thinking I had to do. "Should I walk to the right or left around this table? Should I touch this random object along the way because it might make me feel better? Should I sit on the couch or the chair? The chair seems to give me less anxiety at first glance, so I'll sit in the chair. Wait, no. I just got a bad thought while sitting down in the chair. MUST CASUALLY MOVE TO COUCH NOW." This is a vivid example of how in depth I had to think before making ANY and EVERY decision in my life with severe OCD. I just wanted relief.

Call a friend to *get out of your house and head* and go do something, literally anything. Re-connect with someone you used to hang around, someone who you have separated yourself from because of your OCD. Join book clubs, workout classes, study groups, and support groups. Go solo to events in your city and force yourself to talk to strangers. Reach out to people and be anyone you want to be. Just get yourself involved in the real world instead of our fake world. To this day, when I am feeling extremely anxious and suddenly find myself frequently tempted by OCD, I call a friend and go do something. If you don't have a friend to call, go by yourself. Screw the comfort zones of OCD. I change my location, change my mental state, and I shift my thinking pattern immediately back into the real world before my mind takes me somewhere that *isn't real at all.*

How nice it would be to be able to do the same thing as others without constant paranoia! Order what you want. Dress how you want. Touch people without getting "infected." Embrace bear hugs, shake hands with people without shying away. Hang around the people you want and not be fearful of you doing something vulgar or bad. Say what you want. Walk how you want. Be able to truly shuffle through your day and your passive thoughts without the debilitating thoughts interjecting themselves and taking over. Have a series of thoughts without getting a cringing sting in your stomach, just allowing the thoughts to flow freely without the fear of what is coming next — the fear of the next intrusive thought. It's a beautiful world, but I didn't enjoy any of that for the past seven years. Perhaps that's how you are right now. Trust me, life is so much bigger than it seems right now. Sometimes you'll feel like it's not worth doing what you need to do because you'd rather just stay in your little disturbed world. Which I get...trust me. But boy, I am glad I am not where you might be right now anymore. Use me as an inspiration, please! Understand that I have been where you are right now, and even though we may not have had the same obsessions, and we don't have the same thought processes, it doesn't make any difference. This is a disorder that meets at the same spot in the middle between all of us. We all are going through the exact same thing, regardless of the details. The same basis of fear, worry, anxiety, horror, anger...all the same. We are all scared and plain tired. Tired of this. So tired, yet we cannot let go to save our lives. So that's where the decision comes in, I guess. What's worth more to you in the long run? Not the short run... don't think that way (even though thinking short term and in the moment is all we know). Force yourself to think about your future because we all have one. And it can be so bright and beautiful if we allow it. Create those memories for yourself that are still out there for you. No, it is never too late. If you are still breathing, it is not too late!

This is your chance. This is your time to *wake the hell up*. Every single moment you spend dwelling through life with your OCD is a moment you could have spent with a loved one, creating limitless memories. This whole thing boils down to you having a choice. It was never your choice to have a mental disorder, but do not feel sorry for yourself. The pity party needs to be over because action needs to be taken. That action can only be taken by you, and that action is the very definition of what comes down to your choice. This choice is solely yours to make at any moment from this point forward.

Author's Note: Don't ever expect the people of this world to under-stand what you are going through. Understand that you may not be alone in this battle, but you need to stand alone in this fight. This is between you and your mind. You and OCD. You and the beast. This is *your life*, and OCD has invaded it. I don't know why you have this disorder. I don't know if you will ever feel complete relief, but I do know that you have a purpose with it and a fighting chance to live a normal life. Whether you agree with that or not isn't my concern; my concern is that you see beyond the pain and gear up for the fight. If you are not willing to fight, you have no business reading my book. Seriously. I can do nothing for you if you won't do anything for yourself.

29

"BE ANXIOUSLY AWARE"

My ultimate beast is my anxiety. I have a grip on my OCD now because I know how to manage it day in and day out, but I hardly had a grip on my anxiety before I started Zoloft in the last couple of years. Up until that point, where the medication took the edge off, I spent years focusing on my OCD but not necessarily dealing with my anxiety about life in general.

OCD has long been classified as an anxiety disorder, that is until you look it up in the DSM-5 (Diagnostic and Statistical Manual of Mental Disorders). OCD has always and probably will always be linked as an anxiety disorder for me personally, because that's what it was classified and treated as when I went through the intense program. This was before the DSM changed the official classification of OCD to its own classification after anxiety disorders as Obsessive-Compulsive and related disorders. I often refer to OCD as an anxiety disorder to this day, and probably will continue to because OCD stems from anxiety and anxious thoughts. Because of this, figuring out how to cope with the anxiety by itself is essential. That's where I have been for the past two years.

It seemed as I got older and faced more realities of the real world, my anxiety only got worse. It used to paralyze me. What seemed to be a surmountable issue to one person seemed insurmountable to me. Any factors of change, flexibility, or adjustment were just too much for me to handle most of the time. As soon as I began to get over-whelmed about anything in life, I tended to go into fetal position. I crawled into my bed and didn't get out until I sorted through every area of my mind to find a solution. I have stayed there for too many hours, far too many times. In the past, up until recently, I have spent enormous amounts of time analyzing my anxiety over something but not taken action, thereby prolonging the ruthless circle that is anxi-ety. I would sit for hours, even days, just contemplating the pros and cons of the potential outcomes of the elements that were causing me anxiety. I often became so anxious over making decisions that I stayed where I was and didn't make any decision at all. To get out of the anxiety in the moment, I have always tried to distract myself with some temporary activity or incentive to look forward to because looking at the bigger picture of anything is too overwhelming for me. All this mentality has done is delay life for me.

At times, the anxiety has become so bad that I can't even pinpoint what specifically was crippling me. That only gave me more anxiety since the only way I know out is to break the anxieties down and find real world solutions. I used to get so overwhelmed in the moment; I would break down because I couldn't express myself. Other times my anxiety took me to another world. It catastrophized every little thing, and my mind could go from A to Z within a matter of seconds. I felt like I was going to explode if I didn't deal with it in that very moment. At times it got to a point that scared me. It's like my brain went into a different state for only a moment. It's as though, in that millisecond, I questioned everything, as if I couldn't tell real from not real. These were the times I was afraid of the potential of my own brain. I was terrified in these times of mental detachment that my mind would stay that way, and I wouldn't be able to get it back to where it is now. This all comes back to a mental state of obsessiveness — catastro-phizing things to a point of endless anxiety.

To this day, the best way that I get myself out of the deep holes anxiety pulls me into is to **deal directly** with whatever it is that is causing me the anxiety. I have to break down each anxious thought and face it head on and form an actionable solution immediately. The root of many things that cause me to be anxious is often the unknown. I feel like I need to know everything about a situation so that I can be prepared. Oftentimes, my anxiety blocks my ability to think in that moment if I hit an unexpected roadblock. However, when I am not anxious, I take roadblocks and seem to be able to sort through them quite rationally. So, I started an anxiety journal, where every time I feel overwhelmed, I write down *every single thing* that I am anxious about in that moment. I then *formulate a plan* of how to lower that anxiety. If it is a person causing me the anxiety, I contact that person, and I face whatever issue we have right then. I don't prepare. I just do it. If it is a something health related, I get it looked into. Instead of wandering around my house day in and day out fixating on what could potentially be wrong and trying to figure it out on my own, I remember there are professionals for that. If it is financially related, I make a written plan as to how I am going to move forward. In many cases, once I have addressed the issue itself, especially on paper where I can see it, it wasn't nearly the beast I thought it was. I will have wasted countless hours of anxiety over an issue that could have been dealt with in a much simpler way, much sooner. I don't want to live this short life wasting days just pondering and dwelling. I want so desperately to live a life where I can breeze past things no matter how hard they are to face. I guess what I'm trying to say is, I don't want to waste this life any more than I already have.

Another way I have been dealing with the anxiety is by talking about it out loud to someone I am close to, in hopes they can help me sort through my inflexibility and mental roadblocks. It always helps me to hear how other people deal with life changes and situations, and I try to take notes. Talking about my anxieties with people who greatly care about me has helped me enormously. Once I say the anxieties out loud, it's almost like I am releasing them. It's very similar to how I used to talk through my obsessions and compulsions out loud. As soon as I do so, they don't seem like such an impossible burden to get through. Full disclosure — it even helps me to say these things out loud back to myself in the mirror. There's something about being able to formulate the words out loud that seems to do part of the work itself.

I am constantly trying to find new ways to cope with how I approach anxiety. As soon as I feel my anxiety rising, I do my very best to stop my *flight* mode from going with it. The longer I let the anxiety linger, the harder it is for me to get back to a calm state. As it lingers, the issue itself turns into a much larger, unrealistic problem. I start breathing slower to get my heart rate to come back down and try to just take a moment. If I am not in a position to deal with the anxiety in that moment, I often immediately force myself to change mental gears. If I am out in public enjoying an evening with friends, and I can feel my anxiety rising, my instinct is to want to leave and go straight home, straight into my bed alone to think. But I don't let myself. I force myself to stick out whatever situation I am in at that moment and let the anxiety just stir. It can't kill me. So I let it be and focus on what is in front of me. My anxiety *can wait* during these inconvenient times, even though I want to stop everything and deal with it right then. Just as with OCD, it comes down to a decision. I *choose* to not let it ruin my time with other people. It doesn't deserve that credit. Obviously, this only causes more momentary anxiety, but I wait until I am home and strong enough to rationally face and think through the anxiety headfirst. By this time, I've forced myself to sit with it, so the initial spike of anxiety has lowered significantly. Then I formulate my plan to deal with moving forward on how to address the issue causing me the anxiety.

So it comes down to this. I do my very best to be "anxiously aware," by becoming aware of the root of the anxiety as soon as possible. And then, I do my very best to *let the anxiety part of it go*. Unlike with OCD, I personally have found getting to the root when it comes to anxiety is logical and helpful, as long as you don't obsess over it and don't allow the initial spike of anxiety to completely take over. OCD is senseless, which is why we don't search for the "root" of it; it doesn't have a root, as we have previously well established. If you get to the root of your anxiety, and it comes down to an obsession or recurring irrational thought that you know is OCD (when in doubt — treat it like it's OCD), then you know you need to stop and allow the anxiety to sit with you because we know the anxiety itself will pass. I try to mentally separate my obsessive thoughts from my anxiety. Anxiety is more of a feeling, and the obsessive thought is more of a question.

Being prone to anxiety is a constant fight or flight mode. I am finally learning that I don't have to choose *flight*. I can choose *fight* every time and face it just like I would OCD. Just as with OCD, you always have a choice. It's just about learning how to utilize that choice the right way every time.

***

Author's Note: Every single time I get anxious, which is far too often, I am tempted with performing compulsions. And every single time I have to consciously remind myself I am just anxious, and the compulsion will mean absolutely nothing regardless of what my gut is telling me to do. Don't let bouts of heightened anxiety throw off your hard fought battle with OCD. The truth is, the anxiety itself does nothing for you. It might as well be air, just like the OCD is. However, the reason we need to train ourselves to be "anxiously aware" is because the more anxious we are, the more vulnerable to the OCD we are. This is why we need to be constantly scanning (scanning, not dwelling on) our inner anxiety scales, so we can separate the anxiety from the OCD before we combine the two and go back down the rabbit hole. Without anxiety, OCD feels like nothing to freak out about. Without OCD, anxiety is just a heightened sense and feeling coming over your body. Be strong during these times, and remember who is in control.

30

"RELATIONSHIP STATUS: OCD"

Let me guess, your current relationship status is not with another human being, it's with OCD. Am I right? Let's discuss the inevitable — maintaining any type of relationship with severe OCD. Whether it is an acquaintance, a friendship, a family member, or a romantic partner, the chances of you running into serious relational obstacles solely because of your OCD is very likely. I, for one, rarely had the opportunity of taking any relationship past an acquaintance for years. My compulsions were so evident; I had people running for the hills within moments of meeting me. As soon as I caught wind of the off-putting nature of my compulsions, I maneuvered ways to hide my compulsions for the first few times I was around the same person. I would seem normal to the average person at times, with the exception of the state of my hair, and would slowly incorporate my compulsions into the relationship. I would usually begin by making jokes out of my compulsions, laugh off my OCD in front of the newcomer. The responses I received initially were often "understanding" and positive, as if I was acting like it was no big deal, and therefore, so should they. I think a lot of people thought since I was acting lighthearted about my OCD, it must not be that serious. That is, until it started quite literally getting in the way

196

of our times together. I would often hold people up, having to go back and re-step or go up and down stairs twice when walking somewhere, having to go back and touch something we passed while they patiently waited, or even have to physically touch them or their hair at random times (Sound crazy? I was).

I usually received the exact same responses in the beginnings of my friendships. Once they knew about my OCD, every single new friend wanted to "help" me. It was a consistent theme. My newfound friends would get so excited about helping me get better (as if), and they would inquire and want to know as much as they could about the disorder once they saw my battle. They only ever saw small parts of the battle, and it was embarrassing to explain it again and again, breaking down each compulsion. At first, I was as eager to explain my OCD as they were to learn about it. This phase of interest and desire to help on their end usually lasted a couple of weeks, tops. At that point, either the person realized they didn't understand what the hell was wrong with me, or they gave up hope of ever helping me. They were exhausted, yet they hadn't seen past the first layer of my OCD. Or they just didn't care enough to. Both seem applicable. So there I went, short-lived friendship after friendship.

The truth was, past the OCD, I was a cool girl to be around, but after a short amount of time, my cool factor was *outweighed* by my OCD. It took a while for people to learn I wasn't a freak at all. I was just **misunderstood**. Mentally-misunderstood should be my middle name. In order to know who I was underneath, or see my true funny, compassionate, and loving personality, it would involve that person staying around long enough to shed those layers — layers of OCD. What my friends didn't know was that by standing and waiting for me the times they did or trying to make me feel comfortable about my compulsions, they were enabling me. More often than not, I didn't have it in me to explain how they really should be helping hold me accountable rather than reinforcing my behaviors. But that was completely my fault, not theirs. They were not trained in OCD, and I don't blame any of them for giving up on me. People who don't have our disorder just don't get it. Why would they? Would you understand the complexity of a disease you don't have? Not to the extent the person with it does. And we need to accept that at face value.

So, what's the answer here? Do we, the obsessive outsiders, just go through this life alone? Do we just steer clear of anyone and everyone, so we don't have to go through the torture of being left again? Do we just learn the only company we can ever depend on is our own?

I don't know about you, but I don't want it to have to be that way. I'm so tired of being lonely and let down by people I let in and out of my life. The truth is, just like me, you are someone far beyond your OCD. **You are still you.** You are being grossly inhibited by a torturous disorder, but you are still yourself, a unique and very worthy individual. You still have your very own personality, as well as an imagination *far beyond* the limitations OCD preys on.

A lot of people just can't see past the disorder to remind themselves why they want to be around you, especially if the disorder is directly affecting your relationship with them. I could sit here and say if the person is a good human being they will stick around and be supportive of you. But in all honesty, you are the one with the crippling, misunderstood disorder, a disorder that usually affects one or more relationships around you. You are the one who needs to do the majority of the work to get better. If you are working on getting better, wanting with everything in you to put up the fight against OCD, and taking active measures to do so, there is no reason to blame OCD for your relationship not working out in the end. But your relationship partner, whether that is a close family member, close friend, or significant other should be pulling their weight too. That comes with the territory of being close to someone who has severe OCD. This can happen in a couple of different ways. They can either just be incredibly supportive of your OCD battle but not involved in helping you, or they can be both supportive and involved. Ideally, this person would care enough to help you in any way they can. This help usually surfaces when they better understand your disorder. They can do this by attending a therapy session with you to learn directly from a therapist the extent of OCD, by doing personal research, and by talking in depth with you about your particular case. By them helping you overcome the worst of your OCD, you might be eliminating the majority of the problem in the relationship. The catch is that in order to help and encourage you to *not* give into your compulsions, they must know arguably all about your OCD. They must know what your triggers are, what your main compulsions are, what sparks your anxiety so that they can help hold you accountable, so you don't continue to give into the OCD. This person can call you out directly, help you expose your thoughts, and talk through what you are feeling in the moment. This can seem like the worst idea ever, but it is also great for you. That means that every time you are around this person, they have the potential to verbally hold you accountable when they see you performing a compulsion. This is also the best thing for you because it's like you have another therapist right there with you at times. As hard as it seems to be honest with them about what you are currently facing, it may be what is best for you in the long run. If you want these people to remain in your life, you need to allow this accountability to happen if the person is willing to be active in supporting you through your journey to recovery.

Obviously, this stance can vary based on the type of relationship you have. This system works best if you live with someone because you are often with the same, consistent person. On their behalf, learning to live with someone who has blatant compulsions and rigid ways of doing things at home is obviously very hard. This is all the more reason to get control of your world so that you are not impeding on their home life — like I did to my parents for years. It pushed them over the edge and put me at an utter loss. I continued to choose my OCD over my relationship with them, and if I was going to choose anything at all over my relationship with my parents, it should have solely been fighting my OCD, not choosing it. My parents to this day still help hold me accountable when I am around them. Truly out of pure habit, there are times when I show my OCD tendencies. For example, I often touch things to this day as I walk by for what must feel like good measure. I might go to open the refrigerator but quickly touch the kitchen counter before doing so. My mom or dad will see me do this type of thing and say, "Was that a compulsion?" A lot of the times I stand there for a second and realize it was. I wouldn't even have had a distinct intrusive thought before I did it. I just did it for good measure because something intuitively made me *feel* like I needed to do it. I don't even realize I do it most of the time. As much as I hate them calling me out, I am so thankful when they do because even years later, it still keeps me in check. Since they know my OCD to a certain extent, they are able to help me, which is exactly what I need at times. They obviously don't understand the depths of my ever-changing obsessions and compulsions, but that is solely my responsibility and exactly why I have trained myself to become my own therapist.

Having a relationship that holds you this accountable can be a hardship in itself. When the person decided to have a relationship with you, whatever that relationship may be, they most likely didn't sign up to be your therapist. This can put a strain on a relationship, but at least you are mutually addressing the shallows and extent of your OCD. The truth is, the person doesn't have to help you. They can just be a support system to talk to if you need it, but this just puts more pressure on you and leaves a field of unknown about you to the other person. This approach can indeed add ease to the relationship by not having them feel like they are your therapist but rather your partner or friend. You have to understand the place in which they stand. They didn't ask for this. They might not want to hold you accountable all the time. However, you can choose your reliance on them. *Ultimately, you are the one who is responsible for holding yourself accountable. The other person is simply a crutch. They have their own life to worry about too.*

Perhaps you have a fear that after you share your deepest obsessions with this person, especially a friend or significant other, they may pack their bags and be off. Especially if you have to explain your violent OCD, sexual OCD, or general disturbing obsessions. It is perfectly normal to be very concerned about being so brutally honest in these situations. What I can tell you is that the explanation can help if it comes directly from your therapist. See if this person will attend a session with you, and let your therapist explain to them why you think what you do and why it is just in your head and not a reality. This session will be purely educational and will undoubtedly help them understand more of the facts behind OCD, rather than just the seemingly crazy thoughts a person so close to them is having.

Put yourself in the shoes of this person. If you didn't have OCD, and they came to you and told you they get intrusive thoughts they are going to hurt someone, describe their weird magical thinking, that they may be attracted to someone they know is morally wrong, etc., your instinct would be to run. They need to hear the <u>facts behind OCD</u> and that they are standard thoughts for someone with OCD. They mean nothing — no action will be taken. They are simply obsessions with fears, not within reality. Everything will sound a little more reassuring coming from your therapist and will be less likely to scare the people you love away. The reality is, being honest and not hiding your OCD with the people who you are closest to can seem like a risk, but it is a risk worth taking on your path to getting healthier and maintaining an open, growing relationship.

Maintaining a romantic relationship with severe OCD is a beast unlike any other as far as I'm concerned. The relationship dynamic is completely different when it is someone you are intimate with on many different levels. Because of this, your obsessions and compulsions alone could be off-putting enough to end the relationship or prevent one in the first place. This is an area I am now all too familiar with because I just went through the painful depths of this very thing in the last few years. You want to have attractive qualities, but we all know constant obsessive, seemingly crazy thoughts are far from attractive. To be perfectly candid, up until these past few years, the only area OCD was never able to affect me in was a romantic relationship since I'd never technically been in one.

Conveniently, when I got involved in my first serious, committed relationship at 25, my OCD found a new place in my brain once again, unpacked its bags, and attempted to sign an indefinite lease. As I have mentioned, I turned my emotions off when I was at my worst with OCD. Once I became truly, emotionally invested in the relationship, everything changed. Along came the OCD destruction again, once I was happy for the first time in my life. *THANK YOU, NOT.*

One brisk fall weekend, I was triggered into a state of question for the first time in our relationship by something my boyfriend specifically said on a Friday night. It was in an area I was already slightly sensitive towards — other women. At first, I didn't think much of it. Everything was so blissful, and I was blindly in love. Over the weekend I realized what he told me was something I was uncomfortable with. The more I digested it, the more my OCD crept in to explore every nook and cranny to make *sure* I was uncomfortable with it.

From that point forward, *a seed of doubt was planted* in my OCD mind with him. That small seed of doubt quickly evolved into a massive catastrophe based on the way he was handling things. I quickly became my own Energizer Bunny lit on fire with endless energy and questions. I would approach him daily with a new list of questions on the same subject we had already beaten, quiz him, and run both of us into the ground. It was like my anxiety put me on overdrive, and I never knew when enough was enough. Right when I thought I had addressed it all, a new list evolved. To the average person, I can't imagine how off-putting this must have been. I can obsess until literally no end. When I'm in my obsessive mindset, I can't seem to see outside of it. The worst part was my compulsions began to become pure reassurance, which meant that I no longer felt I had control over the compulsion. I had to rely on *other people,* especially him. If I approached him with my dire need of reassurance and didn't hear EXACTLY — and I mean word for word — what I was looking for, it only would build into further obsessing when I got home. It became similar to therapy, I would feel better in the heat of the reassurance, then come home to spend hours on end obsessing and finding the loopholes in whatever we had *just* talked about. As soon as I thought of a new question, I felt this dire, desperate need to ask it as soon as possible. I began writing down every single question in my phone so I wouldn't forget to ask him. I could feel the questions rise in my throat like I would explode if I didn't get to ask them right then. It was a constant, pulling torture of me never being satisfied and in an everlasting anxious, unhealthy state and him in a twilight zone of endless interrogation. This was because I finally had something in my life I thought was stable. I had unknowingly put my identity and self-worth in him because I didn't know I needed to make a conscious effort not to. This was my first real relationship with emotions I had never felt before. It's not like I expected to put that much of myself into our relationship. By the time I realized I had everything to lose, it was too late.

Although I had basis in the things I was uncomfortable with in the relationship, my OCD took my ability to blow things out of proportion (and run with them around the world, all the planets, and circle the sun) to the point where I felt like it destroyed my relationship. It was like my OCD was directly attached to my heart once I started to fall in love. Every time my heart beat, my OCD began to flare over God knows what. I began to feel every emotion known to man. The harder I fell for him, the more I began to overanalyze *everything*, from his every movement to his every word. I would see certain behaviors, hear certain things he said, and even make intuitive assumptions that I was convinced were accurate. The problem was, most of the time these intuitive assumptions were accurate. I'm just that person who has an intuition that is dead on because I overanalyze so much as it is. I wasn't just coming up with complete, detached craziness. It was all based on what I knew deep down was accurate. I could feel something wasn't right in my gut, and day in and day out, my anxiety over this certain triggered situation became unbearable. I just couldn't let go of it, but I also couldn't let go of him. I took the term "beating a dead horse" to a level I never knew I could. To me, *the horse never died.* I could keep obsessing for hours, which turned into days, and no amount of thinking about something was enough time.

It soon hit me that the intensity of the constant anxiety that I was feeling was the same as it was when I was at my worst with OCD before the intensive program, *but even worse.* The difference was the change of my miscellaneous, physical compulsions to much needed reassurance seeking from someone else. Since reassurance typically comes from others, we drive them into the ground to get it and will always tire out the relationship. Some put up with us longer than others, but no matter how much someone loves us, sometimes it isn't worth it for them — even though it will always seem worth it to us because *we can't let anything go.* Putting up with our OCD sometimes isn't worth it, *even though we are,* deep underneath it all. I was convinced my first adult relationship had crashed and burned, mostly because of what I did to the relationship with my OCD and to myself. I just couldn't take the ever existent, crippling anxiety I was living in every single second, and I needed to get above water, fast. I walked away from the relationship because I wanted to be as far away as possible from this paralyzing anxiety I couldn't shake. I didn't blame my OCD for the wrong that was done on his end, but I did blame the demise of our strong relationship on my OCD to a certain extent. I went on for months believing that my OCD may very well have been the reason for the end of the first thing in my entire life that actually gave me happiness. I realized that as soon as I became emotionally attached, I would be like this in every relationship going forward: this obsessive, clingy, questioning, jealous girl with a mind that creates the worst of every positive scenario and finds a way to sabotage it. I became the girl with "relationship baggage" that I swore I would never be. Although I knew I had good reasons to walk away, I was still scared things would have been different if my mind hadn't destroyed us. Although we both openly knew he initially screwed up, for months he tried to convince me I had made most of what I was accusing him of up in my head and went on to convince both himself, his friends, and his family I was crazy. I began to believe it myself, that I would never hold a healthy relationship again.

Three months later, he contacted me out of the blue only to tell me that everything I "made up," obsessed about, assumed, predicted, and accused him of all that time had all come true. All of it. What I had spent months in crippling fear "making up in my head," all ended up happening exactly as I predicted it would. I knew all along my gut had to be right for me to be that uncomfortable with what was going on, but I had truly believed my OCD had broken us for good.

The truth now is I do still believe my OCD played a massive role in the relationship's end — because of what it did to me and my actions — but ultimately this was far beyond just OCD. Although I know I had firm ground of discomfort to stand on, only I truly know the role my OCD played. Once my OCD stepped up, my approach towards the relationship was never the same. You might be thinking, "See! Your OCD was right all along! This is my worst fear! Your obsessions were all valid. He did exactly what they told you he would do. Listen to your OCD!" Although at first glance, this seems like it could be true, it was the tortuous life I allowed myself to live *because of what the OCD was telling me* that wasn't right. My womanly instincts and fears were valid and right, but my OCD only made each of these more literal, visual, and seemingly all real, enveloping me in a constant state of torture. It would have been nice to just have listened to my gut and instincts instead of having my OCD get so tangled up in this because I had to live in a MUCH more complicated world than I needed to because of it.

These things happen. There will be times when you will be *convinced* your OCD was right, and you think you should have listened to it, that you are so glad you performed all those compulsions. But this mentality is not only wrong — it's deadly. Because even if it seems like it was right in one rare scenario or another, it doesn't mean it ever actually is in itself. Don't confuse reality with what your OCD is simply catastrophizing to a point of delirium. The line here is so fine you may not even be able to see it. You have to step back and separate the OCD before a normal issue and OCD blend together so much, you truly can't tell anymore. I may have ended up being right in my relationship about the core issue I was deathly afraid of, but many of the smaller, crippling, paralyzing things my OCD was picturing and thinking weren't always the case. I had just become so obsessed with the situation, I thought up every single detail imaginable, and of course, to a certain extent when you've thought of everything, you could end up being right. I naturally have great intuition and good foresight, and that has never mingled well with my OCD. But it wasn't right to let myself endlessly obsess about certain things because the only one in the end who was miserable was me. What I blame my OCD for is putting me through a much more tortuous time than I needed to go through during an already horrific time. The situation was already painful enough, but as you know, your OCD will only make anything already hurtful as painful as possible.

Even after all of this, I am terrified that I will never be able to overcome this obstacle in my relationships. The obstacle of doubt and question. The obstacle of obsessing and needing constant reassurance in order to give all of myself to that person. The obstacle of never being able to see the grey area because I only see in black and white. The obstacle of never learning to pick and choose my battles because my OCD picks every single one. With OCD, your brain records and replays everything and anything going forward, and you apply it to all kinds of things you don't need to. I hate that because of this awful ending to my relationship, my OCD will now always replay the mistrust I have for men now. It only takes one time with OCD, and you will never forget it. But I have to constantly remind myself to separate this. I can't let one guy who royally screwed up pave the way for my OCD to screw up every relationship I have going forward.

Each and every person who walked out of my life either because of the disorder or just because of me, I've let them go. The reality was I had a lot of bigger issues going on than to try and salvage a relationship or friendship that didn't feel I was worth sticking around for. I just so happened to have OCD in my adolescence, so my parents played a huge role as my support system. Once they talked with my therapist and knew more about OCD, they wanted to help in any way they could. But they were also family, they weren't going to abandon me. None of my friends or acquaintances truly had the stamina to really try and help me, which has never been my concern. If they walked away, they walked. If they stayed, they stayed. I needed to focus on my relationship with my OCD, first and foremost, before any other relationship in my life.

The bottom line is that the people in your life don't *have* to go through your OCD with you. As I mentioned earlier, they can just be supportive in your journey to getting better. You can choose whatever method works better for you and the dynamic of your relationship. I was someone who needed the accountability from those around me. My relationships have not permanently suffered because of the accountability; they have instead grown because I am now more understood by those who I am closest to. However, I must honestly admit that I was not always upfront in my romantic relationship with my obsessions because of my fear he would think I was crazy. Spoiler alert! *I would probably think I was crazy if I was him and didn't understand OCD, as most people understandably don't.* I was waiting to explain the depths of my case to him after we had been together for a long time, except we didn't even get that far.

A great piece of advice I can leave you with in this territory — which is about as clear as mud — is this: it is not so much about learning how to manage your relationships as it is about learning how to manage your OCD. That comes first, and in turn, leads to healthier relationships. You need to put your OCD first because it is your biggest roadblock to maintaining healthy relationships that result in longevity. When you are in your healthiest state, you will be able to maintain an impeccable relationship, and only then will it feel unquestionably right.

Author's Note: To this day little makes me angrier than when people throw around OCD terminology with the typical stigma. You know, the "Sorry, one second. I just need to fix these papers on my desk because I have OCD!" And then a coworker says, "Oh, no worries. I totally have OCD too!" *This* is how our disorder becomes devalued. How and why would anyone take me or any other person suffering from severe OCD seriously when the term *OCD* is used so commonly? I stopped telling people I have OCD completely unless I get to know the person very well. It's not worth them just thinking nothing of it because of the stigma it has in our world today, blowing it off and/or trying to "relate." Almost every time I tell someone I have

OCD, I can feel myself retract because I know they will have no idea of the seriousness of it. *It's hard to generalize the biggest part of you in one sentence.* Because OCD is taken so lightly today and is so misunderstood, it makes cases like ours seem like they are surface level and not pure torture of unwanted back and forth pounding thoughts in our heads. People always think they might have the "same thing" and find a way to make it about them. People seem to *want* the drama of something wrong with them, and OCD seems like an easy and logical thing to diagnose themselves with. People often use OCD for attention, but anyone with actual OCD knows attention is the last thing we are seeking. Bottom line — don't say you have OCD unless you have been clinically diagnosed with it. If you think you or someone you know has OCD, you should absolutely take the time to be evaluated. This can be compared to the same situation if I were to say to a truly specially challenged person, "Sorry, I'm so retarded. I don't know why I did that!" Can you *imagine* how they would feel? How dare you compare yourself to their daily world and suffering! It makes their condition meaningless, and eventually, they will not be taken as seriously when they *are actually the one with the problem.*

31

"THE CONTINUOUS TEST"

Today, eight years into my recovery, I can honestly say there are days when I don't even think about my OCD. It just isn't the forefront of my life anymore. I still struggle with anxiety pretty regularly and with that comes OCD at times. The difference is that now my OCD is completely manageable, so I don't *allow* it to be the forefront of my life. The intrusive thoughts are more faint, floating thoughts in the back of my mind, but I can think completely clearly at the same time instead of the thoughts overtaking me. When the anxiety is really bad over something specific, the OCD tends to creep forward and crowd into my normal thinking instead of staying in the shadows. I know how to control and work with my OCD, so any time it acts up, I am able to immediately put it back in its place. That's how much my life has changed over the years of persistence. I am not saying that it's always easy for me or that I always refrain from the compulsion. When that anxiety strikes, I am just as tempted as ever, *but I know better now whether I give into the compulsion or not.*

I still have to make a constant and consistent effort to not give into any obsessions. The worse my anxiety or intense fear is, the harder it is for me to resist giving into my OCD. Trust me when I tell you it is still very hard for me at times. In these times, I just have to stop, slow down, and articulate to myself what and why I am doing what I am doing. I articulate the obsession if it is recurring and break down why I shouldn't perform the compulsion. But then I move on. If I don't take the time to do this, I find I get a lot more consistent intrusive thoughts. There have been times when the thoughts begin to pour in again because I haven't taken the time to expose them. I almost immediately can see what is happening in my brain. The OCD is creeping in, little by little, thought by thought. If I don't stomp out the fire then and there, *I will regret it*. It's almost like I have to momentarily put my training wheels back on and retrain my OCD back out of my way. It is much easier to catch the mishaps earlier rather than later because the longer you wait and don't expose the thoughts, the faster and more frequent the thoughts will come. I still find myself having to use ERP all the time. Once you get good and fast at ERP, you are able to do it very unnoticeably, and it becomes a minuscule task. It will not always be as time consuming and overwhelming as when you are in the initial fight and battle with OCD. You get really good at knowing how your brain works, what your triggers are, and you learn to adjust to what methods and mind maneuvers work for you. After a while, you start to be able to just breeze past the obsessions by ignoring them. You're still exposing the intrusive thoughts because you are not covering them up with compulsions. You are just not letting the thought stop you from doing exactly what you want to do in life.

Believe it or not, the thoughts really do start to go away after a while if you persistently do not give in to what your gut is telling you to do based on your obsessions. If you stop acting on the thoughts that you are getting, your life will honestly begin to change before your eyes. OCD thrives on being an entertainer. Stop entertaining your enemy, and it will leave. It gets bored because instead of paying attention to it, you are actually living your life.

Let me give you some real-life examples. Every year my hormones act up, and my hair begins to fall out much more than usual. You know, that *one little detail* that triggered the beginning of my affair with OCD. A while back, I had an experience when I was brushing my hair after the shower. I looked down at my brush and knew instantly that it was happening again. The feeling began creeping over me, and I began to go cold. I mentally went back to years prior within a matter of seconds. My face and body then went hot. I needed air. *"No. No. No. Don't let this be happening again."* I knew I needed to reel myself back in immediately.

Guess what I did next? I kept brushing my hair vigorously. As scared as I was in that moment, I instantly knew that I wouldn't let myself go there again. I knew that regardless of what was happening, I would not let my thoughts begin. I would NEVER go through what I originally went through again. I dealt with it to a point of anger and frustration that this was even happening again. I brushed my hair out like nobody's business that night.

Over the next few days, my hair started to come out. And every single time I saw more hair come out or it got tangled, I went and picked up my brush. I brushed my hair. I let it come out. I didn't do anything to stop it. No compulsions. It was almost like I had to ask myself at first, "What does a normal person do if their hair is falling out?" I've accepted my reality and know with everything in my being that I won't let my brain connect my hair falling out simultaneously with compulsions. There *is* no connection. Absolutely none, and I know that now. How? Because I tested it for the past eight years. I said NO then, and I still say NO. I know that my hair is falling out for the same reason that it used to — because of my hormones, the weather change, stress, or any other possible factor. Not because "it" was testing me to see if I would go right back where I started, to see if I would fall into the same trap I was in before. Because there is no such thing as "it." There is life and reality, and "it" is not part of either of those for me. I am going to live my life, and nothing can stop me anymore. My beautiful life is in full swing.

There is a particular song that I remember playing at Nordstrom when I worked there in 2010, and my hair was falling out at its worst. Fast forward to 2016, when I decided to play music while I was showering one night. This was a couple of nights after I realized my hair was falling out again. All of a sudden, that exact song came on. It always brings me back to that dark place I was in. So even though it's a good song, it still bothers me to hear it. I associated it with my hair falling out, and since I was already going through an episode, you can imagine how much I wanted it turned off immediately. The next thing I knew, thoughts began flooding in that brought me back to that bad place. And I just started...dancing. I danced right there in the shower. I forced myself to forget about all the problems and danced. Hard. Little things like that keep me hanging on. In that moment, I knew I needed to quickly snap into being my own therapist and yell, "OH NO! THAT SONG IS PLAYING RIGHT NOW, AND MY HAIR IS ALL GOING TO FALL OUT! AND OF COURSE, I'M IN THE SHOWER, WHERE THE WATER MAKES MY HAIR FALL OUT EVEN WORSE. I AM GOING TO LOSE MY LOCKS BECAUSE I AM SHEDDING ONCE AGAIN! AND I KNOW I AM NOT ATTRAC-TIVE DURING THESE TIMES." As soon as I let myself go there, speak the words, make my fear a reality, the thoughts started to fade. I exposed the OCD so brutally, there was no chance to let the OCD begin nesting in my head. I didn't perform a compulsion as to allow the thought to tuck into another part of my brain and come back later. I shut that son of a bitch down. I shut down my thoughts so fast because *they have no business with me*. It was only when I shut them down that I replaced them with new thoughts. It's important to first approach the intrusive thoughts, mentally zero in on them, and make a conscious decision to not believe in them.

Nowadays when my hair falls out, I don't let myself confuse the hair loss with the OCD. I don't let myself go there — thinking I have some magical control over the hair loss if I perform certain compulsions. I take more vitamins, wash and brush my hair, and take care of myself. I let myself take the risk that my hair will go thin, and there is nothing I can do about it beyond taking care of myself both mentally and physically.

"The Continuous Test" is what I refer to as the forever fight against OCD. The fight never stops. You might have huge periods of relief in your life, but you must be ready to get back up and fight at any given moment. It comes with the territory of having OCD. I live a very normal life, but I always have my gloves at arm's length, ready to slide on and take OCD down. This continuous test is something you will always need to be prepared for. Although once you fight your OCD, the thoughts will indeed slow down, but they will come around from time and time again. You will always be tested. When I say the thoughts slow down, I don't mean they stop forever. You will always have OCD. Any time your anxiety spikes, expect your OCD to follow. Think of it as if your name is in a master OCD database once you've fought the OCD intensely. Year after year, perhaps month after month, or day after day, thoughts will try and creep in again and test you based on your anxiety. It is solely your responsibility to stay strong and expose the OCD every single time this happens. *Don't let it back in.* You must stay on your path and not let it sway you. Being your own therapist is a full-time job for the rest of your life. BUT life is much more tolerable this way, having your OCD creep up on you randomly, rather than for it to be persistent at all times.

My point to you is you must always be on the lookout for ways OCD will sneak into your life. It will not always take the same path, especially if you are fighting hard. Stay strong, and whatever you do, keep going. If you think you have a handle on one area of OCD, and you find it creeping in your life another way (such as a theme shift from symmetry to cleanliness), you must take a step back and make sure you catch it head on. You must address any behaviors that assume OCD in them, so you can expose those thoughts, and eventually, they will stop. Nip the evolving OCD in the bud. Most of the people I encounter with OCD have had multiple themes of OCD at different times in their life. The themes can change, and it's just something we need to be cognizant of.

I often find myself just powering through my days and often my obsessive thoughts, but every now and then I do stop and evaluate if I notice reoccurring behaviors. If I notice I keep subconsciously brushing up or touching something as I walk by, or avoid certain objects or paths every once in a while, I stop and *make* time to articulate why I am feeling the way I feel and why I am giving into possible OCD tendencies. Take note that I'm articulating what's making me anxious, not the obsession or compulsion. This occasional "check in" with myself really helps keep me centered. Then I purposely watch myself as I go forward with my day, making sure to avoid any of these OCD tendencies, take a new route, or re-focus on something worthwhile. I have to constantly throw off my OCD, so it never, ever gets comfortable.

As you sit there and ponder whether or not you are willing to commit to this lifelong fight, I for one, am off to get my hair cut and colored — *because I want to.*

Author's Note: You will always be tested by OCD. Just because you put up a fight and have a much more manageable life, doesn't mean OCD is done with you. As you move on with life, you will still face anxiety and other triggers, perhaps even regularly. But your learned reactions will be different. It's so important to keep in mind that this fight is intensive for certain periods, but the fight is forever. None of what I talk about will lead to a life of blissful harmony, but it will lead to a much better life than you are living now. There is no snapping out of OCD, but there is such a thing as relief. *It is your job to know your place and continue to be in charge of that lasting relief because now you have a better idea of how.* Stay on your toes.

32

"FLY FREE, MY FRIEND"

I can't explain the feeling that you get when you realize you are finished being controlled. The sense of empowerment is unlike any adrenaline rush out there. Even better, it's the feeling when you finally accomplish something that you have been attempting for a really long time, something you truly never thought you were capable of. It's especially powerful because you have gone so long without that feeling. Life comes back into our souls which seemed dead. And it just comes over you like a wave of cool water that you have been wanting for so long. Relief.

I have a fear of the ocean. An irrational fear, but I love to go to the ocean to think. I always stare out at the water and just want to run and jump in and submerge myself in the cool water without that fear. The feeling of this empowerment over OCD is just like finally overcoming the ultimate fear that you have. For me, it's like submerging myself in the ocean water off the coast of the Bahamas, opening my eyes, feeling light as a feather, and never looking back. You know that rush of cool water that comes over you when you first submerge, as if it were inside of your chest for a brief moment? It's *freeing.* For years I wouldn't allow myself to put my head under water while swimming because of fears that had to do with my hair. In the past couple of years, I have made it a point to not go swimming *unless* I allow myself to fully plunge underwater and just...let go. It has become one of my *favorite feelings* — to let my hair down and swim underwater. It is the most freeing feeling in the world for me, to feel the cool water envelop me without any fear at all in those very brief moments. I recently went snorkeling in Hawaii, and I was afraid I wouldn't be able to truly snorkel because of my fears in the ocean. My brother and I just kept slowly swimming, staring at the wonders of the under-water world. After about an hour, I came up, turned around, and looked back at shore. We were *so* far out. If you had told me even that very day that I would swim out that far, hair down and getting tangled in my goggles and the waters, I would have laughed. Hard. You guys — as I stared back at the shore, I didn't feel one single bit of fear. I didn't feel the need to start swimming closer to shore. As I treaded water, I began to smile to myself. *Look at your life now, Ker.* I realized in that moment that all my fears were underneath dark waters. And when I didn't overthink it and just did it, I realized that my fears were just thoughts. In fact, they were completely wrong thoughts because everything I pictured being underwater couldn't have been farther from it. You need to find what this freeing feeling is like for you and apply it to your own life. Start by listing the activities you fear, and if even the tiniest part of you wonders what it would be like to experience it, write it down. Then look over your list and number them in order from most realistic to most unrealistic. Narrow your eyes in on the most realistic one and make it your damn life mission to do exactly what you wrote. Allow yourself permission to feel this freeing feeling that makes you want to scream with admira-tion because you are fuc*ing *living life*. Life isn't about your work, money, fame, appearance, or what you are doing this weekend. It's definitely not about what compulsion you're going to need to perform next. Life is so much bigger than the mundane day-to-day activities. Truly living like you were intended to live is taking risks and feeling the reward. My goal every single day of my life now is to do something that day that makes me feel alive. I need to feel that sense of accomplishment as I crawl into bed, knowing I deserve to feel happy, knowing I will never allow myself to feel pinned down for years like I once did every night I crawled into that bed.

Everyone who has been bound by OCD should feel this feeling I'm speaking of at some point because it instantly takes you back to the basics. You deserve as a human being to feel that very freeing feeling, as so many do. That feeling of what most call *life*. Maybe you remember life before OCD. Maybe you truly cannot remember a life before OCD. I am so thankful that I do because that is what motivated me. It gave me the one thing that keeps me pumping in life... hope. To be perfectly honest, I think it is so much easier that way. If only you were able to remember what it feels like to love and be loved before OCD, when now, you may not be able to hold a relationship. If only you could remember what it's like to have true friends, when now you may not have any friends that can see past your OCD. I've been working on that one for years. If you can't remember life before OCD, then create it in your imagination. Trust me, you've got an imagination that can solve the wonders of the world. So, create a vision in your mind of your life without OCD and what life looks like from that lens. Close your eyes as you do this and when you open them, intentionally visualize you looking through that lens. That is your end goal.

If you could just remember what it's like to wake up in the morning and not get that overwhelming feeling that something bad is about to happen. If you could just get up and go about your day without knowing the mental intrusions you are about to face. Some days I wake up and right away I have this brief moment of solitude, where I forget about the OCD and all my problems. I lay so still and enjoy that single dashing moment when I haven't been able to figure out quite what's wrong in my world yet. Then all of a sudden, as I begin to wake up, my brain immediately goes to everything that is currently going wrong. My thoughts begin to overwhelm me, and I have the worst obsessions. Mine are always the worst right as I am waking up. They are part of that moment when you are not quite awake yet, so you feel trapped. It could be that when I am waking up from a deep sleep, I am not in control yet. I am weak. My body is exhausted. I might be coming out of a dream, but this is where I am tested the most. I start to get bad obsessions before I even open my eyes, and I have often started performing compulsions before I even fully wake up. These obsessions are at their worst if I wake up from a nap during the day. Something about the balance of being in a mental state of rest always seems to get me. "It" can't stand for me to just be calm and content, even to this day. As I start to wake up, I begin to get control of my thoughts and myself and reflect on how intense they can be during these times. Furthermore, every time I am reminded of how much stronger I need to be during these episodes. I can't allow even these few seconds of weakness to set me off. Occasionally, I perform compulsions in my dreams! I never knew OCD could follow you into your dreams, but it can. However, the less compulsions you are performing in your daily life, the less likely they are to follow you into your dreams. Even days where I go about my life and don't perform any compulsions, my OCD will always still try to find some little slit in the wall. Just knowing and being aware of this helps keep me on my toes.

Certainly, you have particular things that set you off as well, like mornings and naps do to me. There's nothing worse than when the first thing you do when you wake up is to set the tone for your day by performing a compulsion or ten. These times, in which you are set off, are the most essential times of your day. It is so important to be able to recognize what these triggers are and gain control over them immediately. You cannot gain control of the triggers unless you identify exactly what they are. Once you have identified what they are, you have to fight them. Push through them. Work against them. Prove to them and yourself that they have no effect on you. There can definitely be a point where they have no effect on you, but you have to get to a point where you are immune to them. Once you've immunized your triggers, you will decrease your stress and anxiety levels immensely. Most of the reason they are your triggers is because your stress levels rise so high when you are about to face the trigger. The key is getting your stress and anxiety levels down with each of your triggers, so you can train your mind. Since OCD runs off of anxiety, intentionally getting the anxiety down is essential to being able to immunize yourself to your triggers, which is exactly what ERP does.

For example, I have an obsession about fainting. I have had it my entire life. I faint when I see or hear about blood, or I faint because I am afraid I am going to faint. Growing up, I had numerous encounters where I fainted, from once while on a moving escalator to fainting and hitting my head in front of my entire church congregation. The root of my fainting, however, is mental. As I have grown older, I have gained more control over hearing about or seeing blood, but the fear is still evident. I'm not sure where the fear of blood stops and the anxiety of fainting begins. But every so often, I go through a period of fainting for a month or so where I can't be in a confined space because I will think of blood and faint.

During these times, I'm much more sensitive to avoiding situations and places where I could faint. The times when it is the worst is when I know I can't get to cold water, fresh air, or ice immediately and lay down. If I am in a big store, in class, in a meeting, or in an interview (times when it is not appropriate to faint), my anxiety goes out the roof and I panic. It zones into tunnel vision about the *potential* to faint. Sure, I don't like to see blood. And I hate hearing about people getting cut, but it is so much worse on occasions where I can't get to a place to calm my anxiety with cold water or air. However, if I am at home where I am comfortable and not confined, you and I could talk about blood all day, and I am actually fascinated by the different elements of emergency situations. This all comes back to an anxiety of mine that is situational. I've learned to be prepared when I have these episodes and bring an ice water with me if I'm going to be in a position where I know I could faint.

Obviously, this takes a lot of preparation and thinking ahead, and I am not always prepared. This is where I get to a point of which I need to gain mental control of this fear and obsession of mine. I have to identify that the deep-rooted problem is the anxiety of possibly fainting in an unsafe place. The last thing I want is to faint in public, and I absolutely will. One way to handle my fear is to not bring water or any "safety net" with me when I am going into these situations and to mentally tell myself that I am going to have terrible fainting spells when I get to my location. If I tell myself the worst possible thing will happen, especially if I say it out loud, it begins to immunize the triggered reality of fainting. Sometimes it even helps for me to tell whoever I am with that I am going to faint a series of embarrassing times, and that's that. I plan out an exaggerated worst-case scenario. By putting that trigger and obsession out into reality rather than just my head, it helps ease the anxiety. I make sure I have a plan, so I can't have anxiety about not having a plan.

My toned-down way of handling the situation is to just not let my mind go there. Every time I'm in a public place and see an image of blood or someone getting cut, I immediately replace the thought with a different one and focus on that. I distract myself, not because I am trying to run from the fear, but because it is a situational solution that works for me. After a while, I learned how to get myself out of the deteriorating mindset, and the thoughts stopped coming when I was in public. My brain realizes it can't make me break down and faint any longer, so it stops tempting me. Now I am at a point where I feel I have control over the situation and await the next time my OCD tries to go back there because I will be ready. It's mind versus mind. Your mind versus your OCD mind, as I like to call it. My goal in this life is to ensure that my God given, intentional mind will overpower the OCD/doubt side of my mind — every — single — time.

Honestly, I just want to fly free. I want to live the rest of this life without the shackles of OCD. I've done a great job these past few years, and I intend to keep it that way. Life itself has so many struggles that you and I cannot control, which are seemingly only getting worse, and we don't need to add more stress to life by creating our own struggles. That's what OCD does. It creates these unnecessary struggles that overcomplicate your life. *But life is complicated enough.*

I don't want to fly free alone. Who does? I want to fly free with you.

Author's Note: When I reflect on how much time I spent overcomplicating my every move in life, it pushes me to a point of anger. Now that I am healthy and can look back, I realize that I am not ashamed, but I am completely and utterly sad. Life is just so complicated in itself. I took a complicated life and had to subconsciously simplify everything in it so that I could focus the amount of attention and time I needed towards my OCD. I made life so much more difficult than it ever needed to be. I can still sometimes feel the binding force my OCD had on me in my dorm room my freshman year of college when I was at my worst. I have made it my mission to spread my wings and *never feel that way again.*

33

"THE OBSESSIVE OUTSIDERS"

You do need to accept the fact that you may never have a life completely free and separate from this disorder. But if you make a conscious effort to begin and persevere through the fight, you will have the ability to live a happy, functional life. There will eventually be a day when you slowly forget that you have OCD and many of the bad memories along with it. That is, unless you try and write a book about it...

It kills me to this day when I think that some people may not believe that I have this disorder as bad as they do because I am so functional now. There are still people out there who don't understand OCD recovery. It's so hard for some to believe when they see me now, or hear me speak at events and conferences, that I somehow became "so healthy," especially when they feel so far away from it. But my story is true, and my overcoming of severe OCD is all too real.

To be perfectly honest, there will always be a part of me that is scared, deep down. I am distantly scared my OCD is going to somehow creep back into my life, and I am even more scared that I will allow it someday. *Not because OCD has any ground to stand on* but because of my own weakness. Sometimes I feel powerless and realize that I might not have come as far as I think I have. It's been a disappointing realization that perhaps I am no better off than you are, after all this work and all this time. But it is in these exact doubtful moments that I have to come back to my core and remind myself how much control I have gained through my fight with OCD. When I get down and OCD seems to consume me in every way, I *always* get out because I mentally take ownership and remember OCD doesn't control me anymore. I still have control over that even in my weakest moments. It's just a matter of utilizing that control the right way, consistently.

Of course, there are times where I feel the OCD creeping in more than ever. It's so close — so easy to fall back into. That hypothetical drink is sitting on the rocks next to me, that cigarette is burning incense right under my nose. There are days when I feel tempted all day — faced with such blatant, unwelcome, insane thoughts — and they stop me dead in my tracks. They are so sudden, so unexpected, and so powerful. I stop and look to the sky and think to myself, "If only I could go back to three seconds ago, when my mind was at peace." But now, I have to make a conscious decision to not perform a serious compulsion.

Sometimes in that moment, as I break down what exactly it is my obsession wants so I can do the opposite, I realize the opposite is yet suddenly another compulsion. For example, I might get a thought that jolts into my brain saying, "*Don't step* on this next stair if you want this book to be successful." My automatic, healthy reaction would be to stomp right on that specific stair, just to prove to myself that I don't believe that thought for a second. And just in case my book was wildly successful, I would never ever want to think back to that moment and give any credit to me stepping or not stepping on that stair. I know better. That stair has nothing on me! My OCD has evolved over time, and instead of being this black and white, strict intrusive thought/perform specific compulsion, it now gives me ulti-matums and no-win situations. The no-win situation here is just as I was about to skip that step, I would look at the next step and get another thought such as, "If you do *step* on this next stair above this one, you are accepting energy from the universe that your book will be successful." My body can't jump up over two steps, just like that, to avoid both of these thoughts in an attempt to not give in to either. It's in these situations that I know I need to take a moment. "What is the right way out of this?" This all comes back to that continuous test. I have blocked off all of the doors to my brain, so OCD knocks on the windows. It is almost like in order to get out of these situations, I have to unintentionally perform a compulsion one way or another, just like with the staircase. I have to step on one of the two stairs. No matter what step I chose, my brain had an intrusive thought for it. I am not a doctor or therapist — and as much as I have trained myself to hold accountability as my own therapist — I have humps like this all the time. My anxiety is up and down regularly; therefore, I constantly need to re-evaluate newfound obsessions and make sure I am moving past them in the healthiest way I can. Most of the time when I run into these dire ultimatum situations, I have realized I just have to power through them. I can't keep standing on the staircase, trying to justify what my decision should be so as not to give into the OCD. I just take a moment, look up, and start climbing the stairs, directing my mind immediately to something of merit, so I don't dwell deeper or analyze. I power through so that I don't give any more credit to the ultimatum than I absolutely have to.

As I went back through and edited this book, I could see *many* compulsions in my writing from when I first started this project years ago. As you know, I have always struggled with compulsions through spelling and grammar. Throughout the editing process, I couldn't believe how many sentences didn't make sense — how the grammar was *so* intentionally off. I was shocked at how much I let my OCD interfere with this very book. I turned that shock into motivation, and I went through and made every single edit I could to correct all those compulsions. *And boy, did it feel good.* I suppose I am still taken aback how far I have really come in every single year it took me to complete this book.

Just because I seem to have all the answers or a solution to everything doesn't mean I am anything but another obsessive outsider. Except, *I don't want to spend the rest of my days as an obsessive outsider.* I don't want to be obsessive, and I don't want to be an outsider. I have a passion for maintaining the control I have rightly earned over my OCD.

This book is to give you hope. It's to help you hear a story straight from someone who has the same disorder as you do. To hear it straight from someone who goes through the same torture you feel every single minute. It's also because you *need* to see and hear about severe OCD sufferers who have miracle stories stand up and become examples of hope for this beautifully tortured group of obsessive outsiders. But now it's time to write your miracle story.

We are what we are — obsessive outsiders. We are a group of terribly misunderstood people who are sitting on the edge of the pool while all of the others are playfully splashing around in the water. We are the scared kids who can't take the leap. We just want to go home. But at the same time, I can honestly say that I don't. I don't want to just go home. I *want* to splash, feel the cool water wash over me while laughing at the *feeling* of the emotional rush of happiness that comes along with the freeing moments of living life. I don't want to be just another obsessive outsider another day. I want to help lead the pack.

It's no longer just a "want" of mine; it's a reality of mine that I am bringing to fruition.

———

Author's Note: I coined the term "obsessive outsiders" when I realized that I couldn't find a better way to describe us. We are a community of people who are missing out on so many elements of this life because we are caught up in our heads. We are outsiders, and the cause is our very own minds. It's hard to understand ourselves, let alone for other people to understand why we do what we do and think what we think. Sometimes when I am doing really well with my OCD, I think back to the things I used to do or the compulsions my tortured friends do, and I cannot believe it. I wonder how I ever thought that way. But then even an hour later, I get my intrusive thoughts and feel the dire desire to perform a reassuring compulsion to rest my gut, and all of a sudden, it doesn't sound so crazy to me to think that way. It feels so real; it makes so much sense in the moment. How can my mind be in such opposite directions in such a close proximity of time? It just comes along with the territory of being an obsessive outsider. But that is who I was, it is no longer who I choose to be.

34

"RELIEF IS THE CURE"

I never want to make my progress with OCD sound like I walked through a tunnel, and I walked out on the other side cured. There is no cure. What there can be though is relief. And I am proof of that. There *is* a way to manage your OCD so that you keep it on a leash. Think of it like those dog leashes that can extend and release with the push of a button. Some days you will let the beast on the other end take out all the leeway that the leash will extend throughout the fighting process. Other days you will be strong enough to reel it in a bit, and every time you do, you might feel a tug on the other end. A tug in your brain and in your gut to just perform the compulsion, whatever it may be. A tug to wash those hands. A tug to blink a certain number of times in a row. A tug to check something again. A tug to do something to cancel a bad thought. A tug to find relief. But you are satisfying a *momentary* beast if you give in. Beasts are not all ruthless. If you fight them hard enough, they give up. They lose interest fast. Once you show the beast on the other end of the leash who's the boss consistently, they finally register the truth of the matter. It's the same basic concept of what we are taught to do if a bear threatens us while out in nature. We are told to raise our arms high, puff our chests, make loud noises to show the bear we are not weak, and we will not be taken down. When done correctly, the bear doesn't know if it wants to mess with you after all. It may be too much effort.

You are controlling the situation. You can *always control* the situation. It's your brain. God gave it to YOU. They say the brain has a mind of its own, but it's still in YOUR body. You can train your brain to work differently, to think in a new sense, to stop habits you don't like. The brain acts like a muscle, just like any other, and it takes constant attention, improvement, and dedication. The only step before taking action is realizing you have the power and confidence to do so. Keep your ground. You work too hard to give up the ground that you work so hard every day to seed. It's yours to water and constantly watch yourself change and grow.

OCD is a disorder that takes over the mind. Yes — I've fought hard. I've suffered in so many ways for what I consider to be much too long in this short life. I wasn't able to enjoy my adolescent years, and so far, I certainly haven't enjoyed my early adulthood.

I never experienced some of the most crucial years of a young adults life - I didn't experience the growth and youthful happiness and freedom before adulthood sets in and you can never truly go back. I was so busy in my disturbed world that I missed it. I don't know what it's like to feel that exhilaration of the easy going, college lifestyle or have a great, consistent group of friends. I never experienced what it was like to fit in. I will never have the chance to go back in time to get those experiences or years of adolescence back. There are no "re-do's" in terms of time periods in life. But there are second chances. They are just different than the first time around. Every day you have the opportunity to choose how you react to your OCD, and every day you choose it over your life, you have lost yet another day of what could have been. I've taken years upon years away from my quality of life. I kept putting off the fight for as long as possible. I also didn't really understand what the fight was exactly or how to even approach it. If only it could have been so much sooner, and I would have had those precious memories of my college years, like so many people do. Instead, I have regular memories of me crouching on the floor of my dorm room floor, rocking back and forth, balling my eyes out, and crying out to God because I had no hope left. I felt as though I was out of people to talk to. Nobody listened to me anymore because they were sick of me saying my hair was falling out, being socially awkward, and allowing so much negativity into my family from my OCD. I was so alone. I was in a rut because I didn't understand what life was outside of my head anymore. I couldn't grasp it. There were few and far between moments when I identified with the outside world, then I would look at the ends of my hair and see all the loose hairs that were falling out, and my heart would literally sink. I don't think my heart could have sunk any lower than it did. Then I would have to start fresh and build my OCD barrier back up because I became too vulnerable.

As I grow older, I realize I am scarred in so many ways from my battle with OCD. Many of those scars are from how I was treated so poorly in college for being the "bat shit crazy girl." Nothing will ever fully erase those scars, those feelings so deep in my gut they physically hurt when I mentally go back to that place. At the end of the day, even with such horrible memories, I would rather have *scars* than *open wounds*.

You know what has helped, even if it's only the tiniest bit? The countless, and I mean countless, apologies I have received over the years since college. Whether it's because people heard my real story through the grapevine or because I have made such a bold comeback — word gets out. The more I have shared my story through my online platforms, through speaking engagements, and press interviews, the more the apologies came filing in. You wouldn't believe the lengths people go to so they can contact you and apologize! Every single person who has reached out and apologized for the way they personally treated me admitted that they feel *horrible* knowing what was really wrong and that they used to contribute to the gossip and bullying. I don't know these people anymore, but somehow, they know me. I believe that sharing your story is truly that powerful. Being open about the stigma of OCD and showing up unashamed as a walking example of OCD, each and every time you do this, you are impacting at least *one* person's view.

There is nothing, absolutely nothing good about OCD. It doesn't protect you; it doesn't help you. It is toxicity at its finest, and it is slowly killing your livelihood from within. You can't help but break down after a while. The amount of energy you and I have expended is enough for an entire other life to have lived. You are over-complicating life. But life is complicated enough in itself. Look at the way this world is going! It will only get worse. You have to get control of your mind, your power, and your strong will that is *absolutely within you* — now. Tomorrow could be too late. Let this book speak to you right here, right now. Don't set me down after the last page and do nothing. I know this has been a lot, but it is in your hands and your head for a reason. Stop putting things off. Don't wait until Monday. Don't wait until you feel stronger, and don't wait until you're having a better day. Get out a journal and start writing. I don't care what you write, as long as it has to do with ideas or concepts that caught your eye in this book. Write down all your further questions. Write how you really feel about all of this and write feverishly until your hand cramps. But do not get up until you have listed three things you can tangibly do to get a plan in place to START. That could be making calls to therapists and interviewing them to see if they practice ERP. Yes, you know now, you can absolutely interview a therapist. It needs to be a good fit. It could be listing the main compulsion you know you need to start with because it's interfering so incredibly much with your life. It could be downloading the nOCD app (an app that helps aid in effective OCD treatment). It could be finding a local OCD support group to get your feet wet. It could be a deep, meaningful, even tearful prayer that you write down right now, telling God exactly what you feel. Every fear, every hope, ask for direction and guidance on this journey, ask Him anything. It could also be shutting your journal, feeling empowered as all hell and going straight out to do something that scares you. It can be the smallest thing but follow through and *do it for you.*

When you are lying on your deathbed someday, you will hopefully have some time to reflect back on your life. When you do so, I wonder if you will feel immense regret for the time you wasted on this debilitating disorder. I wonder if you will be greatly saddened by all of the quality experiences and opportunities you missed out on because your mind got in your way. I know you might not yet know how to control it, but this is your chance.

I would never write a book like this, only to fall back into all the ways that I am telling you not to. I am showing you that you must understand the bigger picture of what you are battling, instead of just zeroing in on finding the next moment of reassurance. Writing this book has held me accountable in so many ways. Every time I have so desperately wanted to give into an obsession, perform a compulsion, do anything to get relief, I think about you. I think about how you are reading what I have written and how I don't want to be a hypocrite and give into my OCD when I'm telling you not to. We are one in the same. So, whoever you are, I want to say thank you. You have already unknowingly held me accountable, just as I am trying to hold you accountable.

I am twenty-eight years old. And when I look back and reflect, I cannot even begin to tell you the time I have wasted in my so-called short life. I could have taken my life in a completely different direction, could have accomplished so much more by my age. I could have had real relationships, real friendships instead of being so late to the game on all of the above.

But the point is that I fought when I did, and I earned my life back when I did. So, you wasted some time, perhaps you've wasted years. You can't get them back. You can't get back the time you missed out with your family, your relationships, even the time you could have had with yourself in this life, rather than with your OCD. Don't sit there and feel regret and remorse for the time you wasted. Turn that energy into something you can actually use, so it doesn't feel so wasted. Turn that energy into power and control over yourself, beginning with the preparation for the fight. This time in your life will not be wasted if you turn it into your own success story. I **promise you this — at some point, your quality of life becomes** more important than your compulsions, and you will make a change.

I used to think OCD was my "thing." The thing that made me unique, perhaps saving me from getting involved in bad choices in my adolescent years. But the bottom line is that it isn't my OCD that makes me unique. It's my *triumph* of OCD. It's the fact that I can now live this life freely! Yes, I still find myself bound, sometimes frequently, other times infrequently. But I am a free woman, considering the terms I was under a few years ago.

The point of me saying all of this is to show you that among all the success I've had with conquering OCD, I still hurt. I still battle every day with a beast. I may not have bad obsessions every day, but I still have anxiety every day. However, I battle with the cub nowadays, not the bear. It may never go away. But I know in my deepest being that I fought off the worst beast of all. The beast of constant manipulation and luring control. The foundation of Obsessive-Compulsive Disorder. In fact, I kicked its ass. Now I am just dealing with the aftermath.

You must understand the extent of what is trying to overcome your mind. Millions of people feel a physical aching every single day from what we are going through. I was one of them...but now I am aching inside for you. You don't deserve this. You don't deserve to be constantly confused, paralyzed, scared, and unhappy. In fact, you may have no idea how unhappy you really are because you have been restrained by OCD for so long that to you, this is just...life.

I am here to tell you; *this is not life.*

Life is so much more, so much bigger, and light years better on the other side. I still see new things every day that I never saw before because I was so immersed in my head. I am finally near the end of the tunnel, and I want to walk out of it not alone but holding your hand. You deserve to feel the feeling that I feel every day. A feeling of freedom. Not perfect freedom, but freedom from the darkness you were once in. It's like I've been in prison for years. I am just now getting out into the light and trying to re-learn the ways of the world. You deserve to know you are not alone. You deserve to be listened to. You deserve to know what happiness feels like without weight constantly hovering. And most of all, you deserve to live a life of free will that God has granted us. I get you. I get what you are going through. But now it's time for you to get back in touch with yourself.

Before you do so, stop for a moment and give yourself some credit for your strength. People around us have no idea how strong we are to deal with what we do every day inside our heads. People around us have no idea how hard we desperately try to put a smile on, act normal, and go about our days as anyone would, but inside, we are constantly breaking down. We are trying to balance family, friends, work, school, and everyday inconveniences all while trying to decipher our minds.

You know you need to make a change. I may come off a bit abrupt and harsh at times in this book, but it's only because I've already battled what you are about to face. It's because I have had every excuse you have. And it's because I care more about being the friend that pushes you to a better life in the long run than caring if you like me right now or not. You can change the way OCD affects you and your life. You can absolutely live a fully functional life amidst severe Obsessive-Compulsive Disorder if you truly put up a fight.

I hope I get to meet you someday. Whether you are someone who battles everyday as hard as I did or are someone who struggles just as hard by just watching someone you know struggle. In the least, I just pray that I make you think. Think about what life would be like without these limitations. I know every case is different. I know that you may not have related one bit to my case. But I know you related to my struggle. That's what bonds us. Please don't give in to this falsehood another day.

Above all, I want you to know there is a good life to live out there, amidst OCD. There are so many occasions with severe OCD where it might seem like the good life is long gone. But everyone deserves a good life. The beauty of OCD (did I really just say that?!) is that as crippling as it is, it is just in your mind. You are not truly, physically confined as a quadriplegic, nor are you physically paralyzed. The limitations lie within your very own brain, one of which you simply cannot get your own brain to wrap around! But that's okay. You never need to have all the answers. You're not supposed to! You're only human. But you do have to be willing to fight for yourself, for your life. You just have to be willing to *trust* people like me; people who are just like you. You have to move forward with pursuing the life you *want* to live. I will say it to the ends of the Earth — imagine what you could be in this life without OCD controlling you. It may never leave you for good, but you can still lead an incredible life you didn't know was possible once you get a grip on it. You will have to make adjustments where you see fit for your themes of OCD, but my concepts remain.

So this is all for YOU — the obsessive outsiders. I now live for reaching people just like you. You are my inspiration to keep putting up the continuous fight against OCD for the rest of my days. You've already done so much for me, just knowing you've read my book. Now allow me to do something for you. Take my advice. Put up the fight. May we learn to obsess less and live more. May we fight and may we *fly free.*

Author's Note: Go kick OCD's ass.

OCD RESOURCES

To help encourage you to take immediate action while you're still inspired, I am providing a compiled list of resources below. This list is for you to learn more about OCD and related disorders, as well as have concrete places to turn to next. Please note that these are *not* all of the resources available, and I highly encourage you to do your own further and extensive research.

First and foremost, if you are feeling suicidal or need someone to talk to, you can immediately call 911 or the suicide prevention hotline at 800-273-8255. There is always someone to talk to, and there is always hope, even when it doesn't feel like it at all. When in doubt, make a call. Any call.

The 'hub' of OCD information is **The International OCD Foundation** - www.iocdf.org. Throughout the site you can explore everything from informative fact sheets, resource directory's of treatment options for families and caregivers – even how to find a proper OCD specialist in your area, including asking the right questions. You will also find links to IOCDF affiliates throughout the country. This is a great way to get involved in an OCD local community near you. Another great resource is to attend the annual International OCD

Foundation Conference. Details will continuously be updated on the IOCDF website.

The Peace of Mind Foundation is a non-profit organization whose mission is to help improve the quality of life of OCD sufferers and caregivers though education, research, support and advocacy. Visit www.peaceofmind.com for more information.

OCDChallenge.org is an interactive online self-help program for people suffering from OCD. The program is also available in Spanish. Visit www.ocdchallenge.org for more information.

Recovery International is a global organization with four primary specialties: crisis, health, recovery, consulting. This organization is a beast of crisis direction and is worth navigating their website at https://riinternational.com. This is a much larger base to navigate, but is very educational.

Unstuck: an OCD Kids movie is a very educational film of various kids explaining their disorder and how they have learned to over-come many obsessive issues at the worst of OCD. Please note that this is a fantastic movie for adults, not just kids. You learn to love each kid individually and observe their maturity and how far they have come at such young ages. You can view the film in addition to navigating further OCD resources at ocdkidsmovie.com.

Download the *nOCD* app: This app was created by an OCD sufferer himself who originally wanted to find a way to condense all his notes from therapy into one place. Today, it has become an effective tool in OCD therapy for both sufferers and therapists. The team has designed an interactive app, packed with modern prompts and leads that is truly one of the biggest breakthroughs to directly reach and help OCD sufferers in today's society.

Treatment Centers: There are a variety of treatment centers around the US. Some are inpatient, some are only outpatient, some do not take health insurance, and some do. People often email me through my website asking which treatment centers I recommend or for specific OCD Specialists. In my experience, this is a job that is best fit as inside research based off of reputable direction. I can recommend a specific center or support group all day long, but ultimately the sufferer needs to be the one to identify with the place, the people, their potential therapist, etc. I made a point in the final chapters that there is nothing wrong with an "interview" process when it comes to treatment. I made the mistake of not knowing I had the control of interviewing to find the best place to suit me. I haphazardly landed upon it just in time, yet two years late. I don't recommend that – there are far too many resources available these days. I will list some known centers below, but please do your own outside research and make sure to call and ask all the right questions (i.e. Do they use Exposure and Response Prevention specifically?)

Please note that the below are not listed in any particular order. These are centers I have chosen due to my personal experience, if they come highly recommended and have truly helped people I know, or if they have had booths at OCD Conferences I've attended and I have ensured they all practice the proper treatment for OCD. I would advise you to scan through the below, but to be sure and go to the IOCDF website where you can put in your zip code/city and find treatment options that are IOCDF approved nearest you. Let your research begin!

The Gateway Institute
-Locations: Costa Mesa, CA, San Francisco, CA and Scottsdale, AZ
-Specializes in OCD and Anxiety Disorders
-https://www.gatewayocd.com

McLean Hospital: Harvard Medical School Affiliate
- Location: Belmont, MA
- Specializes in residential, outpatients and day programs for OCD and many conditions

- www.mcleanhospital.org/ocd

Rogers Behavioral Health
- Location: Oconomowoc, WI
- Specializes in OCD, along with many other conditions, both inpatient and outpatient options
- https://rogersbh.org

The Houston OCD Program
- Location: Houston, TX
- Specializes in anxiety treatment for adults, adolescents and children
- https://houstonocdprogram.org

OCD Center of Los Angeles
- Location: Los Angeles, CA, Woodland Hills, CA and Orange Country, CA
- Specializes in OCD treatment and related conditions
- www.ocdla.com

OCD Anxiety Program of Southern California
- Location: Santa Monica, CA
- Intensive Outpatient program, adolescent outpatient program and outpatient clinic
- http://Socalocdprogram.org

Spectrum CBT
- Location: Los Angeles, CA
- OCD Adult Intensive Outpatient Program
- www.spectrumcbt.com

Renewed Freedom Center
- Location: Los Angeles, CA
- Outpatient therapy center specializing in the treatment of OCD and Anxiety Disorders in children and adults
- www.renewedfreedomcenter.com

ABOUT THE AUTHOR

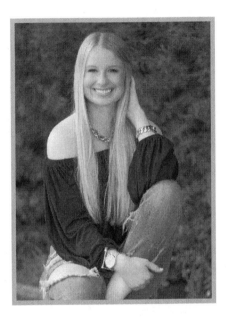

Committed but comical, Kerry Alayne Osborn is a motivational public speaker, writer and mentor in the mental health field. Kerry transitioned from an unhealthy, anxiety ridden life of sending VIP press releases to media outlets in celebrity fashion PR entertainment to becoming the poster child of vulnerability and exposing the intimate, private life of living with a chronic mental disorder in today's society.

Kerry resides in both California and Colorado, and can be found anywhere from her favorite hideout, her bed, to a stage speaking truth to hundreds of people. In her down time, the natural freckle faced, pajama-obsessed writer escapes into a good thriller novel, consumes an unreasonable amount of carbs, and loves redecorating her space of inspiration far too often. If you can't reach her – try calling her local Home Goods.

You can learn more about Kerry and her mission through her website, www.theobsessiveoutsiders.com, or her social media channels, both @kerryalayne and @theobsessiveoutsiders. For contact, press, or speaking inquiries, Kerry prefers to be contacted directly at Kerry@theobsessiveoutsiders.com.

If you would like to join *The Obsessive Outsiders* newsletter and stay in the know of the community, please simply enter your email on the homepage opt-in at www.theobsessiveoutsiders.com. We do not spam and respect your privacy and your influx of emails!

If this book inspired you in any way and you feel compelled to let Kerry and others know, contributing your review on Amazon would be incredibly appreciated. This will allow the book to more likely be seen by other people searching for the same kind of resources you were.

ACKNOWLEDGMENTS

This book is written in honor of God, first and foremost. I would not exist, and this material would not exist, if it weren't for the journey He chose for me. Some people are resentful for the trials and tribulations God puts them through. I do not question His reasoning, nor do I care why. I simply have faith.

My parents. *Obviously.* They did not ask and were not prepared for their lives to turn upside down when their goody two-shoes daughter did a 180 out of nowhere. Although you may never understand me in the sense of my OCD, you have accepted my struggle, and we have always maintained an extremely close relationship, which will always remain a priority. Mom and Dad, thank you for every penny you've spent on this hot mess and for always allowing me to tuck in my wings.

To Jim Sterner, my therapist at The Gateway Institute. Jim, my parents believe you saved my life. But you give *me* that credit, and I am forever grateful for your mentality. You dedicate all of my growth and hard work to me alone and patiently walked with me through the tunnel of darkness in order to break the foundation of OCD itself. For me to discover *for myself.* This book would not exist without you.

To Kerrie Flanagan, my publishing manager and creative wizard. God wove a miracle in order for us to find one another in the circumstances we did. You have provided an integrity filled foundation for me to see this book through to its fullest potential, and I respect you tremendously.

Made in the USA
Columbia, SC
22 October 2020

23297716R00141